The Literature of Delight

The
Literature
of Delight™

A Critical Guide to Humorous Books for Children

Kimberly Olson Fakih

R. R. BOWKER®

A Reed Reference Publishing Company

New Providence, New Jersey

Published by R. R. Bowker,
A Reed Reference Publishing Company
Copyright © 1993 by Reed Publishing (USA) Inc.
All rights reserved
Printed and bound in the United States of America

Library of Congress Cataloging-in-Publication Data

Fakih, Kimberly Olson.
    The literature of delight : a critical guide to humorous books for
children / Kimberly Olson Fakih.
        p.   cm.
    Includes bibliographical references and indexes.
    ISBN 0-8352-3027-9
    1. Wit and humor. Juvenile—Bibliography.   2. Children—Books and
reading.   I. Title.
    Z6514.W5F35   1993
    [PN1009.Z6]
    016.827008'09282—dc20   93-20159
                                                                          CIP

ISBN 0 - 8352 - 3027 - 9

9 780835 230278

Contents

Preface

Children and the concept of humor are almost inseparable. The comic pantheon of children's books is seemingly broad enough to encompass the entire literature of books for young readers. In addition to being the most prevalent, humorous books are among the most popular with children, and it is easy to see the causal relation between their popularity and ubiquitousness. All attempts to highlight and ensure accessibility to these books are worthwhile for those of us interested in issues of literacy and who are ever hopeful that children will spend at least as much time behind a book as in front of a television set. The children's book field, as compared with other areas of literature, is growing very rapidly. The number of books published today is more than double that of a decade ago. There is a dire need for evaluation, classification, analysis, and cataloging that, no matter how imperfect or partial, can only lead to promoting and advancing these important books.

This reference tool is intended to provide a better handle on the stupendous amount of humorous material available. Its purpose is to identify, list, and emphasize those titles that are most representative of the rich variety of humorous children's books. Because most children's books contain some humor, not every title of obvious distinction can be mentioned here because that would mean including a good chunk of the children's literature canon. This volume attempts to present a generous sampling of humorous books—new, recent, and those that have withstood time's test—aimed at various reading levels, with the knowledge that it is a mere plunk in the bucket compared with the sheer number of books available that some reader out there will find amusing according to his or her own standards of literature and laughter.

The 784 annotations are organized according to 17 specific categories designed to include the generally known facets of humor. There are far more books noted than there are entries, since sequels and related titles are mentioned within the annotations.

Following the main listings are five indexes. The Author Index includes author names and titles; the Illustrator Index includes illustrator names and titles; the Title Index contains titles listed as main entries; the Subject Index lists titles under numerous categories; and the Character Index lists the names of beloved and humorous characters that are well known in children's literature.

The book was organized with the recognition that what is truly funny to children may, at the least, bore adults and, at the most, repel them. The literary equivalents to catsup-on-spaghetti and other childish taste treats are therefore included herein, in the form of elephant joke books and some seemingly standard middle-grade readers whose issues matter a great deal more to those fourth-through-sixth graders than they do to adults. Objects (for youngsters) and concerns (for teenagers) of a mundane nature can be found here and throughout children's books, because they are all-important to children.

This volume is intended as a practical tool as well as a critical bibliography of a collection's resources. Unless otherwise noted, all editions are hardcover and still in print. Included are notable fiction or nonfiction English-language titles. Either the library or trade ISBN is included, as well as price, for ordering purposes. When paperback editions are available, whether through the original publisher or a reprint house, there is a notation.

Instead of listing the number of pages in a title, the entries show a format designation. Roughly, picture books are 32 pages long; storybooks are slightly longer, usually illustrated, works; chapter books are those designed as first or easy novels; anthologies may be longer collections of jokes and riddles as well as collected writings; the rest are self-explanatory. (Normally excluded are "fun" books, that is, puzzle and other special-activities books that are closer to toys than texts.) The age range for titles annotated runs from first books—board books, wordless books—to young adult novels, making this a handy volume for those working with both elementary and secondary schoolchildren. The reader will note that far fewer books seem to be available for young adults that can be classified as outright humorous, as compared with the wealth of materials available for young children; when aimed beyond a certain age, books seem to become more serious-minded and sober.

Approximately 65 to 75 percent of the listed books were gleaned from those published in the 1980s and through the first half of 1992. That roughly encompasses the first decade of the recent children's book-publishing boom, particularly the latter part of the 1980s, which, I think, was a truly funny phase in large-scale publishing of children's books, when the mood of the times allowed for an extensive output of most of the humorous books we have today (it seemly coincided with my sojourn at *Publishers Weekly;* some of the annotations are adapted from reviews I had written for that publication and others).

In such endeavors as this one that are true tests of one's mettle, if the only success is in beckoning a child toward the bookshelves, it is energy worth expending. Once kids have located a particular book, a particular author, they can see for themselves how many treats there are to behold, and let personal taste take over. Humor is a valued (and underrated) gift that can be a speedy way to assess children's likes and dislikes. And (unlike the puritanical, pessimistic view of the librarian in *The Name of the Rose,* where "pagan" laughter was deemed the source of all trouble and evil) humor's buoyancy may well be the only balm for the world's toils and troubles.

1: A Confederacy of Laughers

Laughing Together

However spontaneous it seems, laughter always implies a kind of secret freemasonry, or even complicity, with other laughers, real or imagined.
—Henri Bergson

*T*his chapter is mostly about group cohesion. Stump speechmakers and rovers on the rubber chicken circuit have known for years that either their prose must ring with conviction and a distinct elocutionary style or they must rally disinterested listeners with a few good jokes. There is no better way to consolidate a constituency than by roping it in with humor. Laughter is a social impulse, and is more contagious than yawning; every child who has ever sobbed over a playground injustice has learned that "laugh, and the world laughs with you—cry, and you cry alone." Pain and despair are generally private affairs; joy is a communal one, as is joy's little sister, humor. From the sharing of laughter can come social cohesion, or a sense of bonding with others, a communal feeling of well-being.

Rallying the group, though, can come at someone else's expense. In the barbed, competitive world of stand-up comedy, it is clear that making sport of someone is easy if the object of derision is anonymous and stereotypical. Humor is provincial and exclusive when it depends for its punch lines on what "we are" as a society of playmates and what "they are not" (being not like "us," of course) and gives license to prejudice.

Exclusion and homogeneity of group temperament appear to be essential constituents of such "other"-oriented humor; for there to be a like-minded pool of people or a culture-specific humor there must be

1

those outside the fold. Any teenager (in young adult novels or real life) who has ever wanted to be "in" the clique rather than "out" where the risk of scorn is great has assessed the world in fairly realistic terms. Thomas Hobbes regarded humor as an expression of our superiority to others, and in its extreme, this expression is borne out in contempt, ridicule, and subsequently the alienation of those who cannot dip into the common reference we share. The end result of such negative cohesion can be a sort of collective impertinence that leads to nothing less than tribalism and scapegoating.

This category, however, is mostly a blessing rather than an expression of some amoral leviathan; this is reflected in the entries below and in children's books in general.

Alcott, Louisa May. *Little Women.* **Illus. by Jessie Willcox Smith.** Little, Brown, 1968. $19.95 (0-685-47121-7).
FORMAT: Novel   GRADES: 6–up.

Cornelia Meigs, the author of the Newbery Medal-winning *Invincible Louisa*, pens the introduction to this centennial edition of the 1868 story of four sisters and their Marmee at home while Papa is away at war. Jo gives the episodes spunk, but the overall effect is that of a heartwarming classic.

Barbour, Karen. *Little Nino's Pizzeria.* **Illus. by the author.** Harcourt, 1987. $14.95 (0-15-247650-4).
FORMAT: Picture book   GRADES: Preschool–Grade 3.

A pizza joint is the unusual setting for this high-spirited telling of a boy's knowing how important is his contribution to the family. Barbour's flat perspectives and diamond-bright colors make this a feast for the eyes as well as the heart.

Barbour, Karen. *Nancy.* **Illus. by the author.** Harcourt, 1989. $13.95 (0-15-256675-9).
FORMAT: Picture book   GRADES: Preschool–Grade 3.

Nancy the new girl manages to turn a group of four best friends who exclude her into her own four best pals, just by a simple demonstration of her "cool." A simple tale of bonding, with funny touches throughout. (Don't ask why children need to belong, they just do.)

Blos, Joan W. *Old Henry.* **Illus. by Stephen Gammell.** Morrow, 1987. $13.95 (0-688-06399-3).
FORMAT: Picture book   GRADES: Kindergarten–Grade 3.

When Old Henry sees a ramshackle house, he decides to move in, birds and all. The neighbors expect him to fix up the house and yard—

expectations he ignores, thank you very much. But when he moves out, the townspeople feel lost without him, and Old Henry misses them, too. A compromise is achieved. Rainbow-hued paintings by one of the most gifted illustrators working today exalt the simple affirmations of the story, with characters both comic and poignant.

Byars, Betsy. *The Pinballs.* HarperCollins, 1977. LB $14.89 (0-06-020918-6). paper avail.
FORMAT: Novel   GRADES: 4–6.

Newbery Medalist Byars's audience grows ever wider with the popularity of her Blossom family books, but this early comic work takes a look at the lives of three kids in a foster home who band together to save all their souls. Wise and funny.

Carlson, Nancy. *Arnie Goes to Camp.* **Illus. by the author.** Viking, 1988. $11.95 (0-670-81549-7). paper avail.
FORMAT: Picture book   GRADES: Preschool–Grade 3.

Last seen shoplifting some markers (and thoroughly repentant for his impulsive act), Arnie has gone straight and is going to camp. It's all here—the initial homesickness, admiration for the "neat" camp counselor Stretch, hearing scary stories around the campfire, and learning camp songs. When it's over, Arnie is named Best New Camper. In this primer of the concerns and delights of going away from home for the first time, Carlson works in points about getting along with others: a boy named Ted seems a little obnoxious at first, but Arnie learns to enjoy his tricks. The colors of camp with all the ups and downs are bright, the feeling is genial, and the experience is realistically presented and welcome.

Cleaver, Bill, and Vera Cleaver. *Where the Lilies Bloom.* **Illus. by Jim Spanfeller.** HarperCollins, 1969. $12.95 (0-397-31111-7). paper avail.
FORMAT: Novel   GRADES: 6–up.

Mary Call's brothers and sisters were almost accustomed to being without a mother, but now they are fatherless as well, a fact she hopes to hide from interfering outsiders. As the family struggles on in the Great Smoky Mountains, Mary Call's observations on their life together meander from outrageously funny to bittersweet and innocent.

Conrad, Pam. *Seven Silly Circles.* **Illus. by Mike Wimmer.** HarperCollins, 1987. LB $11.89 (0-06-021334-5).
FORMAT: Novel   GRADES: 2–5.

In a sequel to *I Don't Live Here!* by the acclaimed author of *Prairie Songs* and other books, Nicki accidentally has made seven red circles on her face by sticking a suction cup arrow to her skin. She vows not to leave her house until the marks fade, even missing part of the annual leaf-raking party held by her family the next day. Rescue comes; by the end of the party, Nicki has learned to trust her friends, family, and herself. Poignancy underscores this sweetly humorous story. Although the potential for melodrama is here, the author never falters or overstates her case, and her touch is light but sure.

Denton, Terry. *The School for Laughter.* **Illus. by the author.** Houghton, 1990. $13.95 (0-395-53353-8).
FORMAT: Picture book   GRADES: Preschool–Grade 3.

A less than original, still entertaining story of a boy who has lost his laugh. Eddie, previously a happy child, wakes up one morning and cannot manage the smallest smile. He is therefore enrolled in the School for Laughter, where concerned that he is depressing his classmates, he unpacks some jokes of his own. The text is sadly flat, but the illustrations, full of broad and subtle humor, show the madhouse classrooms and sprinting children of the School.

Estes, Eleanor. *The Moffats.* **Illus. by Louis Slobodkin.** Harcourt, 1941. $14.95 (0-15-255095-X).
FORMAT: Novel   GRADES: 4–6.

Estes may be best known for the Newbery Medal-winning *Ginger Pye*, but her tales of the Moffats—including *The Moffat Museum* and *Rufus M.*—are full of fun and good-hearted playfulness. The genuine affection the family members have for one another makes all their adventures worthwhile reading.

Feldman, Eve B. *Dog Crazy.* **Illus. by Eric Jon Nones.** Tambourine, 1992. $13.00 (0-688-10819-9).
FORMAT: Novel   GRADES: 3–5.

Sara Fine is dog crazy—she dreams about them day and night, draws them, talks about them, and tries to ensure that when her next birthday arrives, a puppy of her own will be one of her presents. The heart of this book is in Sara's spirited single-mindedness; she is a charmer in her purely childlike focus on her unwavering goal. This modest pursuit is the inspiration for some very funny scenes, grounded in the real, goal-oriented aspirations of a normal American family.

Härtling, Peter. *Old John.* Lothrop, 1990. $11.95 (0-688-08734-5).
FORMAT: Novel   GRADES: 4–8.

Translated by Elizabeth Crawford. Laura and Jacob's grandfather, who cherishes an oversized poster of Albert Einstein sticking out his tongue, moves in with the family, bringing with him difficult times as they all adjust to his presence. This story of the problems of the elderly is lightened by fluid humor in the relating of Old John's idiosyncrasies, and by the family's warm and winning compassion.

Henkes, Kevin. *Chester's Way.* **Illus. by the author.** Greenwillow, 1988. $13.95 (0-688-07607-6). paper avail.
FORMAT: Picture book   GRADES: Preschool–Grade 2.

Chester has definite likes and dislikes and there is no changing his mind. His friend Wilson is just like he is; they're quite a pair. Then Lilly moves in. She plainly scares them both, until she terrorizes some bullies. Suddenly Lilly's ways don't look so bad. This vision of friendship captures the essence of the childlike. The story unwinds at a deliberate pace and every sentence is either downright funny, or dense with playful, deadpan humor. Behind every Henkes book is a wide open heart, one children can't help but respond to, and which makes all his books— especially this one—of special value.

Honeycutt, Natalie. *Invisible Lissa.* Bradbury, 1985. $13.95 (0-02-744360-4). paper avail.
FORMAT: Novel   GRADES: 4–6.

Lissa enters fifth grade ready to take on the world, but the world is not ready for *her*. A classmate rallies all the "in" girls, leaving Lissa temporarily out in the cold. Although she is ultimately accepted into the group, Lissa retains her right of refusal, bringing this funny and touching middle-grade novel to a satisfying close.

Horvath, Polly. *An Occasional Cow.* **Illus. by Gioia Fiammenghi.** Farrar, 1989. $13.95 (0-374-35559-2).
FORMAT: Novel   GRADES: 3–7.

Horvath's first novel is a flip and funny view of life in Iowa. Imogene, a New York City girl, is astonished when her parents decide to send her to her relatives' home after her summer camp burns to the ground. But Imogene quickly discovers that her cousins have a distinct brand of charm. Iowans may take issue with the decidedly screwball capers that are passed off as regional behavior, but the tone of this anything-goes comedy is wholehearted fun. As exaggerated and comic as the story itself, Fiammenghi's black-and-white illustrations help put that point across.

Lovelace, Maud Hart. *Heaven to Betsy.* **Illus. by Vera Neville.** HarperCollins, 1980. paper $3.50 (0-06-440110-3).
FORMAT: Novel   GRADES: 5–up.

For younger readers, there are all the Betsy-Tacy stories illustrated by Lois Lenski. This is the first illustrated by Neville, taking Betsy and her whole new high school gang through the first heady years of adolescence at the turn of the century. Affectionate fun, cast in an old-fashioned setting but with lessons for our times as well.

Lyon, George Ella. *Come a Tide.* **Illus. by Stephen Gammell.** Orchard, 1990. LB $14.99 (0-531-08454-X).
FORMAT: Picture book   GRADES: Preschool–Grade 3.

A community comes together in Kentucky, as certain as the tides of flood water formed by snow melt and heavy rains each spring. There is fear accompanying these events—one small girl needs reassurance. But there is also robustness, as Grandma faces the crisis head-on and greets the subsequent cleanup with gusto. ("If it was me," she comments in light of the work ahead, "I'd make friends with a shovel.") A witty bonding, between old and young, and among the members of this flood-stricken locale.

McKenna, Colleen O'Shaughnessy. *Too Many Murphys.* Scholastic, 1988. $12.95 (0-590-41731-2). paper avail.
FORMAT: Novel   GRADES: 4–7.

Eight-year-old Collette is tired of being expected to be some kind of "midget mother" to her siblings. As in Felicia Bond's picture book, *Poinsettia and Her Family,* Collette has the chance to be an only child again—temporarily. The plot may not be substantial enough to float an entire book, but McKenna accurately serves up the dialogue and behavior of a houseful of children, and readers in the same boat as Collette will find common ground here. There are plenty of Murphys; there are also plenty of books about them.

Maxner, Joyce. *Nicholas Cricket.* **Illus. by William Joyce.** HarperCollins, 1989. LB $13.89 (0-06-024222-1). paper avail.
FORMAT: Picture book   GRADES: Preschool–Grade 3.

Nicholas and the Bug-a-Wug Crickets lead the throngs of surrounding insects through a joy-filled night of music and dancing. Moody illustrations bring an edge to this rollicking verse, giving it a cinematic look. Children like the bugs.

Naylor, Phyllis Reynolds. *All But Alice.* Macmillan, 1992. $13.95 (0-689-31773-5).
FORMAT: Novel   GRADES: 5–8.

Motherless Alice returns, ready to join the great sisterhood she's sure exists among all females, and finds herself snared in battles of loyalty (to her brother, or to the young women who want to date him?), love, and honor (to help former boyfriend Patrick, or to stick with the group?).

One thing is certain: Readers will pledge their loyalties to all the Alice books and make all her delectably funny escapades their own.

Pearson, Tracey Campbell. *The Storekeeper.* **Illus. by the author.** Dial, 1988. $12.95 (0-8037-0370-8). paper avail.
FORMAT: Picture book GRADES: Preschool–Grade 2.

It is not even dawn, but the amiable storekeeper—a plump, elderly woman wearing a bright red sweater over her blue checkered dress—is up to receive a supply of doughnuts from a deliveryman and to prepare for the busy day ahead. While imparting some information about a storekeeper's tasks, the book captures the essentially social aspects of the general store environment. This has all the appeal of Pearson's other exuberant works, but provides a contrast to the breakneck rhythms she usually conveys. The storekeeper's day unwinds slowly, and the pace is welcome and leisurely.

Peck, Robert Newton. *Soup in Love.* **Illus. by Charles Robinson.** Delacorte, 1992. $14.00 (0-385-30563-X).
FORMAT: Novel GRADES: 4–7.

For some, the "Soup" formula is bound to run a little thin: Soup dreams up impossible schemes, Rob protests but goes along, all ends well. Others, however, will relish all the side dishes that make this formula so easy to swallow. Here, the boys each fall in love, and take the whole town down with them. Fans will enjoy the ride.

Pendergraft, Patricia. *Hear the Wind Blow.* Putnam, 1988. $14.95 (0-399-21528-X). paper avail.
FORMAT: Novel GRADES: 5–up.

The author of *Miracle at Clement's Pond* returns with a second spunky book about life in a small town and the role one person plays to bring the community together. Isadora, who narrates, watches as her best friend Maybelle is good and kind to everyone. Sickly Maybelle dies after being baptized in an icy river. Pendergraft weaves the results of Maybelle's influence through the story of Isadora's own blossoming personality. A rich, rewarding story, replete with witty, winning details.

Pendergraft, Patricia. *Miracle at Clement's Pond.* Putnam, 1987. $13.95 (0-399-21438-0).
FORMAT: Novel GRADES: 5–up.

When Lyon Savage and friends Sylvie and Justin find an abandoned baby, they secretly deliver it to a spinster named Miss Adeline and set into motion events that change Clement's Pond forever. The homey flavor of the writing sets readers down in Clement's Pond and infuses the story with tall-tale elements that are easy to swallow. This portrait of a small town is moving and humorous, with inhabitants that readers will be darn glad they met.

Rathmann, Peggy. *Ruby the Copycat.* **Illus. by the author.** Scholastic, 1991. $12.95 (0-590-43747-X).
FORMAT: Picture book   GRADES: Preschool–Grade 3.

Rathmann pokes fun at issues of conformity by showing the risks of being copied or a copycat. Ruby, who hops everywhere she goes, begins by loving Angela's red bow and finding one of her own, but ends by teaching her classmates how to hop as she does. Never weighed down by its philosophical concerns, this is a festive, jocular tale with an engaging (though reformable) copycat at its center.

Rayner, Mary. *Mrs. Pig Gets Cross and Other Stories.* **Illus. by the author.** Dutton, 1987. $11.95 (0-525-44280-4). paper avail.
FORMAT: Storybook   GRADES: 1–3.

There are 10 piglets in Mrs. Pig's family, so it's no wonder that the woman gets cross. A collection of stories by the always funny Rayner show that piglets and human children have more in common than readers might first suspect. No matter what happens, however, the portraits are always loving. Mischief abounds, but more than that, these are stories that exist in every family.

Rylant, Cynthia. *Henry and Mudge and the Long Weekend.* **Illus. by Suçie Stevenson.** Macmillan, 1992. $12.95 (0-02-778013-9).
FORMAT: Picture book   GRADES: Kindergarten–Grade 3.

The winter blahs have taken over Henry's home, and boredom has descended on the entire family—even Mudge. How Mom brings them together on a fun project and quells the "Pre-spring meanies" makes for a lively weekend that for readers will be all too short. Brightly endearing, as are all the books for beginning readers about these two.

Samuels, Barbara. *Faye and Dolores.* **Illus. by the author.** Macmillan, 1985. $13.95 (0-02-778120-8).
FORMAT: Picture book   GRADES: Preschool–Grade 3.

Even a little sibling rivalry may be inevitable, but it has seldom been presented with such balance and good spirits as in Samuels's first outing for these sisters. Dolores is a wide-eyed troublemaker and Faye a careful, caring type, but their relationship is the star of three generous tales. There's more about the little sister and her spotty friendship with a feline in *Duncan and Dolores.*

Sawyer, Ruth. *Roller Skates.* **Illus. by Valenti Angelo.** Puffin, 1986. paper
$3.95 (0-14-030358-8).
FORMAT: Novel   GRADES: 4–7.

Young rollerbladers will immediately empathize with the freedom Lu-
cinda feels as she sets out to discover the big city, even though the setting
of turn-of-the-century New York will at first be beyond their ken. Since
1936 when this tale was first published, the city has much changed, and
few children would have her freedom these days, but the joys of discovery are timeless.

Schertle, Alice. *Jeremy Bean's St. Patrick's Day.* **Illus. by Linda Shute.**
Lothrop, 1987. LB $12.88 (0-688-04814-5).
FORMAT: Picture book   GRADES: Kindergarten–Grade 3.

Give the green light to Jeremy, who faces up to the taunts of his peers
and his fear of authority in one day. When his classmates tease him for
neglecting to wear green on St. Patrick's Day, he hides out in the janitor's
closet, but is rescued by the principal, wearing green to spare. Small and
reassuring.

Selden, George. *The Cricket in Times Square.* **Illus. by Garth Williams.**
Farrar, 1960. $16.00 (0-374-31650-3). paper avail.
FORMAT: Chapter book   GRADES: 4–6.

Delight in the purely whimsical idea of a mouse and cat in a Times
Square newsstand and a cricket who soothes the savage souls of city
slickers with its two back legs poised in song. This was a Newbery Honor
book, not only for its heart but for its warmth and sense of humor. More
good news: there is an entire array of Selden-Williams collaborations
about Chester Cricket and company.

Seuss, Dr. *Horton Hears a Who!* **Illus. by the author.** Random, 1954. LB
$12.99 (0-394-90078-2).
FORMAT: Picture book   GRADES: 2–3.

Horton has a heart, which he proves when he becomes protector to tiny
living creatures residing on a speck of dust. The juxtaposition of his size
to that of his wards is gratifyingly funny. And, "a person's a person, no
matter how small." Clearly, Dr. Seuss's plea for tolerance was ahead of
his time.

Singer, Isaac Bashevis. *The Fools of Chelm and Their History.* **Illus. by Uri
Shulevitz.** Farrar, 1973. $14.00 (0-374-32444-1). paper avail.
FORMAT: Storybook   GRADES: 4–6.

Others have retold these tales, but this is the standard by which the rest
are judged. Singer's fools bear the most unbelievable burdens, yet de-

spite everything, Chelm is forever on the map. For more of old I.B., try *When Shlemiel Went to Warsaw* and *Stories for Children*.

Staines, Bill. *All God's Critters Got a Place in the Choir.* **Illus. by Margot Zemach.** Dutton, 1989. $13.95 (0-525-44469-6).
FORMAT: Picture book   GRADES: Preschool–Grade 3.

The popular folk song comes to visual life in Zemach's splendid paintings about the children and animals who compose this farmhouse choir. Ebullience in every crowded scene, voices lifted, so serene.

Watanabe, Shigeo. *I Can Take a Bath!* **Illus. by Yasuo Ohtomo.** Philomel, 1987. $9.95 (0-399-21362-7).
FORMAT: Picture book   GRADES: Preschool–Kindergarten.

Taking a bath looks like a pretty dim prospect until Bear finds out that Daddy is already in the tub. A chain of see-and-do events gets them both clean in no time, ready to color together. The white background sets off not only the loving portraits of the bonding between parent and child but also the starkly simple text, perfect for first readers.

Wild, Margaret. *Mr. Nick's Knitting.* **Illus. by Dee Huxley.** Harcourt, 1991. $12.95 (0-15-200518-8).
FORMAT: Picture book   GRADES: Preschool–Grade 3.

Mr. Nick and Mrs. Jolley, the most companionable of souls, knit together. Their skills vary vastly, but the communion is real. Gentle humor informs every page of this purl of a yarn, and young readers will take away an idea or two about friendship.

Wood, Audrey. *Three Sisters.* **Illus. by Rosekrans Hoffman.** Dial, 1986. LB $9.89 (0-8037-0280-9). paper avail.
FORMAT: Chapter book   GRADES: 2–4.

An easy reader about the giddy behavior of three porcine siblings. It makes for the sort of full-blown nonsense children love best: the youngest pig is (of course) left out by the two older ones, but she (of course) knows how to get their attention at just the right moment. With eccentric, idiosyncratic illustrations that enhance the humor on every page.

Zindel, Paul. *My Darling, My Hamburger.* HarperCollins, 1969. $13.89 (0-06-026824-7). paper avail.
FORMAT: Novel   GRADES: 7–up.

One of Zindel's earliest is also one of his finest, as he tackles—in his portrayal of the high school lives of four friends—such issues as intimacy and its consequences and taking responsibility for one's actions. Few readers will settle for just one Zindel, so start them here before plunging them into the headier territories of *The Pigman* et al.

Additional Titles

The following titles, annotated elsewhere in this book (see index), could also fit the "Laughing Together" category.

Berry, James. *A Thief in the Village and Other Stories*
Block, Francesca Lia. *Weetzie Bat*
Hughes, Shirley. *Alfie Gets in First*
Hughes, Shirley. *The Big Alfie and Annie Rose Storybook*
Khalsa, Dayal Kaur. *My Family Vacation*
Modell, Frank. *One Zillion Valentines*
Park, Barbara. *Maxie, Rosie, and Earl*
Pilling, Ann. *The Big Pink*
Rogers, Paul. *Tumbledown*
Schweninger, Ann. *Off to School*
Stevenson, Suçie. *Do I Have to Take Violet?*
Van de Wetering, Janwillem. *Hugh Pine and Something Else*
Yeoman, John. *Our Village*

2: *Cautionary Tales*

Corrective Humor

A teasing reminder, a derisive snort and a smile, a campaign of ridicule—these are manifestations of humor with intent, mostly used to bring a stray member of the group back into the fold. Like a dog nipping at the heels of a wayward sheep, this means poking mild fun at someone in the name of bringing him or her back to their senses, so to speak. Henri Bergson rides this to a logical extreme: "If there exists a madness that is laughable, it can only be one compatible with the general health of the mind—a sane type of madness, one might say."

Some writers of children's books—young adult novels in particular—have used humor gainfully in this way, creating heroes and heroines whose skewed perspectives or ability to comment wryly on their situations prevent the serious problems of adolescence from swinging wildly off the scale and into the arena of tragedy. Where there is excess or imbalance, humor restores some restraint and counterpoise. Thus, potential tragedies become instead tales of the tragicomic, such as Kerr's Dinky Hocker and her last-ditch effort to get her parents' attention, and Zolotow's small dog and his innocent effort in *The Quarreling Book* to restore amiability out of potentially volatile impulses.

Browne, Anthony. *Piggybook*. Illus. by the author. Knopf, 1986. $14.99 (0-394-98416-1). paper avail.

FORMAT: Picture book   GRADES: Preschool–Grade 3.

Declaring her family "pigs," Mrs. Piggott abandons husband and sons to their own slothful habits. In her absence, the house becomes grungier and its inhabitants more porkly with each passing day. Although the message comes late in the feminist movement, it seems it can never be heard (or, in the eerie shifting images of Browne's wallpapers and door-knobs, *seen*) often enough. Brilliant, incisive wit.

Caseley, Judith. *Ada Potato.* **Illus. by the author.** Greenwillow, 1989. $11.95 (0-688-07742-0).
FORMAT: Picture book   GRADES: Preschool–Grade 3.

Ada takes up the cello. She works hard; practicing is no problem. But her path to school is difficult when some older kids call her Ada Potato and make fun of her instrument. It's enough to make Ada abandon her musical aspirations forever. Author Caseley's solution, for once, may strike readers as somewhat unrealistic. But for those willing to suspend belief, the story delivers, especially in scenes of selecting an instrument and enjoying the sounds of making music.

Duncan, Lois. *Wonder Kid Meets the Evil Lunch Snatcher.* **Illus. by Margaret Sanfilippo.** Little, Brown, 1988. $9.95 (0-316-19558-8). paper avail.
FORMAT: Chapter book   GRADES: 2–4.

Brian and Sarah team up with new friends Robbie and Lisa to dethrone a bully, Matt. With the invention of a superhero persona, Wonder Kid, and use of special effects, they scare him off. Matt seems a bit gullible to be falling for these tricks, but the end of a bully's reign is always worth cheering. Duncan here is sharply tuned in to the genuine concerns of third- and fourth-graders.

Fine, Anne. *My War with Goggle-Eyes.* Little, Brown, 1989. $13.95 (0-316-28314-2). paper avail.
FORMAT: Novel   GRADES: 5–up.

Fine leaves the broad satire of her *Madame Doubtfire* behind in this much more realistic and markedly more funny novel of a girl's life with her mother's new boyfriend. Few readers will not have encountered this theme before, but Fine makes it all fresh. Kitty has a winning way of telling a story, and her unbending toward old Goggle-Eyes is slow and grudging enough to have been cut from real life.

Graham, Bob. *Crusher Is Coming!* **Illus. by the author.** Viking, 1988. $11.95 (0-670-82081-4).
FORMAT: Picture book   GRADES: Preschool–Grade 3.

Pete warns his mother not to kiss him after school when he brings home a football hero named Crusher for a visit. But baby sister Claire beguiles the lug. Pete watches helplessly while Crusher gives horseback rides, joins in a tea party, and reads Claire a book. Graham's new slant on sibling rivalry is droll and understated, replete with funny moments. A matter-of-fact tone cleverly underscores the humor of the situation.

Henkes, Kevin. *Jessica.* **Illus. by the author.** Greenwillow, 1989. $11.95 (0-688-07829-X). paper avail.

FORMAT: Picture book   GRADES: Kindergarten–Grade 3.

Jessica is the imaginary friend of a girl named Ruthie, whose parents constantly remind her that "There is no Jessica." But Ruthie knows better—at least until she meets a real little girl named Jessica. The story is characteristically on target in its reflections of the inventive ways in which children play, but the denouement seems hasty—oh, why spoil it? The pictures of Ruthie and her two Jessicas are visions of fun, and despite the ending, readers will find plenty of pleasure within these pages.

Holabird, Katharine. *Angelina and Alice.* **Illus. by Helen Craig.** Crown, 1987. $13.00 (0-517-56074-7).

FORMAT: Picture book   GRADES: Preschool–Grade 3.

Angelina (rhymes with *Angelina Ballerina*) makes a new friend, Alice, and they love to do gymnastics together. But Alice can do a mean handstand, and Angelina cannot. One day, when Angelina falls down again, Alice joins the others who laugh and call her Angelina Tumbelina. Angelina hasn't lost a whit of her enthusiasm since she was first introduced to readers, and Alice is a robust new partner. The festive pictures capture a range of childhood experiences—from shy hanging back to a grand slam performance at the end.

Marino, Jan. *Like Some Kind of Hero.* Little, Brown, 1992. $14.95 (0-316-54626-7).

FORMAT: Novel   GRADES: 7–up.

Ted, attempting to have the best summer ever, goes for extremes and ends up disappointing everyone, including himself. His single-mindedness is so well developed and conveyed that readers will simultaneously be cheering him toward his goals and wondering when his plan will cave in on him. Marino makes Ted's choices multifaceted and true to life, handing him any number of Catch-22s and allowing him no clean getaways. He is spirited and determined, as is the story of his one heroic summer.

Mills, Claudia. *After Fifth Grade, the World!* Macmillan, 1989. $12.95 (0-02-767041-4). paper avail.

FORMAT: Novel   GRADES: 3–7.

Heidi is a fair-minded fifth-grader who is only too anxious to take on the strict, mean-spirited Mrs. Richardson, whose reputation as the meanest teacher at school seems justified. Energetic and imaginative, Heidi takes her zeal to the limits, and with a few well-aimed bad deeds, promptly loses the support of her family, her friend Lynette, and a congenial school principal. Mills chronicles the concerns of this age group with grace and humor, giving their minor problems a just and weighty treatment.

Mills, Claudia. *The One and Only Cynthia Jane Thornton.* Macmillan, 1986. $12.95 (0-02-767090-2). paper avail.
FORMAT: Novel   GRADES: 3–5.

Tireless talker Cynthia's self-confidence takes a dive after she realizes, for the first time, that not everyone is interested in every story she tells. She gets it back, but not without some bruises, and not without the discovery that doling out her talents has its own rewards. Fast-paced, and a good introduction to this author, who brings out another engaging novel each year, such as *After Fifth Grade, the World!* (see above) and *Dynamite Dinah.*

Robinson, Mary. *Give It Up, Mom.* Houghton, 1989. $13.95 (0-395-49700-0). paper avail.
FORMAT: Novel   GRADES: 7–up.

Rayne wants her mother to stop smoking, and the lengths she goes to in order to bring about her goal are comic in the extreme.

Sachar, Louis. *Dogs Don't Tell Jokes.* Knopf, 1991. LB $14.99 (0-679-92017-X). paper avail.
FORMAT: Novel   GRADES: 4–6.

Gary "Goon" Boone tells jokes instead of having conversations, and almost everyone—parents, teachers, schoolmates—is tired of him. Then he goes for stand-up, and succeeds. Readers may feel a bit benumbed by the endless litany of bad jokes; Sachar's talent for original humor is watered down by too-familiar riddles. Still, Gary is a likeable, completely good-hearted boy, who is ultimately refreshingly frank about his own shortcomings.

Sachar, Louis. *Sixth Grade Secrets.* Scholastic, 1987. $12.95 (0-590-40709-0). paper avail.
FORMAT: Novel   GRADES: 4–6.

The author of *There's a Boy in the Girls' Bathroom* shows how easy it is for one secret to become a catacomb of secrets, both harmful and harmless. Laura's club, Pig City, requires secrets of its members as "insurance" against them telling anyone else of the club's existence. Sachar creates a bunch of kids with worries that are quite real; his playful well-paced story proves that he has an impeccable ear for classroom banter.

Scheffler, Ursel. *Stop Your Crowing, Kasimir!* **Illus. by Silke Brix-Henker.**
Carolrhoda, 1988. $12.95 (0-87614-323-0).
FORMAT: Picture book   GRADES: Kindergarten–Grade 3.

Katy has a farm that the neighbors—city-dwellers who moved to the
countryside housing development looking for peaceful surroundings—
consider picture-book perfect. But they hate her noisy rooster, Kasimir,
and the manure Katy spreads in her garden. Katy is forced from her
home and a disco moves in, serving up lots of noise and just desserts.
Reminiscent in many ways of Joan Blos's *Old Henry*, this story is uncom-
promising in its warning of what intolerance breeds. The book's design
is clumsy, but given Scheffler's all-or-nothing perspective, that can be
tolerated.

Spinelli, Jerry. *Maniac Magee.* Little, Brown, 1990. $14.95 (0-316-80722-2). paper
avail.
FORMAT: Novel   GRADES: 6–up.

A Newbery Medal winner, this is an occasionally long-winded, but always affecting, parable about racism and ignorance. Jeffrey Magee is
homeless for the second time, taking to the streets for a year-long flight
that fuels a host of legends and softens the lines of segregation between
two parts of town, the white East End and the black West End. The
illusory writing style is a brave change from the realism of Spinelli's
other books; fans of his tongue-in-cheek, streetwise tone may find it an
integral part of this story, ballast for the mythic shifting portrait of Maniac's year on the run.

Swope, Sam. *The Araboolies of Liberty Street.* **Illus. by Barry Root.**
Crown, 1989. LB $15.99 (0-517-57411-X).
FORMAT: Picture book   GRADES: Preschool–Grade 3.

Symbolism abounds, the messages are clear, but try this book anyway. A
crabby neighbor, General Pinch, restricts all fun in a neighborhood, but
not even he can reign in the exuberance of the newly moved-in
Araboolies. These free-living folk encourage all the children to resist the
General's rules and regulations, and in fact, they stage a coup. Refreshing and upbeat, and kids *like* this lesson.

Additional Titles

The following titles, annotated elsewhere in this book (see index), could
also fit the "Corrective Humor" category.

Blos, Joan W. *Old Henry*
Browne, Anthony. *Willy the Wimp*

Estes, Eleanor. *The Hundred Dresses*
Henkes, Kevin. *The Zebra Wall*
Holmes, Barbara Ware. *Charlotte the Starlet*
Kerr, M. E. *Dinky Hocker Shoots Smack!*
King-Smith, Dick. *Babe: The Gallant Pig*
McNulty, Faith. *The Elephant Who Couldn't Forget*
Montgomery, L. M. *Anne of Green Gables*
Round, Graham. *Hangdog*
Sachar, Louis. *There's a Boy in the Girls' Bathroom*
Zolotow, Charlotte. *The Quarreling Book*

3: Blunting the World's Rough Edges

Healing Humor

*A*ll the clichés are poised to take over: laughter is the best medicine, comedy is a cure, humor resuscitates and heals (carried to excess by Norman Cousins in *The Anatomy of an Illness*). But it is true that through laughter there is a release of energy, a regeneration. Some would say it is the opposite of apathy, nullity, and despair; hence, essential for survival.

Children's joyous play has always been a release of energy, an outlet from the rigidity of serious-minded adults. Kids are mercurial, and can only hold out so long before they must fly in the face of the ominous constraints of logic, reason, consistency, grammar, etc., found in the world of oldlings.

As for teenagers, there may never be a time in life when humor is more important than in the ravages of the adolescent years. It becomes a serious means of bypassing problems—even if only temporarily—when homework, parental pressures, raging hormones, peer troubles, and romantic issues threaten to sink the most buoyant souls. Humor *can* be rejuvenating. Refuge in others—a wink, a wave, a grinning nod, a funny passage in a book about others *just like them*—can help children and teenagers transcend points of pain. There is a healing relief through a relaxation of imperatives as youngsters learn to toy with fixed, seemingly unfathomable, unwavering, inflexible structures.

This is the most praiseworthy aspect of humor, where charity of heart is at work; it transcends barriers and welds together, bringing with it a sense of belonging that is required for any child's ecology of soul and self. No invective, nor malice—it not only heals, but delights. If it did not, "happy endings" would not be such an immutable fixture of story-telling.

Adler, C. S. *Mismatched Summer.* Putnam, 1991. $14.95 (0-399-21776-2).
FORMAT: Novel   GRADES: 5–up.

By alternating Meg's and Micale's first-person narrations, Adler supplies readers with distinct, humorously personal perspectives on (and excuses for) two girls who learn to like each other despite their largely overrated differences. If the outcome is a foregone conclusion, the book gains strength by depicting a realistic bending of two fairly determined wills. Summery, seaside reading.

Alexander, Martha. *Nobody Asked ME If I Wanted a Baby Sister.* **Illus. by the author.** Dial, 1971. LB $10.89 (0-8037-6402-2). paper avail.
FORMAT: Picture book   GRADES: Preschool–Grade 3.

With all the attention new babies need, perhaps it's no wonder that Oliver decides that life would be better if he gave his new sister away. A charming version of an all-too-common problem, and even after all the more elaborate sibling stories of the 1980s, this picture book is still one of the best. See also Alexander's 1979 book, *When the New Baby Comes, I'm Moving,* for another sweetly reassuring comedy about Oliver.

Anholt, Catherine. *Truffles Is Sick.* **Illus. by the author.** Little, Brown, 1987. $9.95 (0-316-04259-5).
FORMAT: Picture book   GRADES: Preschool–Grade 2.

Anholt's distinctive style makes Truffles a piglet to watch. He wakes up in the middle of the night, crying that he doesn't feel well, and the next day he's even worse. He doesn't like the medicine Father tries to give him, but he does like curling up in Mother's lap with tea, cookies, and his favorite book. Slightly offbeat, completely entertaining, this is happily not the only book about Truffles; the other is *Truffles in Trouble.*

Auch, Mary Jane. *Cry Uncle!* Holiday, 1987. $14.95 (0-8234-0660-1).
FORMAT: Novel   GRADES: 4–7.

One of the surprise finds of the season is this relatively quiet story of a city-family-gone-country and their live-in relative, "loony" Uncle Will. He exhibits signs of dangerous senility, but he also saves the family from endless zucchini recipes by inventing an imaginary animal called a "squash ferret" that destroys the crop. He is saved from a nursing home in an inspired, joyful solution. Laden with humor, as dandy as a day on the farm, this tale is heartwarming to boot.

Bate, Lucy. *Little Rabbit's Loose Tooth.* **Illus. by Diane de Groat.** Crown, 1975. LB $15.00 (0-517-52240-3). paper avail.
FORMAT: Picture book   GRADES: Preschool–Grade 3.

The quintessential guide to coping with the loss of that all-important first tooth, this is also a quietly humorous celebration of family togetherness and caring.

Bawden, Nina. *The Peppermint Pig.* HarperCollins, 1975. LB $13.89 (0-397-31618-6). paper avail.

FORMAT: Novel   GRADES: 6–up.

The runt of the litter becomes a prized family pet when a British family moves to the country. Bawden's story, set at the turn of the century, explores the serious themes of growing up with warmth, sensitivity, and humor.

Block, Francesca Lia. *Witch Baby.* HarperCollins, 1991. LB $13.89 (0-06-020548-2).

FORMAT: Novel   GRADES: 7–up.

The sequel to *Weetzie Bat* finds daughter Witch Baby feeling disenfranchised, overlooked, ignored—yes, she's exhibiting classic symptoms found in most teenager-problem novels. The difference is the plugged-in language and sweetly screwball perspectives that made the first book such a late 20th-century knockout. Don't look for deep meanings; let readers fasten their seatbelts and enjoy this open air ride through West Coast adolescence. And don't miss *Weetzie Bat* or the third book about her family, *Cherokee Bat and the Goat Guys.*

Bottner, Barbara. *Let Me Tell You Everything: Memoirs of a Lovesick Intellectual.* HarperCollins, 1989. $12.95 (0-06-020596-2). paper avail.

FORMAT: Novel   GRADES: 7–up.

Even though Brogan says she is a serious girl, with worldly aims and aspirations, she's hard to take seriously as an intellectual. Still, her awakening to the potential of real love is chronicled in a snappy first-person narration that—if full of teenage angst—is also irresistible.

Brown, Marc. *Arthur's Nose.* Illus. by the author. Little, Brown, 1976. LB $14.95 (0-316-11193-7). paper avail.

FORMAT: Picture book   GRADES: Preschool–Grade 3.

This is the first book about the awkward aardvark and his travails, for elementary-age readers. No one could have foreseen that this fellow would become one of the most endearing characters in children's books, but Arthur is a champ. See also *Arthur's Eyes*, among others. Oh, about that nose. He learns to like it. Obviously, readers do, too.

Browne, Anthony. *The Tunnel.* Illus. by the author. Knopf, 1990. LB $12.99 (0-394-94582-4).

FORMAT: Picture book   GRADES: 1–5.

When her brother Jack disappears down a tunnel, Rose is determined to go after him, despite the difference and quarrels that usually divide them. Like Ada in Sendak's *Outside Over There*, the missing sibling provides an opportunity to redress old wrongs and to discover bonds of affection that previously had gone unnoticed. A profusion of dark, surrealistic images give this happy ending an edge.

Carter, Alden. *Wart, Son of Toad.* Putnam, 1985. $13.95 (0-448-47770-X). paper avail.
FORMAT: Novel GRADES: 7–up.

Steve, the son of the most hated teacher in high school, struggles on alone after his mother and sister are killed in an accident. While the themes are serious, this first novel has scenes of wry hilarity in Steve/Wart's darkest moments and quiet humor that underscores the poignancy of his dilemma. Carter's later books (*Sheila's Dying, Growing Season*), though more polished, are not as accessible. This novel is a good introduction to the author's work.

Cassedy, Sylvia. *Behind the Attic Wall.* HarperCollins, 1983. LB $14.89 (0-690-04337-6). paper avail.
FORMAT: Novel GRADES: 3–7.

Imagine Frances Hodgson Burnett writing about an oily little girl who smelled bad, lied, and cheated, and you have an idea of Cassedy's complex, imaginative novel. Before this talented writer died, she proved that she knew a thing or two about a child's ability to heal herself of the many pains inflicted on her by a clumsy, dispassionate world. She also knew plenty about grand finales.

Cassedy, Sylvia. *Lucie Babbidge's House.* HarperCollins, 1989. LB $13.89 (0-690-04798-3).
FORMAT: Novel GRADES: 4–7.

Cassedy's last novel is not as assuredly upbeat as the other two, but it offers children the means for carving out some contentment from any event, no matter how bitter. In the orphanage, Lucie is despised by the others and considered obstinate by her teacher. Secret from everyone is Lucie's house, where she is cherished; secret, also, is her best friend and correspondent, Delia Hornsby. Cassedy's craft is such that she leaves her heroine right where readers found her in the first pages, yet no one will doubt Lucie's quiet, ultimate triumph.

Cassedy, Sylvia. *M.E. and Morton.* HarperCollins, 1987. $13.89 (0-690-04562-X). paper avail.
FORMAT: Novel GRADES: 4–7.

Behind the Attic Wall was the debut of a highly imaginative writer who made readers love a despicable little girl. Now Cassedy writes a more realistic, still humorous story of childhood heartbreaks and solutions.

Mary Ella doesn't appreciate Morton, her mildly retarded older brother, until eccentric, fearless Polly moves to the neighborhood. Cassedy's story unfolds on a canvas of wistful moods and a loner's yearning to belong, showing the complicated emotions that arise from a simple need to be loved. The strokes are broad, textured, and intense.

Conford, Ellen. *The Things I Did for Love*. Bantam, 1987. $13.95 (0-553-05431-7). paper avail.

FORMAT: Novel　GRADES: 5–up.

From the moment Stephanie asks herself, in the form of a school project, "Why do fools fall in love?" her own personal life becomes fraught with disaster and mishap. Her relationships with three boys nearly slay her, and while Stephanie figures out just who she loves, readers will have a fine time trying to outguess Canford's fast moves and broadly comic scenes. For lifting the back-to-school blues.

Cooney, Caroline B. *The Girl Who Invented Romance*. Bantam, 1988. $13.95 (0-553-05473-2).

FORMAT: Novel　GRADES: 7–up.

Cooney's books—in paperback and hardcover—have been pleasing fans for years; she takes the concerns of ordinary suburban teenagers and makes them compelling and often hilarious. This lighthearted novel strikes just the right note about the funny and not-so-funny affairs of the heart.

Crutcher, Chris. *The Crazy Horse Electric Game*. Greenwillow, 1987. $11.75 (0-688-06683-6). paper avail.

FORMAT: Novel　GRADES: 7–up.

Crutcher's tour de force, a story of renewal and hope, confronts the fragility of love and the ways in which people unintentionally inflict pain on one another. Willie, a minor baseball legend, is in an accident that leaves him with strokelike disabilities. This wry, occasionally funny, always honest book resounds with compassion for people tripped up by their own weaknesses. It explores sophisticated themes with both poetic sensibility and gritty realism.

Dabcovich, Lydia. *Mrs. Huggins and Her Hen Hannah*. Illus. by the author. Dutton, 1985. $12.95 (0-525-44203-0). paper avail.

FORMAT: Picture book　GRADES: Preschool–Grade 3.

The premise is anything but funny: Mrs. Huggins's best friend Hannah, a hen, is no more. The kind-hearted woman is bereft and lonely, until she finds Hannah's own child, a baby chick who becomes her welcome companion. Dabcovich's pictures convey the good-spirited fun of this tale and make a tidy, but poignant lesson on loss. Look for her other bold books, *Busy Beavers* and *Sleepy Bear* among them.

Danziger, Paula. *The Cat Ate My Gymsuit.* Delacorte, 1974. $14.95 (0-385-28183-8). paper avail.
FORMAT: Novel   GRADES: 7–up.

Danziger's gifts for humor are well known, but underneath the glib narratives in her books are buckets of compassion for the woes of adolescence. Marcy's life is irrevocably changed by the arrival of a new English teacher, and readers will love Marcy, both before, and after. Other funny bites by this author are this book's sequel, *There's a Bat in Bunk Five*, as well as *The Divorce Express* and *It's an Aardvark-Eat-Turtle World*.

Gallo, Donald R., ed. *Connections: Short Stories by Outstanding Writers for Young Adults.* Dell, 1990. paper $3.50 (0-440-20768-1).
FORMAT: Short stories   GRADES: 7–up.

Infused with warmth and discerning respect for young adults and their concerns, this collection contains both elegant and humorous treats. Robin Brancato, Chris Crutcher, Sue Ellen Bridgers, Colby Rodowsky, M. E. Kerr, and Ouida Sebestyen are among the contributors in this well-executed companion book to Gallo's *Sixteen* and *Visions*. Sampling allowed, but so is a voracious downing of the entire book in one sitting.

Gerber, Merrill Joan. *Handsome as Anything.* Scholastic, 1990. $13.95 (0-590-43019-X). paper avail.
FORMAT: Novel   GRADES: 7–up.

Rachel likes to take issues to their natural extremes in order to see how she feels about them, including areas of romance. Which boy would she marry? Her parents' choice? A motorcycling Zen Buddhist? None of the above? If the angst occasionally seems too strong, it is tempered by flashes of humor and a jolt or two of zaniness that keeps the plot moving.

Henkes, Kevin. *Two Under Par.* Illus. by the author. Greenwillow, 1987. $10.25 (0-688-06708-5).
FORMAT: Novel   GRADES: 2–6.

Wedge is a slightly overweight boy of 10, facing all the adjustments that go along with having a stepfather. The complicated process of learning acceptance and being accepted is one Henkes explores with as sure a novelist's hand as any of his picture-book offerings. In this touching and funny book, there are no easy or sudden solutions. Just a sense of isolation slipping away, as Wedge reaches out and receives much more than he expects.

Henkes, Kevin. *The Zebra Wall.* **Illus. by the author.** Greenwillow, 1988. $10.95 (0-688-07568-1). paper avail.
FORMAT: Novel   GRADES: 3–up.

The watercolor worlds of Henkes's picture books sometimes distract readers from his harsh-world themes. His second novel is even more unflinching and sensitive than *Two Under Par.* Adine doesn't like her Aunt Irene with a whiskery moustache and a habit of smoking narrow brown cigarettes, but the woman is moving into Adine's room while the Vorlobs adjust to a new baby. This is not another new baby story; Henkes understands that every worry in a child's life has many layers. He depicts Adine's concerns with depth and sweetly persuasive touches of compassion, treating the thoughts and feelings of an eight-year-old with uncanny justice.

Hermes, Patricia. *A Place for Jeremy.* Harcourt, 1987. $13.95 (0-15-262350-7).
FORMAT: Novel   GRADES: 3–7.

In a fast-paced and funny sequel to *What If They Knew?*, Jeremy stays with her grandparents in Brooklyn while her parents are in South America adopting a baby. Jeremy is afraid that her parents will love the baby more than they love her and that her grandparents will move to Miami if their house is torn down to make way for a highway. Hermes adds little new to the "place of one's own" theme, but scenes between Jeremy and her grandfather are heartwarming, and classroom antics have been depicted with rib-tickling precision.

Homes, A. M. *Jack.* Macmillan, 1989. $14.95 (0-02-744831-2). paper avail.
FORMAT: Novel   GRADES: 7–up.

Homes's debut novel features a wryly vulnerable, wise-cracking narration by Jack, who is trying to make sense of his father's revelation that a roommate is actually his lover. Compassion underscores the humor in the story; humor illuminates the compassion. Sometimes sharp, often poignant, this story shows how a sense of the comic or the absurd can be merely a signpost for an intellect capable of grappling with life's big questions.

Honeycutt, Natalie. *Josie's Beau.* Avon, 1988. paper $2.95 (0-380-70524-9).
FORMAT: Novel   GRADES: 6–8.

Josie and Beau have known each other most of their lives, and, Beau has confessed, he loved her in fourth grade—for a while anyway. But this is junior high, and she is suffering from near-terminal pangs of ordinariness, which this book ultimately celebrates. Readers will enjoy the story for Josie's budding independence rather than for any message it has to offer.

Hurwitz, Johanna. *Aldo Applesauce.* **Illus. by John Wallner.** Morrow, 1979.
$12.95 (0-688-22199-8).
FORMAT: Chapter book   GRADES: 3–5.

Aldo Sossi, a quiet fourth-grader facing all the pain of moving, makes his
debut in Hurwitz's tale. He later starred in *Aldo Ice Cream;* both books are
warm and humorous. They will win readers with their close-up looks at
ordinary concerns, peppered with relief-bringing chuckles.

Kaye, Marilyn. *Phoebe; Daphne.* Harcourt, 1987. $13.95 each (0-15-200430-0; 0-
15-200434-3). paper avail.
FORMAT: Novels   GRADES: 4–up.

The first two titles in Kaye's enjoyable Sisters series star Phoebe and
Daphne, respectively. Phoebe, returning from camp to find her friends
only interested in boys and clothes, decides to volunteer at the library
and ends up defending banned books. Daphne is a shy seventh-grader
who learns how to act and speak for herself. Breezily written, these
books offer much thoughtfulness and humor, well above most series's
fare.

Keller, Holly. *Lizzie's Invitation.* **Illus. by the author.** Greenwillow, 1987.
$11.75 (0-688-06124-9).
FORMAT: Picture book   GRADES: Preschool–Grade 3.

Everyone gets invitations to Kate's party. Everyone, it seems, but Lizzie.
The day of the party, it is raining, and Lizzie feels terrible. She goes for a
walk and finds a friend, Amanda, who wasn't invited to the party either.
Keller reassures children about one of the most difficult times—being
unwanted. The ending is a little too convenient; being left out can last a
long time. But the pictures make a sad occasion gay, and the girls' resourcefulness is a lesson for all.

Klein, Norma. *Just Friends.* Knopf, 1991. LB $13.99 (0-679-90213-9). paper avail.
FORMAT: Novel   GRADES: 7–up.

This is a humorous novel of the complications that beset four best friends
living in New York City. The late Norma Klein could be serious when she
wanted to be (*My Life as a Body*), but when she wished to laugh with
teenagers—and not at them—about their various angsts, her sense of
comedy was perfectly timed.

Kline, Suzy. *Herbie Jones and the Class Gift.* **Illus. by Richard Williams.**
Putnam, 1987. $12.95 (0-399-21452-6). paper avail.
FORMAT: Novel   GRADES: 2–6.

Hapless Herbie is back with his troublemaking friend Ray, for one last
third-grade adventure before school is out, and the subject is Miss Pink-

ham's end-of-the-year present. Ray and Herbie are put in charge of packaging the gift—a simple task that turns into a fiasco. A heartfelt, funny story to add to the growing list of Herbie Jones titles.

Kunhardt, Edith. *Where's Peter?* **Illus. by the author.** Greenwillow, 1988. $11.95 (0-688-07204-6).
FORMAT: Picture book   GRADES: Preschool–Grade 2.

The creator of *Danny's Birthday* this time shows a loving human family, in sunny pastel washes, adjusting to a new baby. Peter once pretended to be invisible so his parents would search for him. Now that the baby has arrived, Peter feels invisible, but not on purpose. His solution is ingenious. A simplicity in the telling and a realistic time frame make a sweetly persuasive story, aided by low-key humor.

Lobel, Arnold. *Uncle Elephant.* **Illus. by the author.** HarperCollins, 1981. LB $12.89 (0-06-023980-8).
FORMAT: Chapter book   GRADES: 2–4.

Many readers succumb to the charms of *Frog and Toad Are Friends* without ever realizing that Lobel penned and illustrated other endearing tales. When Uncle Elephant takes in his small, apparently orphaned nephew, the affection between the two fairly rolls off the page. Just as heartwarming with a more aggressive humor than the quiet chuckles found here is *Owl at Home*, about a bird whose bouts with small domestic crises are artlessly innocent and recognizable.

Lowry, Lois. *Anastasia Krupnik.* **Illus. by Diane de Groat.** Houghton, 1979. $13.45 (0-395-28629-8). paper avail.
FORMAT: Novel   GRADES: 4–6.

This witty, charming story of an intelligent fourth-grader and her family is the book that launched a series. Now Anastasia's small brother stars in his own books, including *Atta Boy, Sam!* Lowry has a genius for depicting families at both their worst and their loving best, all doled out with humor.

Marshall, James. *George and Martha.* **Illus. by the author.** Houghton, 1972. $13.95 (0-395-16619-5). paper avail.
FORMAT: Picture book   GRADES: Preschool–Grade 3.

The beginning of the story of a beautiful friendship between George and Martha, hippopotami who mostly treat each other with genuine affection. Marshall is never too sweet, and always funny.

Marshall, James. *George and Martha Round and Round.* **Illus. by the author.** Houghton, 1988. $13.95 (0-395-46763-2). paper avail.
FORMAT: Picture book   GRADES: Preschool–Grade 3.

In five stories about these best friends, Martha proves inconsiderate by repainting one of George's artworks, and George proves himself capable of giving a present he'd rather get—and does. These two animals cavort through their arguments with high humor, and perhaps that's why children are so enamored of the pair.

Mazer, Norma Fox. *A, My Name Is Ami.* Scholastic, 1991. paper $2.95 (0-590-43896-4).
FORMAT: Novel   GRADES: 3–7.

Ami's friendship with Mia means the world to both girls; they are inseparable. It is lucky for Ami to have such a constant, because everything else in her life is going wrong, wrong, wrong. In this series of books, which includes *B, My Name Is Bunny* and *C, My Name Is Cal*, Mazer uses humor to pen caring stories about ordinary kids. Likable, lighthearted fare, most of the books are available in hardcover as well.

Miller, Mary Jane. *Me and My Name.* Viking, 1990. $11.95 (0-670-83196-4).
FORMAT: Novel   GRADES: 4–6.

Among Erin Mitchell's many problems is the overriding one of whether she should allow her loving stepfather to adopt her and give her his name. Miller makes this and all Erin's concerns full-bodied issues whose outcomes cannot be predicted. Welcome to real life, Erin's way.

Oppenheim, Joanne. *The Story Book Prince.* **Illus. by Rosanne Litzinger.** Harcourt, 1987. $12.95 (0-15-200590-0).
FORMAT: Picture book   GRADES: Preschool–Grade 2.

A young prince refuses to go to sleep, and that puts the palace and its occupants in a tizzy. Nothing works until a wise woman appears at the gate with a solution—she reads him to sleep. This may be an obvious pitch for bedtime reading, but it is also a clever new-fashioned fairy tale, with bold illustrations that leave the rules of perspective behind and fashion royal personages from flat shapes and exaggerated characteristics.

Pendergraft, Patricia. *The Legend of Daisy Flowerdew.* Putnam, 1990. $14.95 (0-399-22176-X).
FORMAT: Novel   GRADES: 5–up.

Poor unfeminine, unlovely Daisy Flowerdew is raised by her Granny Henry, and then given by her mother and new husband Delbert (along with $10) to Elmer Goots. This is a fairy tale, as lyrically told as Pendergraft's previous books, but full of a snipping, whining, miserable bunch of characters. Blunt, but folksy, and always fine for fans.

Pevsner, Stella. *Sister of the Quints.* Houghton, 1987. $13.45 (0-89919-498-2). FORMAT: Novel   GRADES: 5–8.

It is quite believable that an eighth-grader, the stepsister of quintuplets, would have trouble getting her father's and stepmother's attention. Even though the quints are ultimately just window-dressing for a fairly standard postdivorce story, Pevsner makes some good points about families in disarray, with an always light touch.

Powell, Randy. *My Underrated Year.* Farrar, 1988. $15.00 (0-374-35109-0). paper avail.
FORMAT: Novel   GRADES: 7–up.

What do you do when the girl you love is also your archrival for the top spot on the tennis team? For sophomore Roger Ottosen, any new friendship may come at the expense of the realization of goals set for a great year. This is an understated, surprisingly gentle, and funny look at a boy's first love. More recently, Powell wrote about the joys of distant crushes and up-close encounters of the potentially romantic kind, in *Is Kissing a Girl Who Smokes Like Licking an Ashtray?*

Schotter, Roni. *Captain Snap and the Children of Vinegar Lane.* Illus. by **Marcia Sewall.** Orchard, 1989. LB $14.99 (0-531-08397-7).
FORMAT: Picture book   GRADES: Preschool–Grade 3.

This is a lively, generous tale of good children who in their exuberance have a natural enemy in the meanest man on the lane. But when he falls ill, the children prove the value of being good neighbors, and a glorious understanding is reached.

Seidler, Tor. *The Tar Pit.* Farrar, 1987. $14.00 (0-374-37383-3). paper avail.
FORMAT: Novel   GRADES: 4–6.

The author of the satirical *A Rat's Tale* writes this time of Edward Small, Jr., a boy who thinks the odds in life are stacked against him. However, he has a friend, an allosaurus named Alexander, who will take care of all the idiots in the world if only Edward will point them out. This wry, thoughtful, well-constructed novel of a boy leading a life of quiet desperation is laden with brightly imaginative, healing moments of humor.

Smith, Robert Kimmel. *Mostly Michael.* Illus. by **Katherine Coville.** Delacorte, 1987. $13.95 (0-385-29545-6). paper avail.
FORMAT: Novel   GRADES: 3–7.

Told in diary installments, this story follows Michael from April through December, when his baby brother is born. These are droll, funny entries, about friendship, siblings, and cheating on a book report and ultimately discovering a love for books. Occasionally, Michael sounds far older and wiser than his 11 years. But his is a life of small, but important accomplishments, and readers sympathize with him and cheer him on.

Springstubb, Tricia. *With a Name Like Lulu, Who Needs More Trouble?*
Delacorte, 1989. $14.95 (0-385-29823-4).
FORMAT: Novel   GRADES: 4–6.

The silly title may be misleading. This is an intriguing story of a ten-year-old worrier, who needs to conquer fear and to stand up to her overeager mother. Lulu's first love is Little League, but her greatest "catch" comes when a toddler leaps out a third-story window. A book with one idea— that heroism may come to those who least expect it—serves up comic moments like shiny coins. Not all the loose ends are tied up, but if Lulu's tale is occasionally clumsy, it nevertheless offers effervescent fun.

Stevenson, James. *Fast Friends.* **Illus. by the author.** Greenwillow, 1979.
$10.88 (0-688-84197-X).
FORMAT: Storybook   GRADES: Kindergarten–Grade 4.

The *New Yorker* cartoonist, beloved for his fast and furious picture books, here pens a longer work—two friendship stories

Stevenson, Jocelyn. *O'Diddy.* **Illus. by Sue Truesdell.** Random, 1988. LB $6.99
(0-394-99609-7). paper avail.
FORMAT: Chapter book   GRADES: 2–4.

A lively account of the efforts of a retired imaginary friend, O'Diddy, to get the child he played with to remember he existed. Truesdell brings an exhilarating comic artistic sensibility to the tale; Stevenson's witty telling makes a strong case for keeping good friends, imagined or not.

Swallow, Pamela Curtis. *Leave It to Christy.* Putnam, 1987. $14.95 (0-399-
21482-8). paper avail.
FORMAT: Novel   GRADES: 5–up.

Christy explains that she was a big cheese in sixth grade, but seventh grade isn't so hot. She lands the lead in a play but only because she hams it up, disgracing herself in front of her sister. No matter what happens in this story, readers know Christy will come out on top; she makes happy endings wherever she goes. But it's not slick, or too sweet. Because of the humor in Swallow's writing, Christy is a peach—tart and just right.

Thomas, Joyce Carol, ed. *A Gathering of Flowers: Stories about Being Young in America.* HarperCollins, 1990. LB $14.89 (0-06-026174-9). paper avail.
FORMAT: Short stories   GRADES: 6–up.

Thomas offers a noble collection of stories representing and celebrating various aspects of American culture and people. African-Americans, whites, Mexicans, Native Americans, Latino families, and others populate this eclectic, seemingly encompassing universe. Generous points of view may help defray a reader's dismay that there is no time to linger, savor, and consider each well-realized setting.

Travers, P. L. *Mary Poppins.* **Illus. by Mary Shepard.** Harcourt, 1981. $14.95 (0-15-252408-8). paper avail.

FORMAT: Novel   GRADES: 4–6.

The adventures of Britain's fly-away nanny; don't forget *Mary Poppins Comes Back, Mary Poppins in the Park,* and *Mary Poppins Opens the Door.* For children who believe that Walt Disney had the last word on this magical miss, please send them to the text, where the jolly times truly began.

Viorst, Judith. *Good-Bye Book.* **Illus. by Kay Chorao.** Macmillan, 1988. $13.95 (0-689-31308-X). paper avail.

FORMAT: Picture book   GRADES: Preschool–Grade 1.

A small boy begs, wheedles, and worries through his parents' preparations to go out, without him, for the night. He enumerates all the horrors of baby-sitters and lists the symptoms of his sudden fatal illness. Viorst delivers this soliloquy with just the right amount of lament and fussing; Chorao's pictures soothe away the anger of the words.

Voigt, Cynthia. *Izzy, Willy-Nilly.* Macmillan, 1986. $15.95 (0-689-31202-4). paper avail.

FORMAT: Novel   GRADES: 7–up.

The loss of her legs in a car accident results in changes Izzy believes she is ready to face, as well as those she never anticipated. Newbery Medal-winning Voigt uses Izzy's wry, mocking humor to express some of the most poignant moments in the book; as Izzy cheers the small gymnast she imagines somersaulting around in her brain, so will readers laud Izzy. The books of the Tillerman Saga, also by this author, are incredibly fertile soil for readers to take on next, but Izzy is a heroine they won't soon forget.

Wells, Rosemary. *Shy Charles.* **Illus. by the author.** Dial, 1988. LB $11.89 (0-8037-0564-6). paper avail.

FORMAT: Picture book   GRADES: Preschool–Grade 3.

Just because he prefers the company of himself to others, and just because he seldom speaks, doesn't make Charles a passive dormouse. When he is needed for an emergency, he performs splendidly, comforting the victim and summoning help. A bold argument for allowing children to be themselves, handled with compassion and charm.

Wersba, Barbara. *Beautiful Losers.* Dell, 1990. paper $3.50 (0-440-20580-8).
FORMAT: Novel   GRADES: 7–up.

With integrity and heartbreaking honesty, Wersba relates the third and most joyous of the Rita Formica trilogy. Rita and Arnold are not only reunited, but living together. Arnold, poetic and pure as ever (and maddening in his unflappability), finds beauty in a leaky faucet. But Rita sees nothing lovely about riding through snow on a bike to her jobs just to make ends meet. Will Rita learn to view the world as her parents do and leave her man behind? The ending is very happy and very real—life is not perfect but Rita and Arnold together can meet, head-on, all imperfections in their primrose path. Readers will put this one down with a deeply satisfied sigh; Wersba has humorously melded realism with the romantic.

Wersba, Barbara. *Fat: A Love Story.* HarperCollins, 1987. LB $11.89 (0-06-026415-2).
FORMAT: Novel   GRADES: 6–up.

Wersba's sometimes skewed, always funny view of the outrages of adolescence usually centers on odd parties who love one another, however briefly, and then part. But happy endings abound in this novel about obese Rita Formica's hopeless love for Robert Swann. Fortunately, she survives to find true love in fledgling cheesecake company owner Arnold Bromberg, whom most readers will have loved from his first appearance in the book. Two gentle, wonderfully human souls, without (or in spite of) weight loss, find romance after trodding a path strewn with heartbreak and humor. Wersba's sympathy for her characters and their many faults give this story uncommon depth.

Wersba, Barbara. *Just Be Gorgeous.* HarperCollins, 1988. $11.95 (0-06-026359-8). paper avail.
FORMAT: Novel   GRADES: 7–up.

Two misfits find brief happiness together, then go their separate ways. Heidi falls in love with Jeffrey the first time she meets him, despite his blue eyeshadow, fur coat, and blithe admission that he is gay. This duo will rightly remind many of the pairing in *Carnival in My Mind.* It doesn't break new ground for Wersba, but she brings readers a welcome message: love often goes awry, but is never wasted.

Wersba, Barbara. *Love Is the Crooked Thing.* Dell, 1990. paper $3.50 (0-440-20542-5).
FORMAT: Novel   GRADES: 7–up.

It has all been a mistake, readers learn at the end of this sequel to Wersba's eccentric and funny romance, *Fat.* Arnold has broken up with

Rita Formica at her parents' request. Taken by itself, this is an upbeat story of a young woman's self-discovery. As a sequel—well, those rooting for true love despite the odds would hope that yet another sequel is in the works. (See *Beautiful Losers*.)

Wersba, Barbara. *Wonderful Me.* HarperCollins, 1989. LB $12.89 (0-06-026362-8). paper avail.
FORMAT: Novel   GRADES: 7–up.

Heidi is back, but her romantic batting average is still zero. After recovering from her love for a homosexual man, Heidi gets involved with a handsome, romantic soul—her English teacher—who has wooed her with poetic, anonymous notes. A shocking ending does not detract from Heidi's budding belief that perhaps she is wonderful after all.

Willey, Margaret. *The Bigger Book of Lydia.* HarperCollins, 1988. paper $3.25 (0-06-447049-0).
FORMAT: Novel   GRADES: 7–up.

Each complementing the other's personalities and obsessions, Lydia (who hates being small) and Michelle (an anorexic) heal each other and become whole again. Generous, incisive, and wry.

Wilson, Budge. *The Leaving.* Putnam, 1992. $14.95 (0-399-21878-5).
FORMAT: Short stories   GRADES: 6–up.

Wilson's stories have an aching tautness that will be conveyed to readers in every sensitive, humorous paragraph of this collection. If the curse of adolescence is too many emotions too densely packed, then the blessing is that writers such as this one can capture those feelings on the page.

Zolotow, Charlotte. *The Quarreling Book.* **Illus. by Arnold Lobel.** Harper-Collins, 1963. LB $12.89 (0-06-026976-6). paper avail.
FORMAT: Picture book   GRADES: Preschool–Grade 3.

Like a yawn that travels from yawner to viewer, so travel the bad feelings—that's the world according to this small book. But while there is no way to stop a yawn, a small dog does manage to turn around all those near-quarrels and make everyone's hearts glad once again. Zolotow isn't always this lighthearted, but the affection found in all her books prevents this one from becoming didactic. It has been enjoyed by children for 30 years.

Additional Titles

The following titles, annotated elsewhere in this book (see index), could also fit the "Healing Humor" category.

Blume, Judy. *Otherwise Known as Sheila the Great*
Blume, Judy. *Tales of a Fourth Grade Nothing*
Bond, Felicia. *Poinsettia and Her Family*
Brooks, Martha. *Paradise Cafe*
Browne, Anthony. *Gorilla*
Byars, Betsy. *Bingo Brown and the Language of Love*
Byars, Betsy. *The Burning Questions of Bingo Brown*
Caple, Kathy. *Harry's Smile*
Conford, Ellen. *A Job for Jenny Archer*
Dana, Barbara. *Necessary Parties*
Eastman, P. D. *Are You My Mother?*
Fakih, Kimberly Olson. *Grandpa Putter and Granny Hoe*
Fuchshuber, Annegert. *Giant Story/Mouse Tale*
Greenwald, Sheila. *Give Us a Great Big Smile, Rosy Cole*
Hall, Barbara. *Dixie Storms*
Jenkin-Pearce, Susie. *Bad Boris and the New Kitten*
Kitchen, Bert. *Tenrec's Twigs*
MacLachlan, Patricia. *Cassie Binegar*
Miller, Mary Jane. *Upside Down*
Naylor, Phyllis Reynolds. *The Agony of Alice*
Naylor, Phyllis Reynolds. *Alice in Rapture, Sort Of*
Paterson, Katherine. *The Great Gilly Hopkins*
Pendergraft, Patricia. *Hear the Wind Blow*
Reuter, Bjarne. *Buster's World*
Sendak, Maurice. *Where the Wild Things Are*
Sharmat, Marjorie Weinman. *Helga High-Up*
Smith, Janice Lee. *The Monster in the Third Dresser Drawer and Other Stories about Adam Joshua*
Spinelli, Jerry. *Maniac Magee*
Terris, Susan. *Author! Author!*
White, E. B. *Charlotte's Web*

4: Bonk!

Physical Humor

*T*he best physical humor is a fine art, as anyone who has chortled over the on-the-dime timing of the Keystone Cops or Charlie Chaplin knows. And while some readers might have difficulty defining it, they know it when they see it. The classic mishap in the literature of humor—the sight of a dignified personage felled by a banana peel—is funny because it topples that person from a stable position in the gravitational field. Spectators laugh at the sudden turn of events perhaps because (a) it is a sight in sharp contrast to what preceded it and (b) it produces a feeling of relief that someone other than themselves has been so dehumanized. When faced by such amoral sights (no one was pushed, the banana peel is blameless), the impulse for levity is nearly impossible to stifle.

Any perversion of motion can be funny—collisions, surprises, physical acrobatics, the relaxing of gravitational laws, things going places they don't belong, as in the case of Pinocchio's nose. Before the VCR became a household appliance, even a serious film in fast-forward or rewind mode inspired laughter. Old vaudevillians knew the value of slapsticks and sight gags, and so do such artists as David Macaulay in *Why the Chicken Crossed the Road* and Robin Bell Corfield in *Tumbledown*, in which an entire town is reduced to an aggregate of crumbled structures. Humor offers a Houdini-like freedom of motion that disentangles children and adults from the physical encumbrances of human vulnerability, making it possible to laugh even when it hurts; and more so when conveniently, but harmlessly, it happens to others.

Ackerman, Karen. *Song and Dance Man.* **Illus. by Stephen Gammell.**
Knopf, 1988. LB $15.99 (0-394-99330-6). paper avail.
FORMAT: Picture book   GRADES: Preschool–Grade 3.

An old vaudevillian has the chance to relive his finest moments when his
grandchildren follow him up to the attic and rejoice in his never-rusty
ability to slide, shuffle, and prance across the "stage," just as he did in
the "olden" days. Delightful, eccentric fare, and if readers haven't discovered artist Gammell until now, they're advised to look up this master's
other creations. A Caldecott Medal winner.

Anholt, Catherine. *Chaos at Cold Custard Farm.* **Illus. by the author.**
Oxford Univ. Pr., 1988. $13.95 (0-19-520645-2).
FORMAT: Picture book   GRADES: Preschool–Grade 2.

The creator of *Truffles* and *Truffles Is Sick* goes to the farm for this book.
The day at Cold Custard Farm begins as usual: Fred and Freda run the
place in an orderly fashion, nine animals help out the humans. But when
Fred and Freda have to go into town, the animals get into trouble. Luckily, the farmers return in time to restore everyone's good spirits. The
story is bland, but the pictures are suitably chaotic and sometimes so
busy that the action is hard to perceive. But there are bright colors, odd
perspectives, and an exuberant playfulness. The farm's goodwill will
spread to readers.

Banks, Lynne Reid. *I, Houdini: The Autobiography of a Self-Educated
Hamster.* **Illus. by Terry Riley.** Doubleday, 1988. $12.95 (0-385-24482-7). pa-
per avail.
FORMAT: Novel   GRADES: 5–up.

The title tells all. Slightly pompous Houdini, no slouch when it comes to
vocabulary, seems unaware of his own gift for humor. Houdini relates
the story of his acquisition by a family and the trial runs and trouble
spots that turn him into a great escapologist. Pure fun and full of comic
exaggeration, dramatic moments, and cliff-hangers.

Brock, Betty. *No Flying in the House.* **Illus. by Wallace Tripp.** HarperCollins,
1982. paper $3.95 (0-06-440130-8).
FORMAT: Novel   GRADES: 4–6.

A teacup-sized dog is guardian to a girl who learns, by kissing her elbow,
that she is an enchanted child, and one who can fly. This is the kind of
story that feels warmly familiar the first time readers meet it, full of
affection, fun, and moments of topsy-turvy pleasure.

Brown, Jeff. *Flat Stanley.* **Illus. by Tomi Ungerer.** HarperCollins, 1964. LB $13.89 (0-06-020681-0). paper avail.

FORMAT: Storybook   GRADES: 4–6.

Like the hero in William Joyce's *George Shrinks*, Stanley wakes up one morning to find his physical form slightly altered—he is flat as a magazine, and just as easy to mail. Is he worried? Is this frightening? Not in author Brown's hands. Stanley has a chipper attitude and takes full advantage of his deflated state. The book is instantly engaging and good for newly independent readers. Ungerer's cannily simple drawings provide many silly touches.

Browne, Anthony. *The Little Bear Book.* **Illus. by the author.** Doubleday, 1989. $6.95 (0-385-26006-7).

FORMAT: Picture book   GRADES: Preschool–Grade 1.

With a nod to *Harold and the Purple Crayon*, Browne has created a book for an audience younger than his usual works. A white bear, upon meeting a grouchy gorilla, draws him a stuffed toy to cuddle. After several such encounters, the bear draws a hole through a wall and waves good-bye to readers. Simultaneously tricky and simple, the book highlights this artist's gift for distilling concepts into crisp words, phrases, and pictures.

Chetwin, Grace. *Box and Cox.* **Illus. by David Small.** Macmillan, 1990. $13.95 (0-02-718314-9).

FORMAT: Picture book   GRADES: Preschool–Grade 3.

The broad visual humor of Small's pictures sends soaring this entertaining tale about two men who don't know they share the same boarding room. One has the night shift, one the day shift, and with the energetic machinations of their landlady, each man need never know the other exists. Still, all good things must come to an end, but when this little piece of theatricality comes to a close, most readers will want to go through it one more time.

Coxe, Molly. *Louella and the Yellow Balloon.* **Illus. by the author.** HarperCollins, 1988. $12.95 (0-690-04746-0).

FORMAT: Picture book   GRADES: Preschool–Grade 2.

Coxe's first book is a joy-filled celebration of a baby's innocent confrontations with danger. Patricia Pig takes her baby Louella to the circus and buys her a balloon. "Hold tight to the string," she tells her little pig. But Louella lets go and has to crawl, toddle, and leap after it, encountering nearly every performer, and ultimately tripping across the length of the tightrope. She is saved from a serious turn of events by Patricia, and not a moment too soon. The watercolors are bold and calliope bright; the action is fast and wonderfully far-fetched. Coxe is a newcomer with a welcome, if quirky, sense of humor.

Day, Alexandra. *Carl Goes Shopping.* Farrar, 1989. $11.95 (0-374-31110-2).
FORMAT: Picture book   GRADES: Preschool–Grade 3.

Young consumers will want to head to the mall with everyone's favorite faithful Rottweiler; this may be the first book to turn the inside of a department store into one of three leading characters. The other two characters, of course, are Carl and his baby-sized charge. The results of their antics within the store are invisible to the mother who returns and repeats that now-famous refrain, "Good dog, Carl." Enduring, popular fare.

Denton, Terry. *At the Café Splendid.* **Illus. by the author.** Houghton, 1988. $13.95 (0-395-46476-5).
FORMAT: Picture book   GRADES: 1–3.

The Café Splendid is familiar territory for Adele and her brother Victor, who go there with their mother every Friday. One night, the café becomes a stage for chasing, hiding, running, and noisemaking. Scratchy black lines, eccentric shading, and harlequin colors give the Café Splendid a carnival-like atmosphere not usually associated with the formal, sometimes oppressive world of adult eating-places. Denton makes the café a hospitable place, just another space for hide-and-seek.

Dubanevich, Arlene. *The Piggest Show on Earth.* Orchard, 1989. $13.95 (0-531-05789-5).
FORMAT: Picture book   GRADES: Preschool–Grade 1.

Back from *Pigs in Hiding, Pig William,* and *Pigs at Christmas,* this lively bunch of porcine vaudevillians are up to still more slaphappy antics, in and out of three rings and almost bringing down the Big Top. This festive affair is packed with details, and just like a day at the circus, there's more going on than can be viewed in one showing. Readers will want to nab every corny, breathtaking moment.

Dupasquier, Philippe. *The Great Escape.* **Illus. by the author.** Houghton, 1988. $13.95 (0-395-46806-X).
FORMAT: Picture book   GRADES: All grades.

When a prisoner slips out of jail through the front gate, he is pursued by several policemen down city streets, across rooftops, and through underground tunnels. Pandemonium results wherever he goes. Policemen who must be descendents of the Keystone Cops bumble and stumble after him in a frenzied chase that comes to an end only to begin again. This wordless tale of distractions is energetic, full of boundless comic details and sprawling chains of events. No one will be able to absorb all the fun in just one look.

Ernst, Lisa Campbell. *Walter's Tail.* **Illus. by the author.** Macmillan, 1992. $14.95 (0-02-733564-X).
FORMAT: Picture book   GRADES: Preschool–Grade 3.

It's not Walter's fault that he grew so large, but Mrs. Tully's dog and his rat-a-tat, always-wagging tail have destroyed so many shops that the two of them no longer feel welcome anywhere. The author of *Ginger Jumps* and *When Bluebell Sang* provides plenty of scenes of Walter's sizemic dilemma, his subsequent heroship, and his never-flagging friendliness.

Grossman, Bill. *Donna O'Neeshuck Was Chased by Some Cows.* **Illus. by Sue Truesdell.** HarperCollins, 1988. LB $12.89 (0-06-022159-3). paper avail.
FORMAT: Picture book   GRADES: Preschool–Grade 3.

Donna O'Neeshuck has a hair-raising habit of patting others on the head. Others—cows, people, almost anyone—have unusual reactions to this; they chase Donna to near exhaustion. All they want is more head-pats. Pandemonium reigns in Truesdell's briskly funny pictures of the chase, related in five-line rhyming stanzas. Grossman went on to create the even better *Tommy at the Grocery Store.*

Haas, Dorothy. *Burton's Zoom Zoom Va-Rooom Machine.* Macmillan, 1990. $13.95 (0-02-738201-X).
FORMAT: Novel   GRADES: 4–up.

Boys will enjoy this cartoony portrait of a wacky family of inventors, starring Burton Bell Whitney Knockwurst. Burton wants to make the fastest skateboard in the world, and so sets to work learning about aerodynamics. He makes the mistake of involving a suspicious character named Professor Savvy. A grand sense of humor and an intriguing array of characters lift this madcap scramble up to snuff and put it over the top.

Hennessy, B. G. *The Missing Tarts.* **Illus. by Tracey Campbell Pearson.** Viking, 1988. $12.95 (0-670-82039-3). paper avail.
FORMAT: Picture book   GRADES: Preschool–Grade 3.

The Knave of Hearts' theft of tarts launches the Queen of Hearts on a search that involves Jack and Jill, Old King Cole, Old Mother Hubbard, and other Mother Goose characters. Hennessy has turned familiar nursery rhyme landscape splendidly upside down (except for one clunky piece of verse), and he is generously aided by Pearson's zany, racing gang. Cherubic faces adorn this happy, well-paced, and well-placed crowd.

Hoban, Lillian. *Silly Tilly and the Easter Bunny.* **Illus. by the author.**
HarperCollins, 1987. LB $12.89 (0-06-022393-6). paper avail.
FORMAT: Picture book   GRADES: Preschool–Grade 2.

A gloriously funny tale about the most absentminded of moles, Silly
Tilly, whose lapses in memory will tickle readers.

Hughes, Shirley. *Alfie Gets In First.* **Illus. by the author.** Lothrop, 1982. LB
$13.88 (0-688-00849-6). paper avail.
FORMAT: Picture book   GRADES: Preschool–Grade 3.

British author Hughes knows how to take a childhood dilemma and race
it to the finish. Alfie gets home first, but accidentally locks himself inside
and his mother, out. All Hughes's books draw children into a lively
neighborhood where warmth, goodness, and occasional mischief reign.
The Alfie books never disappoint.

Jarrell, Randall. *The Gingerbread Rabbit.* **Illus. by Garth Williams.** Macmillan, 1972. paper $2.95 (0-02-043900-8).
FORMAT: Storybook   GRADES: Preschool–Grade 3.

First published by Macmillan in hardcover, this spin on the old gingerbread boy tale is a delight from beginning to end. Worth rediscovering in
paperback, and lucky are those who still have the well-loved original on
the shelves.

Kellogg, Steven. *Pinkerton, Behave!* **Illus. by the author.** Dial, 1979. LB
$13.89 (0-8037-6575-4). paper avail.
FORMAT: Picture book   GRADES: Preschool–Grade 3.

Kellogg's wit is renowned, but his Great Dane puppy may be even more
widely recognized. This first of the Pinkerton stories shows how bad
habits might sometimes come in handy; it's a terrific comedic feast. See
also his illustrations for Trinka Hakes Noble's school stories, *The Day
Jimmy's Boa Ate the Wash* and *Jimmy's Boa Bounces Back.*

Korman, Gordon. *MacDonald Hall Goes Hollywood.* Scholastic, 1991.
$12.95 (0-590-43940-5).
FORMAT: Novel   GRADES: 4–6.

The charm of Korman's latest Bruno and Boots book is in his ability to
make total chaos and slapstick comedy utterly believable. Beyond that,
the formula is readable and easy: A movie is being directed at the boys'
boarding school, and Bruno is determined to be an "extra." A grand
finale at a remote camping spot is hilarious.

Lyon, David. *The Runaway Duck.* **Illus. by the author.** Lothrop, 1985. LB $14.88 (0-688-04003-9).
FORMAT: Picture book   GRADES: Preschool–Grade 3.

It begins as such a grand idea: Sebastian ties his wooden duck to the bumper of the family car. But Egbert doesn't stay attached for long once the car is in motion. When the family goes one way and Egbert another, a witty and tension-fraught adventure is under way. One of the brightest and funniest books published that year.

Macaulay, David. *Why the Chicken Crossed the Road.* **Illus. by the author.** Houghton, 1987. $13.95 (0-395-44241-9). paper avail.
FORMAT: Picture book   GRADES: All grades.

Which came first, the chicken or the egg? Macaulay doesn't try to answer that question but ventures to demonstrate the circularity and the humor of the ensuing anomaly. When the chicken crosses the road it triggers a domino effect on events and readers end up at the beginning again. The chicken, first a prime mover, becomes merely a consequence. Macaulay's story shows a justified and true belief in the fun, innocence, and irony inherent in the turning of the wheel. This undoubtedly will delight children and confuse adults. His art, unlike that in such books as *Cathedral* and *Pyramid,* is flushed with color and zaniness; he demonstrates canny timing with the rapid-fire action.

McCann, Helen. *What Do We Do Now, George?* Simon & Schuster, 1991. $13.00 (0-671-74688-X).
FORMAT: Novel   GRADES: 5–up.

This is a hearty, hilarious story of a precocious young fund-raiser and his group of dupes. George has heard that charities are not only about gathering contributions but about skimming off the profits for personal use. He sets to work immediately as a do-gooder. McCann relies on zippy dialogue, a keen understanding of young minds, and a sure hand with slapstick comedy to depict George's travails. Readers will love it.

Marshak, Samuel. *The Pup Grew Up!* **Illus. by Vladimir Radunsky.** Holt, 1989. $13.95 (0-8050-0952-3).
FORMAT: Picture book   GRADES: Kindergarten–Grade 3.

Translator Richard Pevear and artist Radunsky deliver Marshak's 1926 tale into the hands of American audiences in this offbeat offering. A lady going on a train trip registers her belongings with the conductor: "The pan, the divan, the basin, the box with three locks, the valise and a tiny Pekingese." But during the journey, a Great Dane is substituted for her Pekingese. Children will delight in the surprise, explained away in the most childlike of rationales. Radunsky's sophisticated art is sharply daring.

Nygren, Tord. *The Red Thread.* **Illus. by the author.** R&S, 1988. $12.95 (91-29-59005-1).

FORMAT: Picture book   GRADES: Preschool–Grade 4.

The red thread appears endless as it winds through the wordless pages of this original, color-drenched book. Onlookers of any age and temperment will find themselves in a loop that they may jump in and out of at will, for every spread is a little world with its own rules, logic, and dimensions. The thread's travels inspire readers to flip back or forward, looking for ties that bind. Nygren beckons one and all to follow his thread, and the discoveries within these pages will please and challenge both sophisticated and homespun tastes.

Ormerod, Jan. *The Story of Chicken Licken.* **Illus. by the author.** Lothrop, 1986. $13.00 (0-688-06058-7).

FORMAT: Picture book   GRADES: Preschool–Grade 3.

After readers have been weaned on Omerod's baby board books such as *Reading*, they can move on to this feast, as an enthusiastic group of schoolchildren performs the famous tale. In silhouette is the audience and the unfolding antics of a baby who has escaped from its parent's lap.

Pryor, Bonnie. *Mr. Munday and the Rustlers.* **Illus. by Wallop Manyum.** Prentice Hall, 1988. $12.95 (0-13-604737-8). paper avail.

FORMAT: Picture book   GRADES: 1–4.

Mr. Munday is a mailman who recognizes that he may be in a rut. In search of an adventure, he accepts Cousin Arthur's offer to farm-sit, but ends up facing Big Bad Bob and Sneaky Pete. How Mr. Munday brings the bad guys home and returns to his safe former life is the gist of this humorous tale. Manyum has a cartoonist's flare for expressing the antics and action of the text. The story, sort of a chapter/picture book, will get beginning readers ready for their next foray—novels.

Rey, H. A. *Curious George: A Pop-up Book.* Houghton, 1987. $14.95 (0-395-45347-X).

FORMAT: Picture book   GRADES: Preschool–Grade 3.

This is a pop-up version of the beloved title. By opening a page or yanking the right tabs, readers can watch George put on the yellow hat (the act that leads to his capture), get rescued from his attempt at flying, and teeter on the telephone lines. The firefighting sequence (when George accidentally calls the fire department) is action packed, and the final pop-ups, of the monkey with his balloons, is inspired. This really flies, and children will delight in manipulating the action themselves.

Robertson, Keith. *Henry Reed, Inc.* **Illus. by Robert McCloskey.** Viking, 1958. $14.95 (0-670-36796-6). paper avail.
FORMAT: Novel　GRADES: 4–6.

Henry Reed, entrepreneur, has been delighting readers for more than 30 years. This self-sufficient young man, paired with his neighbor, Midge, comes up with one logical scheme after another, only to have them go artfully, hysterically astray. There are many more books starring Henry.

Rogers, Paul. *Tumbledown.* **Illus. by Robin Bell Corfield.** Macmillan, 1988. $12.95 (0-689-31392-6).
FORMAT: Picture book　GRADES: Kindergarten–Grade 3.

When things go wrong in the village of Tumbledown, no one fixes them, until the townspeople get word that the Prince is passing through. But despite all their fix-ups, there is royal crash that readers will find amusing. The easy flow of the musical text and the overall idea of this mythic village are quite charming, but the premise isn't really fulfilled. Corfield, however, creates unforgettable vistas of crumbling buildings, pebbly lanes, and busy befuddled villagers running hither and yon.

Rylant, Cynthia. *Henry and Mudge: The First Book of Their Adventures.* **Illus. by Suçie Stevenson.** Macmillan, 1987. $12.95 (0-02-778001-5). paper avail.
FORMAT: Picture book　GRADES: 1–3.

When an oversized dog comes into a small boy's life, the joy has just begun. Henry and Mudge have starred in several easy-to-read books since this one was published, and each one seems, impossibly, to be wiser, funnier, and more tender than the last. Start readers here, and they won't need to be nudged to the rest.

Schmidt, Julie Madeline. *The Apartment House.* **Illus. by Anita Riggio.** Abingdon, 1988. $12.95 (0-687-01533-2).
FORMAT: Picture book　GRADES: Preschool–Grade 3.

The internationally famous tenants in the apartment building are all working up to a grand, as yet unnamed, event while Mr. Wong, the building superintendent, is distressed because no one has remembered his birthday. Though predictable, this piece has its heart in the right place, and children will love the up-and-down, cutaway views of apartment and its tenants' cumulative efforts to stage the finale.

Seuss, Dr. *The Cat in the Hat.* **Illus. by the author.** Random, 1957. LB $7.99 (0-394-90001-4).
FORMAT: Storybook　GRADES: 2–4.

When the Cat in the Hat comes to play, nothing is ever the same again; throughout a rainy day his feats astonish and entertain. Children will simply go along with the fun, but adults will marvel at the wordplay and pace that never slackens. And to think that it all started with such books as *And to Think That I Saw It on Mulberry Street.*

Sharples, Joseph. *The Flyaway Pantaloons.* **Illus. by Sue Scullard.** Carolrhoda, 1990. $12.95 (0-87614-408-3).
FORMAT: Picture book   GRADES: Preschool–Grade 3.

The sight of pantaloons soaring along on a wind current past the architectural fittings of an Italianate Renaissance city distresses the citizens, but will lasso the imaginations of readers. Opulent illustrations, beautifully composed, do nothing to dampen this high-spirited flight.

Sis, Peter. *Waving.* **Illus. by the author.** Greenwillow, 1988. $11.95 (0-688-07159-7).
FORMAT: Picture book   GRADES: Preschool–Grade 2.

This is a jolly counting book, highly original and a terrific greeting card from a big city. Mary and her mother wave for a cab; two bicyclists wave back. Soon a chain reaction of people waving consumes the city with warmth and friendliness. Covers numbers from 1 to 15.

Stevenson, James. *"Could Be Worse!"* **Illus. by the author.** Greenwillow, 1977. LB $13.88 (0-688-84075-2). paper avail.
FORMAT: Picture book   GRADES: Preschool–Grade 3.

When this book came out, almost everyone agreed that Stevenson had never been funnier. That old codger Gramps regales one and all with tall tales of difficulties that never got him down. A joy, matched by Stevenson's other, more curmudgeonly old guy, *The Worst Person in the World.*

Voake, Charlotte. *The Ridiculous Story of Gammer Gurton's Needle.* **Illus. by David Lloyd.** Crown, 1987. $13.95 (0-517-56513-7).
FORMAT: Picture book   GRADES: All grades.

This 16th-century frolic is livelier than a Punch and Judy show. Voake's gesticulatory cartoons are wildly funny and give the excellent retelling the setting it deserves. The plot is complicated, but it involves Diccon the Bedlam, Gammer Gurton's crooked house, the servant Hodges's trousers, a cat named Gibb, and a series of misunderstandings that lead to a terrific knock-down fight. Grand entertainment.

Additional Titles

The following titles, annotated elsewhere in this book (see index), could also fit the "Physical Humor" category.

Bradman, Tony. *Look Out, He's Behind You!*
Brown, M. K. *Let's Go Swimming with Mr. Sillypants*
Elish, Dan. *The Worldwide Dessert Contest*
Goble, Paul. *Iktomi and the Berries*
Goffstein, M. B. *Laughing Latkes*
Graham, Bob. *Has Anyone Here Seen William?*
Himmelman, John. *Montigue on the High Seas*
Hissey, Jane. *Little Bear's Trousers*
Horvath, Polly. *An Occasional Cow*
Joyce, William. *A Day with Wilbur Robinson*
Macaulay, David. *Black and White*
Marshall, James. *The Cut-Ups*
Marshall, James. *The Cut-Ups Carry On*
Marshall, James. *The Three Little Pigs*
Pearson, Tracey Campbell. *Old MacDonald Had a Farm*
Peck, Robert Newton. *Soup in Love*
Sendak, Maurice. *In the Night Kitchen*
Slobodkina, Esphyr. *Caps for Sale*
Stehr, Frédéric. *Gulliver*
Trivas, Irene. *Emma's Christmas*
Wood, Audrey. *The Horrible Holidays*

5: Anthropomorphic Fun

Mechanical Life

Even though this category belongs to Henri Bergson, it is centered on the aspect of comedy that readily appeals to children's lot—that (roughly) when an object imitates real life, it is funny. This can be the animation of inanimate objects (ever seen a banana do the conga? a brave little toaster take on planet Mars? a dish pirouette in "Beauty and the Beast"? the banter between R2-D2 and 3-CPO?) and the anthropomorphization of tin woodsmen, scarecrows, gingerbreadpersons, and puppets of all sizes and denominations as in, say, a marionette named Pinocchio. Concurrently, humor arises when the absent-mindedness of human beings renders them nearly robotic in their ability to perform tasks. It sounds more complicated than it is, until the name Amelia Bedelia is invoked. Parish's literal-minded maid performs her tasks with a machinelike interpretation of language, from "pairing" the vegetables to "dressing" the fowl. The resulting mistakes are always whimsical, if not downright hilarious. Bergson's idea that any incident is comic that calls our attention to the mechanicalness of life is part of a tried-and-true formula in the world of children's books.

Agee, Jon. *The Incredible Painting of Felix Clousseau*. Illus. by the author.
Farrar, 1988. $15.00 (0-374-33633-4). paper avail.
FORMAT: Picture book   GRADES: Preschool–Grade 3.

The painter Clousseau is blessed and cursed by his artworks' penchant for coming to life, bursting out of their frames, and regaling him with troubles. The funny doings in the paintings will not amaze children for whom all objects have a secret animation, but they will be amused. See also this author's *Ludlow Laughs*.

Babbitt, Natalie. *Nellie: A Cat on Her Own.* **Illus. by the author.** Farrar, 1989. $14.00 (0-374-35506-1). paper avail.

FORMAT: Picture book   GRADES: Preschool–Grade 3.

When a wooden marionette cat is "released" from any further manipulation of strings by the death of her owner, a wise and experienced cat named Tom gives her advice that puts her on her own road to freedom. Nellie's newly animated form dances in the light of the moon in this celebration of independence and creativity.

Browne, Anthony. *Gorilla.* **Illus. by the author.** Knopf, 1985. LB $13.99 (0-394-97525-1). paper avail.

FORMAT: Picture book   GRADES: Preschool–Grade 3.

Left on her own much of the time by her parents, Hannah has developed an imagination that sees her through lonely times. When her toy gorilla comes hugely to life, he becomes the best of companions. Control over their environments is elusive to so many children. But Hannah with ingenuity achieves some grasp of events. Compelling, free-spirited.

Cameron, Polly. *"I Can't," Said the Ant.* **Illus. by the author.** Putnam, 1961. $8.99 (0-698-20197-8).

FORMAT: Storybook   GRADES: Preschool–Grade 3.

For a dishy nonsensical story, look to this one about poor Miss Teapot and her broken spout. But she can count on her friends—ants and spiders alike—to help out when she is in need, and children will love the kitchen camaraderie that transpires.

Cecil, Laura, ed. *Stuff and Nonsense.* **Illus. by Emma Chichester Clark.** Greenwillow, 1989. $15.95 (0-688-08898-8).

FORMAT: Poetry   GRADES: Preschool–Grade 3.

A read-aloud companion to this duo's *Listen to This,* but this time, the focus is on inanimate objects that prove quite animate after all. Classic stories and poems (Andersen's *The Shepherdess and the Chimney Sweep,* Lear's *The Table and the Chair*) appear next to lesser-known works. The concept that binds these is that human and animal attributes can be applicable to *things,* perhaps easier done by a child than a shaman. The well-chosen, mostly funny offerings are accompanied by Clark's blithe watercolors. Deliciously absurd.

Cleary, Beverly. *The Mouse and the Motorcycle.* **Illus. by Louis Darling.** Morrow, 1965. LB $13.88 (0-688-31698-0). paper avail.

FORMAT: Novel   GRADES: 3–6.

This rip-roaring adventure of Ralph S. Mouse and his toy motorcycle (which really *goes!*) has been entertaining children for nearly 30 years; it was followed up by two popular sequels, *Runaway Ralph* and *Ralph S. Mouse*. For many boys, the road to reading Beverly Cleary begins with these three books.

Collodi, Carlo. *Pinocchio.* **Illus. by Roberto Innocenti.** Knopf, 1988. $18.95 (0-394-82110-6).
FORMAT: Storybook   GRADES: All grades.

Innocenti's luminous interpretation of Collodi's melodrama carves the action out of 19th-century Italian landscapes. Clearly shown as a mocking marionette, this Pinocchio races through cobbled city scenes and then prostrates himself at the person—the blue fairy or Geppetto—whom he has most recently offended by his hasty, thoughtless behavior. Enchantment reigns in the pictures, each a perfect takeoff on the text. Innocenti and Collodi are equally at home in a place where puppets have life beyond human hands, and where souls may die and live again, resurrected by the power of love.

Couture, Susan. *The Block Book.* **Illus. by Petra Mathers.** HarperCollins, 1990. LB $12.89 (0-06-020524-5).
FORMAT: Picture book   GRADES: Preschool–Grade 3.

Two blocks spend their days in fairly ordinary fashion, drinking cocoa and washing their socks. They are also collectors, and any child will relate to the treasures Ben and Betsy have accumulated. Whimsical, animated, high living.

Disch, Thomas M. *The Brave Little Toaster.* **Illus. by Karen Lee Schmidt.** Doubleday, 1986. $12.95 (0-385-23050-8).
FORMAT: Chapter book   GRADES: 4–6.

This witty piece is about appliances who miss their master, sort of a *Velveteen Rabbit* with electric cords. Readers will short-circuit over the doings in this story, but loopy as it is, it also has a heart (or perhaps that was simply a heating coil).

Disch, Thomas M. *The Brave Little Toaster Goes to Mars.* Doubleday, 1988. $11.95 (0-385-24162-3).
FORMAT: Novel   GRADES: 5–up.

Those who believed that all that could be said about a band of loyal appliances was stated with electrifying eloquence in *The Brave Little Toaster* will find there is new territory to cover; they will follow this crew to Mars where a force of warring appliances is planning to invade Earth. What is Disch talking about? In fact, while he seems to be amusing himself, much of what he writes will entertain readers, too. The epic elements will appease, but the most exuberantly funny scenes are those in which the appliances wile away the time on gossip.

Field, Eugene. *The Gingham Dog and the Calico Cat.* **Illus. by Janet Street.** Putnam, 1990. $14.95 (0-399-22151-4).
FORMAT: Picture book   GRADES: Preschool–Grade 1.

This is an old, old tale, and most readers will have heard it at least once, but Street opens up the humor in the verse, setting the story in an antique shop and enlisting the watchful presences of the other objects. And of course, the two animated adversaries eat each other up. Delicious!

Fleming, Ian. *Chitty-Chitty-Bang-Bang.* **Illus. by John Burningham.** Knopf, 1964. paper $2.95 (0-394-81948-9).
FORMAT: Novel   GRADES: 5–6.

Adventure follows adventure when the Potts's previously mild-mannered automobile becomes a flying machine with global ambitions. Highfalutin' fun—and yes, it's *that* Ian Fleming.

Goffstein, M. B. *Laughing Latkes.* **Illus. by the author.** Farrar, 1980. $6.95 (0-374-34364-0).
FORMAT: Picture book   GRADES: Preschool–Grade 3.

Many books about holidays fall into a trap that makes instruction the first order of the day; fun, the second. Goffstein's childlike look at Hanukkah uses the perspective of potato pancakes to create a cheerful chortling season of lights. Perhaps of all her esteemed works, this one is her most purely funny.

Hissey, Jane. *Little Bear's Trousers.* **Illus. by the author.** Putnam, 1987. $14.95 (0-399-21493-3). paper avail.
FORMAT: Picture book   GRADES: Preschool–Grade 2.

Hissey's textured illustrations, so lifelike that they resemble hand-tinted photographs, are as remarkable here as in her *Old Bear.* The toy characters have returned to help Little Bear locate lost trousers, which everyone has used differently: Camel as hump-warmers, Dog as a two-bone boneholder, etc. A forgivably weak ending is offset by the snug household scenes; Hissey's world makes readers believe that Old Bear could be just around the next corner.

Leroe, Ellen W. *Robot Raiders.* HarperCollins, 1987. $11.95 (0-06-023835-6).
FORMAT: Novel   GRADES: 6–9.

Bixby Wyler is back for another ripping technological farce, this time involving NASA, M.I.T., an anticomputer group known as "Men, Not

Monsters," his robot Max, his humanoid Ally Tonerds, and Frani, the stellar girl from back home. Bixby, Max, and Frani tell the witty story, all of them impatient to have their turns at getting the facts straight. That keeps the story crackling along, from one short circuit, happily, to the next.

Lester, Alison. *Ruby.* **Illus. by the author.** Houghton, 1988. $13.95 (0-395-46477-3).
FORMAT: Picture book   GRADES: Preschool–Grade 3.

Ruby's patchwork quilt is more than a source of security and warmth. One night when Ruby rescues it from the clothesline, she discovers it flies, just like a magic carpet. She rides it to an island where she saves some animals from a vicious serpent and wins the gratitude and hospitality of one and all. This fanciful flight is standard entertainment, but Lester's illustrations are a treat. Try it as a mild introduction to *Where the Wild Things Are.*

Lionni, Leo. *Alexander and the Wind-Up Mouse.* **Illus. by the author.** Knopf, 1969. LB $15.99 (0-394-90914-3). paper avail.
FORMAT: Picture book   GRADES: Preschool–Grade 3.

Any child who has ever wished he was a robot will have compassion for poor Alexander—he's met his match in a mechanical rodent. This volume, a Caldecott Honor book, is a blissful introduction to the art of Lionni, whose old books and new ones continue to please children with their colors, collage forms, and wonderful sense of space. Dreamy good times, and lessons for youth as well.

McKee, David. *Snow Woman.* Lothrop, 1988. $12.95 (0-688-07674-2).
FORMAT: Picture book   GRADES: 1–3.

McKee brings his avant-garde views on the question of gender to playtime. Two children build a pair of snowpeople, male and female, and the next morning the snowy couple appear to have run away together. It is McKee's superb humor—conveyed almost solely in the illustrations—rather than his intentionally ambiguous ending, that wins the day, particularly a set of framed pictures in the background, one of which depicts Adam and Eve cutting down the apple tree.

Milne, A. A. *Winnie the Pooh; The House at Pooh Corner.* **Illus. by Ernest H. Shepard.** Dutton, 1926; 1928. $9.95 each (0-525-44443-2; 0-525-44444-0).
FORMAT: Chapter books   GRADES: 1–4.

Dorothy Parker aside, these two volumes have been entreating young children into the Thousand Acre Wood for generations. They have been called masterpieces of tenderness and wit, whether read aloud or enjoyed independently, and no child ever forgets the toy who was incarnated as the Bear of Very Little Brain, or any of his friends.

Parish, Peggy. *Amelia Bedelia.* **Illus. by Fritz Siebel.** HarperCollins, 1963. LB $12.89 (0-06-024641-3). paper avail.

FORMAT: Picture book　GRADES: Preschool–Grade 3.

For over 25 years Amelia Bedelia has been giving children the green light to enjoy her literal-mindedness, her obvious mistakes, and the way she, nevertheless, makes everyone around her happy. This housekeeper never loses her job—as long as her job is to keep readers laughing. Other books about her run longer, closer to the I Can Read format for independent readers. Start children with this one, and they'll graduate themselves to *Merry Christmas Amelia Bedelia, Amelia Bedelia and the Baby,* and *Come Back, Amelia Bedelia,* among others.

Parkin, Rex. *The Red Carpet.* **Illus. by the author.** Macmillan, 1948. $14.95 (0-02-770010-0).

FORMAT: Picture book　GRADES: Preschool–Grade 3.

The Duke of Sultana expects a royal welcome, but no one ever believed that a runaway carpet would travel all the way from the hotel to the dock by itself, and just in time. Splendid, enduring fun, with a rhythm that will have listeners bouncing along to the beat.

Pelgrom, Els. *Little Sophie and Lanky Flop.* **Illus. by The Tjong Khing.** Farrar, 1988. $11.95 (0-374-34624-0).

FORMAT: Storybook　GRADES: 4–6.

Lanky Flop and three other of Sophie's toys come alive one night and take the previously bedridden girl on a journey to discover the meaning of life. Profound, witty, suspenseful, and satisfying.

Schneider, Howie, and Susan Seligson. *The Amazing Amos and the Greatest Couch on Earth.* **Illus. by Howie Schneider.** Little, Brown, 1989. $13.95 (0-316-78033-2).

FORMAT: Picture book　GRADES: Preschool–Grade 3.

In this first sequel to *Amos,* the pooch drives his couch to the park one morning but finds that a circus has taken up residence there. As might be expected, he ends up in center ring. This is a far-fetched and funny follow-up to the first book. Amos's antics are comically drawn—readers will love the pictures of him revving up for a stunt.

Schneider, Howie, and Susan Seligson. *Amos: The Story of an Old Dog and His Couch.* **Illus. by Howie Schneider.** Little, Brown, 1987. $13.95 (0-316-77404-9).
FORMAT: Picture book   GRADES: Preschool–Grade 3.

Each day Mr. and Mrs. Bobson leave Amos, their old dog, on his couch while they run errands. These trips mystify Amos; just once he'd like to know where his masters go. When he bonks a certain spot on the couch and it roars to life like a small upholstered car, he gets his chance. A rivetingly fast pace and tongue-in-cheek tone will tickle even the most skeptical reader. The illustrations convey Amos's satisfaction on the day of his discovery, apparent in every smug bone of his tired old body.

Shepperson, Rob. *The Sandman.* **Illus. by the author.** Farrar, 1990. $13.95 (0-374-36405-2). paper avail.
FORMAT: Picture book   GRADES: Preschool–Grade 3.

Is the Sandman supposed to be frightening? Reassuring? A pragmatist? Here is the ultimate lullaby, as Shepperson's nighttime visitor relies not on somnambulistic sand but on simply wearing a child out with highly animated play—toys and books join the romp. A goofy guy, an action-packed book.

Steig, William. *The Amazing Bone.* **Illus. by the author.** Farrar, 1983. $17.00 (0-374-30248-0). paper avail.
FORMAT: Picture book   GRADES: Preschool–Grade 3.

A talking bone falls out of (escapes from?) a witch's basket and into the hands of a piglet named Pearl. This witty book has been pleasing children for 15 years, and even though adults continue to claim Steig as their own, it is his youngest readers who have made him justifiably famous for his humor, use of language, and ability to reveal both the epic and the essential of childhood's experiences. See *CDB!*, the Caldecott Medal-winning *Sylvester and the Magic Pebble, Amos and Boris, Doctor De Soto,* or, for older readers, *Abel's Island.* With any of them, laughter will soon begin.

Tennyson, Noel. *The Lady's Chair and the Ottoman.* **Illus. by the author.** Lothrop, 1987. LB $12.88 (0-688-04098-5).
FORMAT: Picture book   GRADES: Kindergarten–Grade 3.

Eccentric black-and-white pictures upholster this finely crafted story, written with originality, sensibility, and charm. Quite surprisingly, it's a story about furniture that raises several thought-provoking and witty questions: What do you do if you are a chair or an ottoman misplaced as part of a set, unable to move by yourself? The red velvet ottoman, though equipped with brass wheels, cannot move a solitary inch closer to the chinaberry-covered lady's chair he loves. It's a moving drama about the loss of security, of separation and reunion, of hopes and aspirations, of powerlessness in the face of fate, and of the exhilaration of chance occurrence. Visual references—to a wind-up toy, a gramophone, real animals, and people—add to the story an uncluttered set of pictorial allusions that will enrich and delight any who enter these rooms.

Additional Titles

The following titles, annotated elsewhere in this book, (see index), could also fit the "Mechanical Life" category.

Banks, Kate. *Alphabet Soup*
Fuchshuber, Annegert. *The Cuckoo-Clock Cuckoo*
Jarrell, Randall. *The Gingerbread Rabbit*

6: *Language That Tickles*

Jokes, Riddles, Puns, Poems

*I*n this category, language games take center stage. Few things delight children more than the scrambling of language and the unfolding of nonsense poems and playful prose, from the oldest of knock-knock jokes to Edward Lear to the latest verseful mirthful lines of Shel Silverstein.

Alliterative abecedaria are just the beginning; the Scroobious Pip makes an appearance, as do groan-worthy joke collections that have adults shaking their heads even as children gobble up the pages. The real rib-ticklers come in the poems, where humor and a masterful use of sentence structure, logic, grammar, and vocabulary combine in joyful expulsion of images and ideas. Children have a fresher ear for language and speech than adults. Children appreciate the juggling of words and the clucking of tongues, and have a miniature memory palace for unsavory utterances, silly spoonerisms, and "Jabberwockies."

Bang, Betsy. *The Old Woman and the Rice Thief.* **Illus. by Molly Garrett Bang.** Greenwillow, 1978. $11.88 (0-688-84098-1).
FORMAT: Picture book   GRADES: Preschool–Grade 3.

This is a rollicking version of a Bengali tale about a quick-witted old woman and a not-so-lucky rice thief. It carries readers along with a cumulative style and use of repeating words and phrases, excellent for group-sharing.

Berry, James. *A Thief in the Village and Other Stories.* Orchard, 1988. $12.95 (0-531-05745-3). paper avail.
FORMAT: Short stories   GRADES: 6–up.

The phrases in these stories set in Jamaica are musical in print, even before they are spoken. "I know total-total that if I had my own bike . . ." Becky tells readers in "Becky and the Wheels-and-Brake Boys," and her determination is established. Berry's writing is liquid and cool; in "Fanso and Granny-Flo" and elsewhere his descriptions are so original that the language is rendered meaningful and new: "Fanso's comings and goings and concerns were so well woven in with his granny's, it was hard to tell he had a big secret worry." How better to express the feelings on a young adult beginning to pull away from childhood? The collection is epiphanic; each story wraps itself around ordinary incidents and transforms them into lore.

Bodecker, N. M. *Hurry, Hurry, Mary Dear! and Other Nonsense Poems.* Illus. by the author. Macmillan, 1976. $10.95 (0-685-45603-X).
FORMAT: Poetry   GRADES: 4–6.

The noted poet and sketch artist creates a funny confusion from nonsense poems, brilliant wordplay, and upside-down doses of humor. Those enchanted by this collection won't mind finding more of Bodecker on the shelf: *Snowman Sniffles and Other Verse* and *Carrot Holes and Frisbee Trees.*

Brewton, Sarah, and John E. Brewton. *Laughable Limericks.* Illus. by Ingrid Fetz. HarperCollins, 1990. LB $12.89 (0-690-04887-4).
FORMAT: Poetry   GRADES: 3–6.

An acclaimed assembly of limericks, organized with care and illustrated with high-spirited drawings that, like the text they accompany, are amusing and fun.

Brewton, Sarah, John E. Brewton, and George Meredith Blackburn, III, comps. *My Tang's Tungled and Other Ridiculous Situations.* Illus. by Graham Booth. HarperCollins, 1989. LB $13.89 (0-690-04778-9).
FORMAT: Poetry   GRADES: 5–up.

T. S. Eliot, Ogden Nash, and others are included in this compilation of nonsense poems, accompanied by blithe, silly illustrations.

Brewton, Sarah, John E. Brewton, and George Meredith Blackburn, III, comps. *Of Quarks, Quasars, and Other Quirks: Quizzical Poems for the Supersonic Age.* Illus. by Quentin Blake. HarperCollins, 1977. LB $13.89 (0-690-04885-8).
FORMAT: Poetry   GRADES: 4–6.

The nonsense of Ogden Nash, Shel Silverstein, Eve Merriam, and others is applied to the space age, both mocking and regaling technology in line after line of verse. Readers have been known to recite from this book before, during, and after giving oral science reports, just to enliven the scene.

Brown, Marc. *Party Rhymes.* **Illus. by the author.** Dutton, 1988. $13.95 (0-525-44402-5).

FORMAT: Picture book   GRADES: Preschool–Grade 3.

This book features familiar rhyming games that children sing and act out, with diagrams of movements and festive illustrations of all the fun.

Carlstrom, Nancy White. *Jesse Bear, What Will You Wear?* **Illus. by Bruce Degen.** Macmillan, 1986. $13.95 (0-02-717350-X).

FORMAT: Picture book   GRADES: Preschool–Grade 3.

These are recitable rhymes about a most endearing bear, who, like all toddlers, makes the simplest tasks in an ordinary day wholly exciting and new. Catchy and fun, with illustrations that some find too sweet, but others believe are "just right."

Cassedy, Sylvia. *Roomrimes.* **Illus. by Michele Chessare.** HarperCollins, 1987. LB $12.89 (0-690-04467-4).

FORMAT: Picture book   GRADES: Preschool–Grade 3.

This collection features 26 poems, from Attic to Zoo, about spaces and places: Basement, Fire Escape, Closet, Nest, Tunnel, etc. Lively illustrations complement the rhymes, but language and rhythm are center stage. Chantable, too.

Ciardi, John. *You Read to Me and I'll Read to You.* **Illus. by Edward Gorey.** HarperCollins, 1961. LB $12.89 (0-397-30646-6). paper avail.

FORMAT: Poetry   GRADES: Preschool–Grade 4.

The title quite literally describes the way in which this book of 35 inventive poems is to be used; the adult and child take their parts and create an oral verse-making experience. Great for laptime sharing, and Gorey can be counted upon for injecting further levity into each selection. Nonsense rhymes for older readers can be found in this team's *The Man Who Sang the Sillies.*

Cole, Joanna, and Stephanie Calmenson. *The Laugh Book.* **Illus. by Marylin Hafner.** Doubleday, 1986. $15.95 (0-385-18559-6).

FORMAT: Anthology   GRADES: 2–6.

Loads of laughs can be found in these pages, featuring jokes, riddles, tongue-twisters, poetry, and prose. Excerpts from works by Judy Blume and Beverly Cleary burble next to the writings of Shel Silverstein, Mark Twain, and Lewis Carroll. A good browsing title, sure to lead children to other books as well.

Cole, William. *Oh, Such Foolishness!* **Illus. by Tomie dePaola.** Harper-Collins, 1991. LB $13.89 (0-397-32502-9).
FORMAT: Poetry   GRADES: 4–6.

It's not foolishness at all to present this array of nonsense poems and humorous rhymes. Children who love their poetry sunnyside up will find this collection divine.

Corbett, Scott. *Jokes to Read in the Dark.* **Illus. by Annie Gusman.** Dutton, 1980. $12.95 (0-525-32796-7).
FORMAT: Storybook   GRADES: 4–6.

Here Corbett presents knock-knocks, one-liners, limericks, funny epitaphs, riddles, and puns. Adults may find them tiresome, but children never do.

Day, Alexandra. *Frank and Ernest.* **Illus. by the author.** Scholastic, 1990. $13.95 (0-590-41557-3). paper avail.
FORMAT: Picture book   GRADES: Kindergarten–Grade 3.

An elephant and a bear take over a diner for a day, and unearth for readers food talk the likes of which they've never heard before and will never forget. What a command of English!

Day, Alexandra. *Frank and Ernest Play Ball!* **Illus. by the author.** Scholastic, 1990. $12.95 (0-590-42548-X). paper avail.
FORMAT: Picture book   GRADES: Kindergarten–Grade 3.

Frank and Ernest are back to take on sports lingo, perplexing even to some adults but always charming to children. Fast-paced and funny.

de Regniers, Beatrice Schenk, et al. *Sing a Song of Popcorn: Every Child's Book of Poems.* **Illus. by 9 Caldecott Medal artists.** Scholastic, 1988. $18.95 (0-590-43974-X). paper avail.
FORMAT: Poetry   GRADES: Kindergarten–up.

This winning collection of poems, mostly humorous, some serious, is bound to make children rethink the idea that poetry equals boring, or infatuate them anew if they are already fans. Plentiful illustrations make this a gem to pore over, browse through, or settle into for an entire afternoon.

Greenfield, Eloise. *Honey, I Love and Other Love Poems.* **Illus. by Leo Dillon and Diane Dillon.** HarperCollins, 1978. LB $12.89 (0-690-03845-3). paper avail.
FORMAT: Poetry   GRADES: Preschool–Grade 3.

This triumphant collection of poems by the well-known writer touches on children's most intimate experiences. The poems burble with the joy that for most youngsters is never far from the surface. Not all the poems contain humor, but setting the theme of love to laughter makes many of these small poems classics.

Gwynne, Fred. *A Little Pigeon Toad.* **Illus. by the author.** Simon & Schuster, 1988. $12.95 (0-671-66659-2). paper avail.
FORMAT: Picture book   GRADES: 1–5.

Following up his successful books on homonyms (*A Chocolate Moose for Dinner, The King Who Rained, The Sixteen Hand Horse*), Gwynne allows a bewildered girl to narrate some perplexing developments. "Grandma says our four bears came from Scotland" is paired with a picture of four bears in kilts, doing a Highland fling. That's but one of the amusing twists of the language that Gwynne illustrates with the literal-minded images of a child. With a rapid-fire pace, this is fun and inventive fare for all ages.

Hall, Katy, and Lisa Eisenberg. *Buggy Riddles.* **Illus. by Simms Taback.** Dial, 1986. LB $9.89 (0-8037-0140-3). paper avail.
FORMAT: Picture book   GRADES: Preschool–Grade 3.

The authors, who also wrote *Fishy Riddles*, sting children's funnybones with creepy crawly riddles on every possible insect and spider. For inducing laughter among those too impatient to wade through plots.

Haswell, Peter. *Pog.* Orchard, 1989. $13.95 (0-531-05843-3).
FORMAT: Picture book   GRADES: Preschool–Grade 1.

A few philosophical points and much humor are put across in Haswell's wry book. Pog is a pig who, espying his image in a mirror, ponders, "That's not me . . . WHO WAS IT?" When he finds a banana, he assigns several uses to it, until he hits upon the most appropriate one. Playful puns and intriguing ideas are tangled and twirled with. Haswell is more intent on raising questions than answering them, and this he does with flair. The loose, cartoony illustrations are appealing.

Heller, Nicholas. *Happy Birthday, Moe Dog.* **Illus. by the author.** Greenwillow, 1988. $11.95 (0-688-07670-X).
FORMAT: Picture book   GRADES: Kindergarten–Grade 3.

Moe Dog's birthday is literally a happy one. He is greeted by a friendly "H" near his bed and a flying orange "A" outside his window. "P" cooks breakfast, "B" runs a bubble bath, another "A" and a "Y" carry in the cake. An emphasis on patterns here is skillfully spelled out as a contrast to the simple line forms of the letters. Heller's kaleidoscopic color variations are sure to snare even the most ambivalent reader.

Juster, Norton. *As: A Surfeit of Similes.* **Illus. by David Small.** Morrow, 1989. $9.95 (0-688-08139-8).
FORMAT: Picture book GRADES: All grades.

It would be a grievous insult to Juster's and Small's hard work if this book were passed over by those who misunderstand the grim black jacket or those who ignore the black-and-white illustrations before they notice each picture's hilarious content. Readers will love the rollicking batch of similes and wordplay: "As patient as lizards/As heavy as lead/As slow as the ketchup/As safe as your bed." For "As different as noses/As fickle as luck," such notable schnozzes as those of W. C. Fields and Pinocchio gather around a "Wheel of Fortune." Side-splitting fun. Small's contribution is immense.

Keller, Charles. *Remember the a la Mode!* **Illus. by Lee Lorenz.** Prentice Hall, 1986. $10.95 (0-13-773358-5). paper avail.
FORMAT: Anthology GRADES: 3–6.

This is perhaps Keller's punniest book, with real groaners and innovations children will cherish and repeat.

Keller, Charles. *Tongue Twisters.* **Illus. by Ron Fritz.** Simon & Schuster, 1989. $13.95 (0-671-67123-5). paper avail.
FORMAT: Picture book GRADES: Preschool–Grade 3.

A festival of tongue twisting feats greet readers on every page. Try this pair's *Belly Laughs!* when young tongues get tired of twisting and would prefer to laugh their way through a meal of food jokes and riddles.

Kitamura, Satoshi. *What's Inside? The Alphabet Book.* **Illus. by the author.** Farrar, 1985. $14.00 (0-374-38306-5). paper avail.
FORMAT: Picture book GRADES: Preschool–Grade 3.

This offbeat alphabet book will be appreciated by those who mastered their ABCs long ago. Unfolding like a cinematic extravaganza, the book intrigues and amuses with its splendid use of whimsy and its tacit vow to entertain. *When Sheep Cannot Sleep*, Kitamura's counting book, is just as goofy and appealing with its twist on the old "counting sheep" cure for insomnia.

Komaiko, Leah. *Annie Bananie.* **Illus. by Laura Cornell.** HarperCollins, 1987. LB $13.89 (0-06-023261-7). paper avail.
FORMAT: Picture book GRADES: Preschool–Grade 3.

Annie has long since moved away, but the narrator of this bouncy, jazzy paean to friendship can remember all the great times they had, right down to summers in the outdoor wading pool. Readers will practically skip rope to the beat of the verse—and find their fondness for poetry growing.

Komaiko, Leah. *Earl's Too Cool for Me.* **Illus. by Laura Cornell.** Harper-Collins, 1988. LB $13.89 (0-06-023282-X). paper avail.
FORMAT: Picture book   GRADES: Kindergarten–Grade 3.

Fresh from their collaborative success on *Annie Bananie*, Komaiko and Cornell bring humor and rhapsodized zaniness to this story of misconceptions that become friendship. A narrator lists just why Earl is so cool, in jingles that are dandy for reading aloud. Cornell brings to this budding friendship an inventive use of dress and hairstyles to convey "cool" status. With finger-snapping rhythm, this is sprightly and hip.

Lear, Edward, and Ogden Nash. *The Scroobious Pip.* **Illus. by Nancy Ekholm Burkert.** HarperCollins, 1987. paper $5.95 (0-06-443132-0).
FORMAT: Picture book   GRADES: Preschool–Grade 5.

Nash completed this verse by Lear, brought fantastically into focus by the images in Burkert's generous, splendid paintings. Turn this over to young readers and ask them just what is the Pip. Or, what is he not?

Levine, Caroline Anne. *Knockout Knock Knocks.* **Illus. by Giulio Maestro.** Dutton, 1985. $6.95 (0-525-33255-3).
FORMAT: Storybook   GRADES: 2–4.

Simple vocabulary and ready word associations make this a fine choice for newly independent readers. The 61 jokes are clever; more humor can be found in this pair's *The Silly Kind Joke Book*.

Lobel, Arnold. *The Book of Pigericks.* **Illus. by the author.** HarperCollins, 1983. $14.89 (0-06-023983-2). paper avail.
FORMAT: Poetry   GRADES: Kindergarten–Grade 3.

Readers young and old will enjoy the artist's pig's-eye view of limericks. Surprising and original, these will inspire confidence in newly independent readers.

MacCarthy, Patricia. *Animals Galore!* **Illus. by the author.** Dial, 1989. $11.95 (0-8037-0721-5).
FORMAT: Picture book   GRADES: Preschool–Grade 3.

Delightful shocks underscore the happy batiked canvases of this volume; think of a child's discovery that "a murder of crows" describes a bunch of birds. Brilliant, diaphanous colors and craft meld with an invisible lesson-book on collective nouns, whose only, minor, flaw is the graceless title.

McCord, David. *The Star in the Pail.* **Illus. by Marc Simont.** Little, Brown, 1976. paper $5.95 (0-316-55521-5).
FORMAT: Poetry   GRADES: Preschool–Grade 4.

For the very youngest listeners, these are lightly engaging, often humorous poems about their world—from small details to large vistas—by the award-winning poet. His earlier work, *Every Time I Climb a Tree,* was also illustrated by Caldecott Medal-winning Simont. Older readers may find solace and humor in *One at a Time* and *All Day Long.*

Mahy, Margaret. *Nonstop Nonsense.* **Illus. by Quentin Blake.** Macmillan, 1989. $12.95 (0-689-50483-7).
FORMAT: Anthology   GRADES: Preschool–Grade 4.

What a combination—two masters of nonsense in one book! This is an excellent collection for introducing readers to Mahy, who supplies jubilant verse and ebullient stories to laugh over, and to Blake, whose vintage loose lines and quirky compositions are sure to please.

Martin, Bill, Jr. *Brown Bear, Brown Bear, What Do You See?* **Illus. by Eric Carle.** Holt, 1992. $14.95 (0-8050-1744-5).
FORMAT: Picture book   GRADES: Preschool–Kindergarten.

This book is perfect for preschoolers, who will find its thumping good rhythm worthy of a giggle or two. Splendid collages fill each page.

Martin, Bill, Jr., and John Archambault. *Chicka Chicka Boom Boom.* **Illus. by Lois Ehlert.** Simon & Schuster, 1989. $13.95 (0-671-67949-X).
FORMAT: Picture book   GRADES: Preschool–Grade 1.

The alphabet dances to a syncopated beat in this lively three-way collaboration. Every child will join in on the eponymous chorus, and even adults will chant along with the bouncy, exuberant rhythm.

Milnes, Gerald. *Granny Will Your Dog Bite? And Other Mountain Rhymes.* **Illus. by Kimberly Bulcken Root.** Knopf, 1990. LB $15.99 (0-394-94749-5).
FORMAT: Anthology   GRADES: All grades.

This is a collection of mountain and holler rhymes, most with a foot-tapping beat and all of them surprising. A scholar's effort has gone into this book, accompanied by vibrant pictures of the kind of folk who might have kept these selections alive—in the best oral storytelling tradition—by passing 'em on.

Opie, Iona, and Peter Opie. *Tail Feathers from Mother Goose: The Opie Rhyme Book.* **Illus. by various artists.** Little, Brown, 1988. $15.95 (0-316-65081-1).
FORMAT: Poetry   GRADES: All grades.

Dinner rhymes, verses for "awkward moments," poems about love, seafaring, and the devil in the garden, nonsense lines loved by a family member and handed down—these have been culled from the vast Opie Collection and published, in many cases, for the first time. These are mysterious sing-song phrases that have fascinated and delighted so many generations; words that have proven of lasting importance to children and adults. A rare project for collectors, it will bring hours of discovery and mirth to any child.

Patz, Nancy. *Moses Supposes His Toeses Are Roses: And 7 Other Silly Old Rhymes.* **Illus. by the author.** Harcourt, 1983. $13.95 (0-15-255690-7). paper avail.
FORMAT: Picture book   GRADES: Preschool–Grade 3.

Patz illustrates nonsense rhymes from English and American traditions in the style of 18th- to 19th-century paintings of the Pennsylvania Dutch. The mood is rapturously buoyant, the poems lilting, and the pictures uproarious.

Petersham, Maud, and Miska Petersham. *The Rooster Crows: A Book of American Rhymes and Jingles.* **Illus. by the authors.** Macmillan, 1969. $13.95 (0-02-773100-6). paper avail.
FORMAT: Anthology   GRADES: Preschool–Grade 3.

This Caldecott Medal-winner holds familiar treats—songs, games, and rhymes that are part of America's tradition. The illustrations are an old-fashioned delight and will charm a new generation of readers.

Prelutsky, Jack. *For Laughing Out Loud: Poems to Tickle Your Funnybone.* **Illus. by Marjorie Priceman.** Knopf, 1991. LB $15.99 (0-394-92144-5).
FORMAT: Poetry   GRADES: 1–5.

The funny works of contemporary poets are assembled in this ticklish anthology, featuring the antic illustrations of the very energetic Priceman.

Prelutsky, Jack. *Poems of A. Nonny Mouse.* **Illus. by Henrik Drescher.** Knopf, 1989. LB $14.99 (0-394-98711-X). paper avail.
FORMAT: Poetry   GRADES: Preschool–Grade 6.

This is a collection of more than 70 poems that over the years have been falsely attributed to "Anonymous," according to A. Nonny Mouse.

Prelutsky has collected familiar lines and added a few new ones, most of them funny, and all sure to please.

Rosenbloom, Joseph. *The Funniest Dinosaur Book Ever!* **Illus. by Hans Wilhelm.** Sterling, 1988. $12.95 (0-8069-6624-6).
FORMAT: Picture book   GRADES: 1–3.

Take almost any elephant joke, substitute the word "dinosaur," and that's the source for most of the little ditties in this book. Adults may groan, but these are just the kinds of worn-out jokes that seem to appeal to children most. Wilhelm's pictures of giggling beasts, shivering bones, and several attentive children relating jokes to one another are the freshest part of this package.

Rosenbloom, Joseph. *Twist These on Your Tongue.* **Illus. by Joyce Behr.** Dutton, 1978. $10.95 (0-525-66612-5).
FORMAT: Storybook   GRADES: 3–6.

Rosenbloom has published many joke books, but this collection of tongue twisters—part compilation of familiar entries, part original material—has always been a favorite.

Schwartz, Alvin. *The Cat's Elbow: And Other Secret Languages.* **Illus. by Margot Zemach.** Farrar, 1982. $15.00 (0-374-31224-9).
FORMAT: Storybook   GRADES: 4–6.

The famous punster, prankster, and riddle-regaler goes global for a look at the "ecret-say" "anguages-lay" of the world's children. It's the ripest kind of fun, with material ready for readers to bite into. More passive souls can just sit around and laugh with Schwartz's *There's a Carrot in My Ear, Tales of Trickery,* and more.

Seuss, Dr. *Green Eggs and Ham.* **Illus. by the author.** Random, 1960. LB $7.99 (0-394-90016-2).
FORMAT: Picture book   GRADES: 1–2.

Readers love this debate, as Sam-I-Am makes a persuasive case for the eating of green eggs and ham to a listener who is dead certain of his own likes and dislikes. A rollicking rhythm arises from very few words, ingeniously used.

Seuss, Dr. *Hop on Pop.* **Illus. by the author.** Random, 1963. LB $7.99 (0-394-90029-4).
FORMAT: Picture book   GRADES: 1–3.

This is one of the best teaching tools around, despite its popping, bopping text and appearance of playfulness.

Shaw, Nancy. *Sheep in a Shop.* **Illus. by Margot Apple.** Houghton, 1991. $12.95 (0-385-53681-2).
FORMAT: Picture book   GRADES: Preschool–Grade 3.

This is the most recent of three books about these rollicking woolsters; the others are *Sheep on a Jeep* and *Sheep on a Ship.* Comical tongue-twisting wordplay and a rat-a-tat rhythm will have children clamoring to go along on this shipping trop—make that *shopping trip*—again and again.

Steig, Jeanne. *Consider the Lemming.* **Illus. by William Steig.** Farrar, 1988. $9.00 (0-374-31536-1). paper avail.
FORMAT: Poetry   GRADES: 4–6.

This collection of 25 brief poems and limericks is crafted with simplicity and exhibits a word-lover's ability to turn a phrase. At once wise and witty, these pieces on animals give children a little to bite off and lots to roll over their tongues. Satisfying and classy.

Steig, William. *CDB!* **Illus. by the author.** Simon & Schuster, 1987. paper $3.95 (0-671-66689-4).
FORMAT: Picture book   GRADES: 1–4.

Actually, the title is "See the bee!" Steig reduces words to letter sounds and the results are edifying and often uproarious. Clever through and through.

Terban, Marvin. *Guppies in Tuxedos: Funny Eponyms.* **Illus. by Giulio Maestro.** Houghton, 1988. $12.95 (0-89919-509-1). paper avail.
FORMAT: Picture book   GRADES: Preschool–Grade 2.

The origins of words based on names are explained. The backdrop of cartoony illustrations contains silly, kid-pleasing asides and jokes.

Wolf, Janet. *Adelaide to Zeke.* **Illus. by the author.** HarperCollins, 1987. $11.95 (0-06-026597-3).
FORMAT: Picture book   GRADES: Preschool–Grade 2.

It all starts when Adelaide bothers Benny, then all the letters of the alphabet are introduced one by one in a chain reaction of events. Dr. Dan delivers Edwina; Father (cooing over Edwina) neglects Gretchen who growls at Horace the dog which in turn hounds Ichabod the cat. . . . The transitions are not always logical, but this alluring book with its playful idea of contiguity will have a place in the minds of readers.

Yeoman, John. *Our Village.* **Illus. by Quentin Blake.** Macmillan, 1988. $13.95 (0-689-31451-5).
FORMAT: Poetry   GRADES: 1–3.

Yeoman and Blake create an entire village, from the maps on the endpapers to the the poems within the pages, introducing both people and places. The smallest man in town gardens oversized plants, a busy tailor neglects his own clothing, etc. The characters frolic on the pages in Blake's loose-lined, flowing art. The overall result is a strong sense of place, where readers will meet town eccentrics and ordinary folk tumbling through the book, busy with their lives.

Zimmerman, Andrea Griffing. *The Riddle Zoo.* **Illus. by Giulio Maestro.** Dutton, 1981. $9.25 (0-525-38300-X).

FORMAT: Picture book   GRADES: Preschool–Grade 3.

A small book in all ways but in the laughs it will bring, this is a riddle book for the youngest reader who is putting together words, ideas, and puns for the very first time.

Additional Titles

The following titles, annotated elsewhere in this book (see index), could also fit the "Jokes, Riddles, Puns, Poems" category.

Block, Francesca Lia. *Weetzie Bat*
Bloom, Suzanne. *We Keep a Pig in the Parlor*
Cole, Babette. *The Smelly Book*
Corbalis, Judy. *Porcellus, the Flying Pig*
Duke, Kate. *The Guinea Pig ABC*
Fox, Mem. *Possum Magic*
Gomi, Taro. *Seeing, Saying, Doing, Playing*
Grossman, Bill. *Tommy at the Grocery Store*
Hennessy, B. G. *The Missing Tarts*
Kalman, Maira. *Ooh-La-La (Max in Love)*
Kennedy, X. J. *Brats*
McCaughrean, Geraldine. *A Pack of Lies*
Martin, Bill, Jr., and John Archambault. *Here Are My Hands*
Merriam, Eve. *Halloween ABC*
Nash, Ogden. *Custard the Dragon*
Parkin, Rex. *The Red Carpet*
Prelutsky, Jack. *The New Kid on the Block*
Sandburg, Carl. *Rootabaga Stories*
Seuss, Dr. *The Cat in the Hat*
Silverstein, Shel. *Where the Sidewalk Ends*
Soto, Gary. *Neighborhood Odes*
Stadler, John. *Cat at Bat*
Tryon, Leslie. *Albert's Alphabet*
Willard, Nancy. *East of the Sun & West of the Moon*
Young, Frederica, and Marguerite Kohl. *More Jokes for Children*

7: Instructive Humor

"Didactic, Yet Entertaining"

We can't help it, we are teachers and students all. The insatiable need—altruistic or meddlesome—to guide others to life's secret truths has fired up storytellers for centuries, and this impulse has not escaped writers and illustrators of books for children. If the word "didactic" hadn't taken such a bad rap over the years, it would perfectly describe some truly wonderful instructive books for children, as well as some occasions for well-intentioned, humble attempts (from the clumsy to the tacky) to mold young minds.

The Just So stories of Kipling bring wisdom "even while they entertain," and the cautionary tales of Belloc and his latter-day followers have never been shy about making children think twice. Then there are tales that tacitly ask "Get it?" as they seek to edify children by illuminating concepts, from the epiphanic peek-a-boo of lift-up flaps to the revelatory punchline of a pithy fable. Surprise can be a sort of mnemonic device.

When it is goal-oriented, when there is a lesson at the end of a laugh, humor can be an effective way to help children digest ideas, to coax conformity and cultivate culture. Still, the best teaching comes when the readers—guided by whatever provocations, incarnations, or inspirations a book offers—figure things out for themselves, switching on that old inner lightbulb.

Aesop. *Aesop's Fables.* **Illus. by John Hedjuk.** Rizzoli, 1991. $17.95 (0-8478-1364-9).
FORMAT: Picture book   GRADES: Preschool–Grade 3.

In naïve paintings with patterned backdrops, 14 familiar fables are enacted again. Strikingly designed and composed, the pictures are some of the most directly childlike ever to be paired with these ancient "wisdomisms."

Aesop. *Aesop's Fables.* **Retold and illus. by Fulvio Testa.** Barron's, 1989. $12.95 (0-8120-5958-1).

FORMAT: Picture book   GRADES: 1–4.

For 20 of the famous fabulist's stories, Testa offers robustly colored paintings with many whimsical flourishes. All the tales are simply told; instead of being dealt some obviously stated moral, children are left to think out the lessons themselves. Cheerful.

Aliki. *Manners.* **Illus. by the author.** Greenwillow, 1990. LB $13.93 (0-688-09199-7).

FORMAT: Picture book   GRADES: Kindergarten–Grade 3.

Etiquette is hard to spell for the young, and even harder to reason with. After all, why must everyone have manners? The truth is, many people don't; this book deals with an ideal child, in an ideal world. Etiquette books all exhibit a certain amount of denial, found even in the writings of saucy Miss Manners. Aliki explains how manners grease the world's many transactions and allow others to know that one is thinking kindly of them. Playful pictures spell out the dos and don'ts; the book is intended as a teaching tool.

Arnosky, Jim. *Crinkleroot's Guide to Knowing the Trees.* **Illus. by the author.** Macmillan, 1992. $13.95 (0-02-705855-7).

FORMAT: Picture book   GRADES: Preschool–Grade 3.

Hearty, wise Crinkleroot stops by the woods and offers youngsters lessons in wildlife, with the emphasis on trees. His ways are thorough; no one will regret his company on this or any nature hike.

Ashabranner, Brent. *I'm in the Zoo, Too!* **Illus. by Janet Stevens.** Dutton, 1989. $12.95 (0-525-65002-4).

FORMAT: Picture book   GRADES: Preschool–Grade 4.

The title is a declaration that leads to all kinds of loop-de-loops of thinking and head-scratching. A squirrel named Burl lives in a tree inside a zoo. But *he* doesn't get regular drop-offs of food from the zookeeper! Isn't *he* in the zoo, too? Children may or may not flip past the logistical implications as fearless Burl's tale of trial and error comes to a close. Despite the somewhat awkward illustrations, this remains a bright, appealing tale.

Barton, Byron. *Dinosaurs, Dinosaurs.* **Illus. by the author.** HarperCollins, 1989. $7.95 (0-694-00269-0).

FORMAT: Picture book   GRADES: Preschool–Grade 1.

Barton's economical book does not scrimp on details or ebullient color. In colors straight out of a crayon box he provides children with a genuine "first" dinosaur book. One painting, of a dinosaur in a storm, offers readers a reassuring glimpse of the mighty creatures and implies that they were probably afraid of the same things that children are.

Barton, Byron. *I Want to Be an Astronaut.* **Illus. by the author.** Harper-Collins, 1988. $7.95 (0-690-00261-5).

FORMAT: Picture book   GRADES: Preschool–Grade 1.

Barton shades his characteristic bold shapes with streaks of gray in pictures that express the very essence of children's wishes to be astronauts. The accompanying text is minimal and beautifully precise: "I want to be up there/on a space mission" shows two pilots at the controls of the space shuttle and the rest of the crew functioning (in a cutaway view) in the rest of the ship. An ode to the sort of child's play that leads to dreams-come-true.

Base, Graeme. *Animalia.* **Illus. by the author.** Abrams, 1987. $16.95 (0-8109-1868-4).

FORMAT: Picture book   GRADES: All grades.

Base has created an alliterative ABC book that goes far beyond a simple listing of items in alphabetical order. There are captions or headlines accompanying each letter's scene, such as "Eight Enormous Elephants Expertly Eating Easter Eggs," and each picture is replete with an apparently random choice of objects that have something in common. Although an incredible visual feast, this lacks a clear conceptual coherence, or unity of action or meaning on every page. Readers will nevertheless have a fine time guessing at objects and searching; the meticulous artistry is far-reaching in its innovation, detail, and humor.

Belloc, Hillaire. *Jim, Who Ran Away from His Nurse and Was Eaten by a Lion.* **Illus. by Victoria Chess.** Little, Brown, 1987. paper $4.95 (0-316-13816-9).

FORMAT: Picture book   GRADES: 2–4.

Parents who will stop at nothing to make their children behave may want to present—in good spirits—this Victorian cautionary tale. Naughty Jim's story is all in the title; Chess's art shows off the splendor of zoo life and presents very personable bears, anteaters, and a zoo keeper. The images make a lasting impression.

Bolliger, Max. *Tales of a Long Afternoon.* **Illus. by Jindra Capek.** Dutton, 1991. $13.95 (0-525-44546-3).

FORMAT: Picture book   GRADES: Preschool–Grade 3.

An animal community of near-enemies-turned-friends is the setting for this retelling of six fables by Aesop. Nuances in the pictures add an extra dimension to these well-trod paths of instruction.

Bradman, Tony. *Look Out, He's Behind You!* **Illus. by Margaret Chamberlain.** 1988. $11.95 (0-399-21485-2).

FORMAT: Picture book   GRADES: Preschool–Grade 3.

A lift-the-flap version of a familiar tale. The animals of the forest keep warning Red Riding Hood with the refrain of the title, but all the characters contribute funny asides that add much charm. The irreverence will appeal to children as much as the paper engineering does.

Brown, Laurene Krasny, and Marc Brown. *Dinosaurs Alive and Well! A Guide to Good Health.* **Illus. by Marc Brown.** Little, Brown, 1990. $14.95 (0-316-10998-3).

FORMAT: Picture book   GRADES: Preschool–Grade 3.

Dispensing advice on fitness, nutrition, and other aspects of health, the Browns present cavorting dinosaurs in comic cartoons. Readers will swallow all of it, hook, line, and sinker.

Brown, Laurene Krasny, and Marc Brown. *Dinosaurs Divorce: A Guide for Changing Families.* **Illus. by Marc Brown.** Little, Brown, 1988. $14.95 (0-316-11248-8). paper avail.

FORMAT: Picture book   GRADES: Preschool–Grade 3.

This advice book for children neither diminishes nor underestimates their feelings about their families, but it may help them understand and talk about their pain. Practical help, too, for simple social interactions. Surprisingly funny, despite the serious subject.

Brown, Laurene Krasny, and Marc Brown. *Dinosaurs to the Rescue: A Guide to Protecting Our Planet.* **Illus. by Marc Brown.** Little, Brown, 1992. $14.95 (0-316-11087-6).

FORMAT: Picture book   GRADES: Preschool–Grade 5.

The format is now familiar; the stars of *Dinosaurs Divorce* return to teach young readers the need for environmental awareness and resourcefulness, even on a small scale. Comic cartoons, sound advice, and infectious enthusiasm will persuade even stalwart litterbugs to change their trashy ways.

Browne, Anthony. *Look What I've Got!* **Illus. by the author.** Knopf, 1988. LB $11.99 (0-394-99860-X).
FORMAT: Picture book   GRADES: Preschool–Grade 3.

Jeremy has it all, so it seems. Sam does not. While Jeremy brags, Sam seems quiet and content. And when Jeremy's many valuables cause trouble, Sam is there to help. Browne creates, in porcupine-haired Sam, a genuine hero with unwavering good character and a sound, imaginative mind; he is a comic contrast to that very familiar type, Jeremy. As usual, Browne includes amusing visual puns and jokes, for those with eyes to see.

Burningham, John. *John Patrick Norman McHennessy.* **Illus. by the author.** Crown, 1987. $14.95 (0-517-56805-5).
FORMAT: Picture book   GRADES: Preschool–Grade 2.

Subtitled "The boy who was always late," this book is primarily concerned with the life of the imagination, and its skeptics. The hero never gets to school on time, and his excuses—though absolutely true—are considered too outrageous to believe by his teacher. A brilliant comeuppance awaits that teacher, however, on the one day that John Patrick Norman McHennessy accidentally gets to school right on the dot. A funny tale for children; a cautionary one for adults.

Cole, Joanna. *The Magic School Bus at the Waterworks.* **Illus. by Bruce Degen.** Scholastic, 1986. $13.95 (0-590-43739-9). paper avail.
FORMAT: Picture book   GRADES: 1–4.

A fantastic blend of facts and fictions make this exploration of a town's major utility a joyful study in learning. The kids, traveling with their nutty teacher into the heart of the waterworks, make the sort of snide, wise-guy cracks that most field trippers indulge in, but come away with real knowledge. So will readers.

Conford, Ellen. *A Job for Jenny Archer.* **Illus. by Diane Palmisciano.** Little, Brown, 1988. $9.95 (0-316-15262-5). paper avail.
FORMAT: Chapter book   GRADES: 2–4.

Jenny takes her mother's wish for a fur coat—and the impossibility of her getting one—as a measure of their poverty, and she resolves to earn the money herself. A light lesson in the value of family love over material possessions, Conford's story is at its best when depicting the friendship between Jenny and her best friend Wilson. With witty line drawings in every chapter, the book will inspire other young entrepreneurs and remind them that it's okay to fail.

dePaola, Tomie. *Bill and Pete Go Down the Nile.* **Illus. by the author.**
Putnam, 1987. $14.95 (0-399-21395-3). paper avail.
FORMAT: Picture book   GRADES: Preschool–Grade 3.

On their journey down the Nile, dePaola's celebrated duo transport the reader from the mummified past to a living present. Time distinction is abolished as the Nile Queen, the Grand Hotel, cars and umbrellas, sarcophagi, sacred jewels, and sphinxes are all part of the setting for an ancient story that still bears retelling, especially in such a comic fashion.

Dubanevich, Arlene. *Pigs in Hiding.* **Illus. by the author.** Macmillan, 1983.
$13.95 (0-02-732140-1). paper avail.
FORMAT: Picture book   GRADES: Preschool–Grade 3.

The title tells all in this riotous, laughter-inducing work about a frenetic case of hide-and-seek. Readers will chuckle all the way back to the shelf, where they will also find this author's *Pigs at Christmas* and *Pig William.* All three books are full of porcine splendor.

Duke, Kate. *The Guinea Pig ABC.* **Illus. by the author.** Dutton, 1983. $12.95
(0-525-44058-5). paper avail.
FORMAT: Picture book   GRADES: Preschool–Grade 3.

This first book about Duke's guinea pigs was a phenomenal success, and for excellent reasons; these critters roll and tumble and clamber every-where at once, with barely-contained zeal that will bring smiles to all onlookers' faces. By the way, the book also teaches the alphabet. For more hijinks involving this exuberant bunch in a domestic setting, pass the Guinea Pig board books: *Bedtime, Clean-Up Day, The Playground,* and *What Bounces?*

Duvoisin, Roger. *Petunia, Beware!* **Illus. by the author.** Knopf, 1958. LB
$12.99 (0-394-90867-8). paper avail.
FORMAT: Picture book   GRADES: Preschool–Grade 3.

Another eye-opening glimpse of the world from innocent Petunia's per-spective is provided. She learns by every silly situation she gets into, and never loses her sense of childlike wonder.

Eastman, P. D. *Go, Dog, Go!* **Illus. by the author.** Random, 1961. LB $7.99 (0-
394-90020-0).
FORMAT: Storybook   GRADES: 1–3.

Canines in all shapes and sizes plunge into activities herein. New read-ers weary of Dick and Jane texts find this a refreshing change of pace, even after 30 years. The cartoons are simple, action-packed, and lovable.

Ehlert, Lois. *Fish Eyes: A Book You Can Count On.* **Illus. by the author.**
Harcourt, 1990. $14.95 (0-15-228050-2).
FORMAT: Picture book   GRADES: Preschool–Kindergarten.

In jubilant colors and carefully crafted forms, Ehlert offers a lesson on counting, a fishly mystery, and page after page of visual gusto, akin to that found in her earlier *Growing Vegetable Soup.*

Ehlert, Lois. *Growing Vegetable Soup.* **Illus. by the author.** Harcourt, 1987.
$13.95 (0-15-232575-1). paper avail.
FORMAT: Picture book   GRADES: Preschool–Grade 3.

The title explains the story. First there is the idea to garden, then the actual work right up to the harvest, and then the cooking of soup. This is a healthy way for any child to digest a primer on growing and nurturing living things. It is also a zesty introduction to vivid abstract art.

Flack, Marjorie. *Angus Lost.* **Illus. by the author.** Doubleday, 1941. LB $12.95
(0-385-07214-7). paper avail.
FORMAT: Picture book   GRADES: Preschool–Grade 3.

Angus the Scottie terrier has delighted children for generations: in this title, he spends the night in the great outdoors, with surprisingly chilly results. Other favorites are *Angus and the Ducks* and *Angus and the Cat.*

Fleming, Denise. *Count!* **Illus. by the author.** Holt, 1992. $14.95 (0-8050-1595-7).
FORMAT: Picture book   GRADES: Preschool–Grade 1.

Fleming's text commands the animals of her count to stand still, but sometimes they just won't. Numbers from 1 to 10, then 20, 30, 40, and 50. A blissful rebellion of the animal kingdom, right down to the worms, but worthy lessons as well.

Fox, Mem. *Possum Magic.* **Illus. by Julie Vivas.** Harcourt, 1987. $13.95 (0-15-200572-2). paper avail.
FORMAT: Picture book   GRADES: Preschool–Grade 2.

Apparently the marsupials Down Under take quite literally the expression "you are what you eat." This is the story of two possums—Hush and Grandma Poss—and the magic serves as food for thought. A lesson in geography as well as language, this will introduce readers to two of the more inspired characters in children's books. Cheeky, bouncy fun.

Fradon, Dana. *Harold the Herald: A Book about Heraldry.* **Illus. by the author.** Dutton, 1990. $14.95 (0-525-44634-6).
FORMAT: Picture book   GRADES: 3–6.

Puns and visual funny business underscore the information provided on that most medieval of journalists, the herald.

Freeman, Don. *The Chalk Box Story.* **Illus. by the author.** HarperCollins, 1976. $13.95 (0-397-31699-2).

FORMAT: Picture book   GRADES: Preschool–Grade 3.

This is a small, imaginative charmer about a small boy stranded on an island drawn in chalk. The author of *Corduroy* has created a quiet lesson in colors that never overwhelms the story. Childlike pictures, too.

Fritz, Jean. *And Then What Happened, Paul Revere?* **Illus. by Margot Tomes.** Putnam, 1973. $13.95 (0-698-20274-0). paper avail.

FORMAT: Biography   GRADES: 4–6.

Nonfiction can be funny, when placed in the witty hands of Fritz, known for the spirited, curious approach she brings to all her biographies, *Why Don't You Get a Horse, Sam Adams?* and the timely *Where Do You Think You're Going, Christopher Columbus?* among them. This book was acclaimed for "humanizing" the man most readers will have met only through Longfellow's ringing but somber poem.

Giganti, Paul, Jr. *Each Orange Had Eight Slices.* **Illus. by Donald Crews.** Greenwillow, 1992. LB $13.93 (0-688-10429-0).

FORMAT: Picture book   GRADES: Preschool–Grade 3.

Story problems create a funny text of mathematical somersaults for youngsters. Bright paintings make multiplication a colorful process. Throw out the dull old textbooks of yore.

Gomi, Taro. *Bus Stops.* **Illus. by the author.** Chronicle, 1988. $10.95 (0-87701-551-1).

FORMAT: Picture book   GRADES: Preschool–Grade 1.

As a bus progresses on its route to the garage where it will park for the night, various travelers—actors, commuters, families—hop off at their stops. Readers can count along, and the text suggests different objects to pick out on each spread. Gomi's pictures are beautifully composed, with funny, peppy shapes, and use white space to carve out the horizon. With appeal for children and adults.

Hennessy, B. G. *The Dinosaur Who Lived in My Backyard.* **Illus. by Susan Davis.** Viking, 1988. $12.95 (0-670-81685-X). paper avail.

FORMAT: Picture book   GRADES: Preschool–Grade 1.

About midway into this story, it will dawn on readers that this is no fantasy excursion and that Hennessy is packing in a lot of facts about dinosaurs in an absolutely charming fashion. Davis, illustrator of *When Daddy Comes Home* and *Waiting for Mom,* adds odd, humorous perspectives.

Hirst, Robin, and Sally Hirst. *My Place in Space.* **Illus. by Roland Harvey with Joe Levine.** Orchard, 1990. LB $13.99 (0-531-08459-0). paper avail.

FORMAT: Picture book   GRADES: Preschool–Grade 2.

Henry knows exactly where he lives and, like Emily in *Our Town*, can give directions right down to the Virgo Supercluster of galaxies. While his thoughts are in space, his town's Main Street becomes the setting for raucous scenes of earthly residents. Witty and thought-provoking.

Hoban, Lillian. *Arthur's Pen Pal.* **Illus. by the author.** HarperCollins, 1976. LB $12.89 (0-06-022372-3). paper avail.

FORMAT: Chapter book   GRADES: 2–4.

When a chimp named Arthur, first spotted in *Arthur's Christmas Cookies*, finds himself in the middle of hot correspondence with a new pal who likes karate and playing the drums, how is he supposed to guess that his pen pal is a girl? Not the first pen pal story to go awry, but one of the funniest for the beginning reader set.

Hoban, Russell. *Bread and Jam for Frances.* **Illus. by Lillian Hoban.** HarperCollins, 1964. LB $13.89 (0-06-022360-X). paper avail.

FORMAT: Picture book   GRADES: Preschool–Grade 3.

Bread and jam—that's what Frances wants for every meal, and that's what she gets. Not surprisingly, everyone's favorite badger finds out that a little variety in life is not such a bad thing. This wasn't the first Frances story, but it is one of the funniest. Most readers can't resist all the books once they've tried one.

Hoban, Tana. *Look! Look! Look!* **Illus. by the author.** Greenwillow, 1988. $12.95 (0-688-07239-9).

FORMAT: Picture book   GRADES: Preschool–Grade 2.

This book offers three chances to see ordinary objects in an enticing setting. What is that wrinkled, hairy gray thing? Turn the page and see the back end of an elephant; turn one more page and there it is in its entirety. Wordlessly, Hoban entertains as she provides her apparently random choice of the things patterned. Unlike many of her other books, such as *26 Letters and 99 Cents*, this one doesn't hold up to repeat viewings, except as a catalog of familiar items. But a sense of humor guides Hoban's selections, and that may inspire children to spot texture and pattern in all objects.

Jonas, Ann. *Aardvarks, Disembark!* **Illus. by the author.** Greenwillow, 1990. LB $14.88 (0-688-07207-0).

FORMAT: Picture book   GRADES: Preschool–up.

A procession of animals, with names beginning with letters from A to Z, march out of Noah's ark and down into the world. The book opens vertically, so that each upturn of the next page reveals more creatures, many from a list of endangered and extinct species. Inventive and useful.

Joslin, Seslye. *What Do You Say, Dear?* **Illus. by Maurice Sendak.** HarperCollins, 1958. LB $13.89 (0-06-023074-6). paper avail.
FORMAT: Picture book   GRADES: Preschool–Grade 5.

Absurd situations aside, this is an entertaining introduction to manners and companion title to *What Do You Do, Dear?*, published the same year. Sendak's illustrations received a Caldecott Honor award, but it is Joslin's tongue-in-cheek questions and answers that will have the slothful young sitting up straight and refining their ways.

Kalman, Maira. *Hey Willy, See the Pyramids.* **Illus. by the author.** Viking, 1988. $14.95 (0-670-82163-2). paper avail.
FORMAT: Picture book   GRADES: Preschool–Grade 3.

The stories Lulu tells in the middle of the night are weird and funny— one part imagination, one part facts gleaned from a mysterious adult world, and one part pure silliness. The pictures have the deceptive look of child's drawings, but are really a sophisticated pandemonium of idiosyncratic shapes, colors, and perspectives.

Kalman, Maira. *Sayonara, Mrs. Kackleman.* **Illus. by the author.** Viking, 1989. $14.95 (0-670-82945-5). paper avail.
FORMAT: Picture book   GRADES: Preschool–Grade 3.

A travelogue of Japan is presented, through the distinctly skewed perspectives of Kalman, who illustrated David Byrne's *Stay Up Late* as well as her own *Hey Willy, See the Pyramids.* Lulu and her brother Alexander glean some facts about this country, while adding their wildly funny surmisings to the plot.

Kellogg, Steven. *Johnny Appleseed.* **Illus. by the author.** Morrow, 1988. LB $14.88 (0-688-06418-3).
FORMAT: Storybook   GRADES: Preschool–Grade 3.

A retelling of the legend of John Chapman—a.k.a. Johnny Appleseed— is doubly invigorated with Kellogg's snappy pictures.

Kellogg, Steven. *Paul Bunyan.* **Illus. by the author.** Morrow, 1984. LB $15.88 (0-688-03850-6). paper avail.
FORMAT: Picture book   GRADES: Preschool–Grade 3.

All of Kellogg's tall tales are genuine child-pleasers; this one is slightly longer than *Pecos Bill* and packs in a lot of legend about the mighty big guy. Don't worry, there's still room for Babe, the bright blue ox.

Kellogg, Steven. *Pecos Bill.* **Illus. by the author.** Morrow, 1986. LB $15.88 (0-688-05872-8). paper avail.

FORMAT: Picture book   GRADES: Preschool–Grade 3.

The author of the Pinkerton saga and other tales brings rip-roaring illustrations and an anecdotal tone to this exaggerated Texas legend. A hoot and a half.

Kipling, Rudyard. *The Best Fiction of Rudyard Kipling.* Doubleday, 1989. $24.95 (0-385-26090-3).

FORMAT: Anthology   GRADES: All grades.

A massive volume of the author's best-known works, including his pourquois stories: *Just So Stories, The Jungle Book, Kim, Rikki-Tikki-Tavi, Wee Willie Winkie,* and many others. His merits do not need to be sung here. Best for read-alouds or older readers.

Kipling, Rudyard. *The Elephant's Child.* **Illus. by Lorinda Bryan Cauley.** Harcourt, 1983. $14.95 (0-15-225385-8). paper avail.

FORMAT: Picture book   GRADES: Preschool–Grade 3.

Many critics consider this unabridged version of Kipling's classic to be the finest illustrated edition available. The humor of the tale is wonderfully intact and extended by award-winning Cauley.

Knutson, Barbara. *Why the Crab Has No Head.* **Illus. by the author.** Carolrhoda, 1987. $9.95 (0-87614-322-2).

FORMAT: Picture book   GRADES: Preschool–Grade 3.

Knutson retells the African folktale about how the crab must live forever without a head, and how he brought this fate upon himself. This is more of a cautionary tale than a pourquoi story, and readers who occasionally find themselves swollen with pride will do well not to take this *too* seriously.

Krause, Ute. *Pig Surprise.* **Illus. by the author.** Dial, 1989. $11.95 (0-8037-0714-2).

FORMAT: Picture book   GRADES: Preschool–Grade 3.

The illustrator of *The Santa Clauses* and *A Package for Miss Marshwater* does a solo turn. When Nina asks an aunt for a guinea pig, she ends up with a genuine pig. A real porker. A beautiful friendship blossoms, but ultimately the pig needs his freedom, and Nina understands. Wonderful contrasts in every scene, into which Krause instills a solid sense of place.

Lattimore, Deborah Nourse. *The Prince and the Golden Axe: A Minoan Tale.* **Illus. by the author.** HarperCollins, 1988. LB $12.89 (0-06-023716-3).

FORMAT: Picture book   GRADES: Kindergarten–Grade 3.

Lattimore constructs a tale of the destruction of Thera around a young prince's unholy boasting about his own powers instead of paying respect to the Goddess Diktynna. Ultimately, through his folly, Minoan civilization is lost. Each frame has the look of a fresco painting. The storytelling is sure and steady, as though this were a familiar myth retold, rather than a novel creation. Despite the choice of stylized forms, the remote past is animated again and its players dance freely through the pages.

Lawson, Robert. *Ben and Me.* **Illus. by the author.** Little, Brown, 1988. $14.95 (0-316-51732-1). paper avail.
FORMAT: Novel   GRADES: 3–6.

Amos, a mouse, narrates this "true" story of Ben Franklin—yes, that Ben—and brings his compelling point of view to bear on a number of historic occasions. Amusing through and through, and perhaps once children have read Lawson's takes on famous figures (*Mr. Revere and I* and *I Discover Columbus* among them), they will move easily into Jean Fritz's nonfiction favorites.

Leedy, Loreen. *Big, Small, Short, Tall.* **Illus. by the author.** Holiday, 1987. $12.95 (0-8234-0645-8).
FORMAT: Picture book   GRADES: Preschool–Grade 3.

Readers have learned, in a short space of time, to expect humor and boundless energy from Leedy's books. This brightly colored concept book will not disappoint anyone looking for a memorable way to put across opposites, involving a circus of comical animals. Fun for all and painlessly educational—unless it hurts to laugh.

Leedy, Loreen. *A Dragon Christmas: Things to Make and Do.* **Illus. by the author.** Holiday, 1988. $13.95 (0-8234-0716-0).
FORMAT: Picture book   GRADES: Kindergarten–Grade 3.

This round of energetic holiday activities stars bug-eyed blue dragons. The pages are packed with information, but this time, the instructions for crafts seem too sketchy for many younger readers. Still, to pick on the specifics is being mean to this gang, for they score points simply for mustering up enthusiasm with their ever-expressive eyebrows and endless innovations.

Lester, Julius. *How Many Spots Does a Leopard Have? And Other Tales.* **Illus. by David Shannon.** Scholastic, 1989. $14.95 (0-590-41973-0).
FORMAT: Storybook   GRADES: 2–6.

A sterling collection of African and Jewish folktales is communicated with this storyteller's natural eloquence and grace. He has also retold *The Tales of Uncle Remus,* the adventures of Brer Rabbit.

Lionni, Leo. *Tillie and the Wall.* **Illus. by the author.** Knopf, 1989. LB $13.99 (0-394-92155-0). paper avail.
FORMAT: Picture book   GRADES: Preschool–Grade 3.

This is a lovely, humorous fable about a determined mouse who wants—no, *needs*—to know what is on the other side of the high wall.

Lobel, Arnold. *Fables.* **Illus. by the author.** HarperCollins, 1980. LB $14.89 (0-06-023974-3). paper avail.
FORMAT: Storybook   GRADES: All grades.

Even Aesop himself might have laughed over this Caldecott Medal–winning book. Lobel pokes fun at all our human failings with the cast of guileless creatures that troop through these pages.

MacDonald, Betty. *Hello, Mrs. Piggle-Wiggle.* **Illus. by Hilary Knight.** HarperCollins, 1957. $14.00 (0-397-31715-8). paper avail.
FORMAT: Novel   GRADES: 3–7.

Mrs. Piggle-Wiggle loves all children, but she is realistic enough to know that they must be cured of misbehavior and bad habits. Her cures are refreshingly old-fashioned—let the child who won't bathe not bathe until there is enough dirt on her skin in which to plant radish seeds. Sendak illustrated the first of these adventures—*Mrs. Piggle-Wiggle's Farm*—but Knight's comic drawings splendidly decorate three of the four available, including *Mrs. Piggle-Wiggle* and *Mrs. Piggle-Wiggle's Magic.*

McNulty, Faith. *The Elephant Who Couldn't Forget.* **Illus. by Marc Simont.** HarperCollins, 1980. LB $12.89 (0-06-024146-2). paper avail.
FORMAT: Chapter book   GRADES: Preschool–Grade 3.

In this amusing tale, Congo, the smallest elephant in his family, has an excellent memory, but finds out that remembering and holding a grudge are two very different things.

Mahy, Margaret. *The Great White Man-Eating Shark: A Cautionary Tale.* **Illus. by Jonathan Allen.** Dial, 1990. $12.95 (0-8037-0749-5).
FORMAT: Picture book   GRADES: Preschool–Grade 3.

Resembling, slightly, a shark, Norvin takes to wearing a fin off the coast of Caramel Cove to scare swimmers. Then a real lady shark falls in love with him and demands he marry her. Hey, he's only a child—but just desserts are served up by this favorite author's brimming wit, and Allen's suitably droll illustrations.

Mazer, Anne. *The Yellow Button.* **Illus. by Judy Pedersen.** Knopf, 1990. $12.95 (0-394-82935-2).
FORMAT: Picture book   GRADES: Preschool–Grade 3.

This is an eccentric story of a yellow button, in a pocket, in a blue dress worn by a girl who is shown to be part of a "big picture"—a universe where the earth is no more than a speck. Clean, clear prose matches Pedersen's scumbled, iridescent paintings and brave, simple shapes. Readers will be charmed by the provocative ideas, and smile at the simple unfolding of scenes.

Miller, Margaret. *Whose Hat?* **Illus. by the author.** Greenwillow, 1988. $13.95 (0-688-06906-1).
FORMAT: Picture book   GRADES: Preschool–Kindergarten.

In an almost identical concept to *Whose Hat Is That?* by Ron Roy, photographs show nine different hats. They are worn by adults in situations with which the hats are identified and by children who like to pretend. There is a spirit of playfulness and fun to the pictures—even the adults aren't entirely serious about putting in a hard day's work.

Mills, Claudia. *Dinah for President.* Macmillan, 1992. $12.95 (0-02-766999-8).
FORMAT: Novel   GRADES: 4–6.

Middle school may swallow up others, but not dauntless Dinah. She is ready to make a name for herself, even as an entering sixth-grader, by running for class president. With the guts, the need for glory, and a budding awareness of environmental concerns, she almost pulls it off. Rip-roaring in some places, quietly funny in others.

Minarik, Else Holmelund. *No Fighting! No Biting!* **Illus. by Maurice Sendak.** HarperCollins, 1958. LB $12.89 (0-06-024291-4). paper avail.
FORMAT: Chapter book   GRADES: 1–3.

In this splendid story-within-a-story, children Rosa and Willy are squeezing and pinching each other when Cousin Joan tells them about little alligators who behave in a remarkably similar fashion. The author and illustrator of the well-loved *Little Bear* tales turn bickering gators into high comedy, and at the end, Willy and Rosa sit quietly reading books. Good stuff.

Norman, Howard. *How Glooskap Outwits the Ice Giants: And Other Tales of the Maritime Indians.* **Illus. by Michael McCurdy.** Little, Brown, 1989. $14.95 (0-316-61181-6).
FORMAT: Chapter book   GRADES: 3–7.

Glooskap is one of the most endearing gods to come down the folkloric pike in some time. Curious as a child despite his gigantic size and great powers, he makes himself available to help out his creations, the Maritime Indians. He is the subject of good-natured, polished storytelling that enhances his reputation with the turn of each humorous page. McCurdy's striking woodcuts present Glooskap's funny, noble face. These stories will have readers laughing as they bellow "More!"

Oram, Hiawyn. *Ned and the Joybaloo*. Illus. by Satoshi Kitamura. Farrar, 1989. $11.95 (0-374-35501-0). paper avail.
FORMAT: Picture book   GRADES: Preschool–Grade 2.

Ned is impatient for Fridays, when he and the Joybaloo—the size of a dragon, closely resembling a white dog with confettilike spots—play together. But Ned demands the attention of the Joybaloo so often that it loses its joy. Kitamura interprets Ned's plight in offbeat perspectives of a zanily cluttered, chaotic household. A provocative lesson in independence.

Poortvliet, Rien, and Wil Huygen. *The Book of the Sandman and the Alphabet of Sleep*. Illus. by Rien Poortvliet. Abrams, 1990. $19.95 (0-8109-1524-3).
FORMAT: Storybook   GRADES: 4–6.

This faux reference book rivals these creators' *Gnomes*. It contains footnotes that sound like logical explanations. Using equations that invoke terms like "speed of thought," the book may persuade readers that its *jultomten*-like man really can travel into every single home each night, in 12 short hours.

Raskin, Ellen. *Nothing Ever Happens on My Block*. Illus. by the author. Aladdin, 1966. paper $3.95 (0-689-71335-5).
FORMAT: Picture book   GRADES: Preschool–Grade 3.

This small paperback will elicit sympathy from readers who have also complained of living on too-quiet streets. But then they'll be wise to what Chester is missing. While he complains, the whole world is agog with activities, if only he looked around. The author's pictures are crammed with details to be pored over and savored.

Sachar, Louis. *Sideways Arithmetic from Wayside School*. Scholastic, 1989. paper $2.75 (0-590-42416-5).
FORMAT: Short stories   GRADES: 2–6.

After they read *Sixth Grade Secrets* and *There's a Boy in the Girls' Bathroom*, tease children into going after this collection, all funny stories loaded with brainteasers.

Schweninger, Ann. *Off to School!* Puffin, 1989. paper $3.95 (0-14-050661-6).
FORMAT: Picture book   GRADES: Preschool–Grade 1.

Irrepressible Button Brown is facing school for the very first time. Soon he's involved in drawing, milk time, the playground, and making new friends. The rabbit world is a genial one, which touches on—sometimes in pictures alone—many of the concerns all schoolbunnies have. Fresh and amusing, this book is alive with the paints, crayons, pencil sharpeners, and tears of any first day.

Sendak, Maurice. *Nutshell Library.* **Illus. by the author.** HarperCollins, 1962. $14.95 (0-06-025500-5).
FORMAT: Picture book   GRADES: Preschool–Grade 3.

This palm-sized library (a boxed set of four books) offers children almost everything they need to know to survive and thrive in life: the months (*Chicken Soup with Rice*), counting (*One Was Johnny*), the alphabet (*Alligators All Around*), and how to care (*Pierre: A Cautionary Tale in Five Chapters and a Prologue*). Divinely funny, these books are available separately in library editions.

Sharmat, Marjorie Weinman. *Helga High-Up.* **Illus. by David Neuhaus.** Scholastic, 1987. $11.95 (0-590-40692-2).
FORMAT: Picture book   GRADES: Preschool–Grade 2.

Long-necked and awkward, Helga is the tallest giraffe in her family and has bad posture, too. Still, her height arrests a robbery in midcrime, and a mild lesson of self-acceptance becomes engaging through Sharmat's typically bouncy prose. With sight gags to tickle anyone's sense of the absurd.

Sheppard, Jeff. *The Right Number of Elephants.* **Illus. by Felicia Bond.** HarperCollins, 1990. LB $12.89 (0-06-025616-8). paper avail.
FORMAT: Picture book   GRADES: Preschool–Grade 3.

Perplexing problems of ordinary existence can be unraveled, if one just knows the correct number of elephants to bring in for the solution. For example, if a child is reading a book and having a snack, then the right number of elephants is one. A companionable counting book, featuring endearing pachyderms.

Sis, Peter. *Beach Ball.* **Illus. by the author.** Greenwillow, 1990. $12.88 (0-688-09182-2).
FORMAT: Picture book   GRADES: Preschool–Grade 1.

Several concepts are joined under one sun by Sis's electrifying seascapes, crowded with details and energetic beachcombers: the alphabet, opposites, sounds, counting, and more.

Snape, Juliet, and Charles Snape. *The Boy with the Square Eyes.* **Illus. by the authors.** Simon & Schuster, 1990. paper $5.95 (0-671-69445-6).
FORMAT: Picture book   GRADES: Preschool–Grade 7.

From watching television constantly, Charlie's eyes become square, and everything he looks at becomes geometric. There is a cure—kids reading this book will already have one up on Charlie. A purely cautionary tale.

Stadler, John. *Cat at Bat.* **Illus. by the author.** Dutton, 1988. $9.95 (0-525-44416-5).
FORMAT: Picture book   GRADES: Preschool–Grade 3.

This easy reader by an established comedian in the field of children's books uses a limited, rhythmic text and complementary illustrations to make its point: it's fun to learn how to read. Children will be delighted as the visual clues and words combine to help them to read, perhaps for the very first time. Stadler is a good name to know; children will seek out his other books for their boisterous good humor.

Stehr, Frédéric. *Gulliver.* **Illus. by the author.** Farrar, 1988. $10.95 (0-374-30865-9).
FORMAT: Picture book   GRADES: All grades.

This is a reassuring look at separations and reunions through the eyes of a kitten with wanderlust. Gulliver, a gray cat, gets out of his family's car at a rest stop. When they innocently drive away without him, Gulliver lives through a night of terror that would be funny if it weren't also frightening. There are cautionary elements in this tale; however, most spreads allow readers to look ahead in the story and see Gulliver safely meet each ordeal.

Stolz, Mary. *Zekmet the Stone Carver.* **Illus. by Deborah Nourse Lattimore.** Harcourt, 1988. $14.95 (0-15-299961-2).
FORMAT: Picture book   GRADES: Preschool–Grade 3.

This is a fanciful attempt to re-create the story of the building of the Great Sphinx at Giza. Zekmet, the stone carver, is approached by the Pharoah's vizier to build a monument for his majesty's "deathless splendor." Inspired by a fearsome lion, Zekmet suggests the Sphinx—half lion, half man. The timeless riddle that rises from the desert sand may prove inspirational to some readers, although the details here are purely fictional. Stylized paintings against a marbled background add a sense of awe and authenticity; with light touches in text and art, the past is encapsulated, but not entombed.

Tryon, Leslie. *Albert's Alphabet.* **Illus. by the author.** Macmillan, 1991. $13.95
(0-689-31642-9).
FORMAT: Picture book   GRADES: Preschool–Grade 3.

A construction site is the arena for a feathered hero's race against time in
a book that builds toward insight and offers tacit revelations on each
page. A clever goose becomes an architect of alphabets by manufacturing
a no-stone-unturned ABC, by transforming the theoretical (and raw materials of his workshop) to the practical world of action and experience—
a playground for children.

Van Allsburg, Chris. *The Wretched Stone.* **Illus. by the author.** Houghton,
1991. $17.95 (0-395-53307-4).
FORMAT: Picture book   GRADES: All grades.

The eponymous stone has one glowing side that transforms into apes
sailors who can't tear themselves away from its flickering light. Readers
will triumphantly guess the obvious nature of this rock, but the book's
real lessons are in the subtle ideas crafted in scene after scene. Imaginative and hard-hitting, though not for every taste.

Viorst, Judith. *Alexander and the Terrible, Horrible, No Good, Very Bad
Day.* **Illus. by Ray Cruz.** Macmillan, 1972. $13.95 (0-689-30072-7). paper avail.
FORMAT: Picture book   GRADES: 1–3.

Alexander's bad day is good news for readers, who learn along with him
that there simply *are* days like that, and there's no use running away
from them. Sophisticated wit, accompanied by handily appealing drawings, make this accessible both to listeners and beginning readers alike.
Viorst's other books are also recommended for funny doses of real life:
Alexander, Who Used to Be Rich Last Sunday and *I'll Fix Anthony* are but
two.

Walsh, Ellen Stoll. *Mouse Paint.* **Illus. by the author.** Harcourt, 1989. $11.95
(0-15-256025-4).
FORMAT: Picture book   GRADES: Preschool–Grade 1.

Three white mice get into some primary hued paint pots and emerge as
artful members of a lesson on color and camouflage. When they were
white mice, on white paper, the cat couldn't see them. But when they
find jars of paint, they begin a flirtation with color that provides them
with nearly all the hues in the spectrum. Simplicity reigns in Walsh's
brief tale, and a feeling of joyful discovery pervades her broad lines and
expressive figures. Her message is clear, and one readers will respond to:
Paints have many purposes, at least one of which is fun.

Watson, N. Cameron. *The Little Pigs' First Cookbook.* **Illus. by the author.**
Little, Brown, 1987. $12.95 (0-316-92467-9).
FORMAT: Picture book   GRADES: 1–3.

Charles, Bertram, and Ralph are the three pigs, all just learning how to
cook. The recipes are clearly written, the food is appealing and healthful,
and dessert is not overlooked. But the real treats are Watson's pictures,
full of bright, bold shapes and sweet schematics to help in the assembly
of ingredients. The design is outstanding, incorporating small poetic
asides, suggestions for alternate ingredients, and definitions of some of
the hard words. For cooking up meals, and fun.

White, E. B. *Charlotte's Web.* **Illus. by Garth Williams.** HarperCollins, 1952.
LB $11.89 (0-06-026386-5). paper avail.
FORMAT: Novel   GRADES: 3–6.

Few children will not have come across this enduring classic, which uses
both broad humor in the barnyard squabbles of Wilbur's fellow creatures
and a more gossamer kind of comedy to explain and ennoble themes of
friendship and loyalty. Ever-felicitous. Don't forget *Stuart Little,* of
course.

Wood, Audrey. *Elbert's Bad Word.* **Illus. by Audrey Wood and Don Wood.**
Harcourt, 1988. $13.95 (0-15-225320-3).
FORMAT: Picture book   GRADES: Preschool–Grade 3.

Elbert shocks everyone at a garden party by using a bad word; it seems
just to have come to him, without any thought on his part. Despite the
moral, children will find this funny.

Young, Ed. *The Other Bone.* **Illus. by the author.** HarperCollins, 1984. LB
$14.89 (0-06-026871-9).
FORMAT: Picture book   GRADES: Preschool–Grade 3.

This delectable fable from Aesop—about the dog who went after the
bone reflected in the water, only to lose his own bone—shows the imp-
ish humor of the beloved, normally more serious Caldecott Medalist.
Completely wordless, it speaks volumes.

Young, Ed. *Seven Blind Mice.* **Illus. by the author.** Putnam, 1992. $16.95 (0-
399-22261-8).
FORMAT: Picture book   GRADES: Preschool–Grade 3.

In a tale that harkens back quite deliberately to the fable of the blind men
and the elephant, seven blind mice each venture out on consecutive days
of the week. They each encounter "Something" but draw short-sighted
conclusions—all but one, the white mouse, who unifies all the informa-

tion the others gathered and comes up with a solution. Rewarding and funny on all counts.

Zavos, Judy. *Murgatroyd's Garden.* **Illus. by Drahos Zak.** St. Martin's, 1988. $9.95 (0-312-01629-8).

FORMAT: Picture book   GRADES: Kindergarten–Grade 3.

This is the ultimate cautionary tale for all those children out there who refuse to undergo a good shampoo now and then. Murgatroyd is allowed to grow his dirty hair into a garden, complete with vegetables, fruits, birds, and an apple tree; he soon becomes miserable. Told with theatrical touches and a good, bouncy tone, this tall tale will amuse those who wash and impress those who don't.

Additional Titles

The following titles, annotated elsewhere in this book (see index), could also fit the "Didactic, Yet Entertaining" category.

Ahlberg, Janet, and Allan Ahlberg. *Starting School*
Anno, Mitsumasa. *Anno's Aesop*
Arkin, Allan. *The Lemming Condition*
Base, Graeme. *My Grandma Lived in Gooligulch*
Bible, King James Version. *The Nativity (Vivas, illus.)*
Bradman, Tony. *Not Like This, Like That*
Brown, Marc. *Arthur's Nose*
Carroll, Lewis. *Alice's Adventures in Wonderland*
Dahl, Roald. *Charlie and the Chocolate Factory*
Gwynne, Fred. *A Little Pigeon Toad*
Heller, Nicholas. *Happy Birthday, Moe Dog*
Jabar, Cynthia. *Alice Ann Gets Ready for School*
Juster, Norton. *As: A Surfeit of Similes*
Juster, Norton. *The Phantom Tollbooth*
Kennedy, Richard. *The Boxcar at the Center of the Universe*
Kitamura, Satoshi. *What's Inside?*
Lattimore, Deborah Nourse. *Why There Is No Arguing in Heaven*
Martin, Bill, Jr., and John Archambault. *Chicka Chicka Boom Boom*
Meigs, Cornelia. *Invincible Louisa*
Modesitt, Jeanne. *Vegetable Soup*
Nunes, Susan. *Tiddalick the Frog*
Nygren, Tord. *The Red Thread*
Scheffler, Ursel. *Stop Your Crowing, Kasimir!*
Sis, Peter. *Waving*

8: Text and Subtext

Parody, Wit, Irony, Spoofs, and Send-Ups

Kids enjoy Samuel Clemens and James Thurber as much as grown-ups enjoy the likes of George Bernard Shaw and Noel Coward. There are countless others who serve up wit to rival any Shavian play and who dish out drollery deadpan enough to make the most naive readers shriek. The playful dexterity found in these books includes humor to evoke laughter not only for the text but also the elusive "subtext," not only by the openly stated barbs, but also by the larger picture of insults, allusions, or commentary. Children's humor, when self-mocking, implies some self-awareness—a child may be innocently silly, or knowingly silly, in hopes of inducing laughs. The latter behavior, in the best tradition of comedy, can fall under wit. Children and teenagers who enjoy spoofs, parodies, and send-ups revel in two kinds of knowledge at once: a familiarity with the original story being "spoofed" and the discovery of a new "stacked, squeezed in, dangling" version. The more sophisticated reader will gain most from the entries in this section but almost all readers will find something here in which to delight.

Aardema, Verna. *Princess Gorilla and a New Kind of Water.* Illus. by Victoria Chess. Dial, 1988. LB $10.89 (0-8037-0413-5). paper avail.
FORMAT: Picture book   GRADES: Preschool–Grade 3.

A barrel of vinegar is about to become the deciding factor in the question of who Princess Gorilla will marry—but can any creature in the kingdom gulp its acidic contents down? Aardema, who has written such other funny books as *Rabbit Makes a Monkey of Lion,* and such lyric ones as *Bringing the Rain to Kapiti Plain,* has created a text that is grandly served by Chess's always witty, often deadpan, pictures.

Ahlberg, Janet, and Allan Ahlberg. *The Jolly Postman.* **Illus. by the authors.** Little, Brown, 1986. $15.95 (0-316-02033-8).
FORMAT: Picture book   GRADES: Preschool–Grade 3.

The Ahlbergs fracture several fairy tales, simply by putting all the most familiar storybook characters in one great neighborhood. There, an amiable postman delivers expressive missives from door to door, envelopes and pull-out notes included. Will elicit chuckles even upon rereadings. Biting, funny stuff.

Alexander, Lloyd. *The Book of Three.* Holt, 1964. $16.95 (0-8050-0874-8). paper avail.
FORMAT: Novel   GRADES: 4–6.

This funny adventure foreshadows the combination of wit and fantasy for which Alexander has become known. Set in an imaginary kingdom, it should enchant readers and get them ready for the Newbery Honor Book *The Black Cauldron.* Older children will enjoy the travels of Vesper Holly in *The Illyrian Adventure.*

Arkin, Alan. *The Lemming Condition.* **Illus. by Joan Sandin.** HarperCollins, 1976. $13.00 (0-06-020133-9). paper avail.
FORMAT: Novel   GRADES: 4–6.

What do you do if you are a somewhat skeptical lemming, facing, with all your comrades, a suicidal march into the surf? Bubber has his doubts about the wisdom of this impulse. Arkin asks all the right questions about his young hero, and presents a true parable for our time. Funny, and poignant. In the years beyond childhood, some readers will come across Ionesco's scathing *Rhinoceros* and fondly recall Arkin's tale.

Asbjørnsen, Peter Christen, and Jørgen Moe. *Norwegian Folk Tales.* Pantheon, 1982. paper $14.00 (0-394-71054-1).
FORMAT: Anthology   GRADES: 7–up.

Richly rewarding and endlessly funny, this fine anthology has been carefully translated by Pat Shaw Iversen and Carl Norman to preserve the nuances and bold strokes of the original collection. Readers will meet trolls, of course, but also the transformed creatures of the Scandinavian landscape, heroes and villains alike. Other volumes in this worthwhile series include *The Old Wives' Fairy Tale Book,* edited by Angela Carter; *Italian Folktales* by Italo Calvino; *The Treasury of Jewish Folklore,* edited by Nathan Ausubel; and *Arab Folktales* by Inea Bushnaq.

Base, Graeme. *My Grandma Lived in Gooligulch.* **Illus. by the author.** Abrams, 1990. $12.95 (0-8109-1547-2).
FORMAT: Picture book   GRADES: All grades.

Gooligulch is "nowhere much near anywhere," but Grandma puts the area on the map, for she is more famous than it is. Why? Among the reasons: she is known to ride atop a kangaroo or "in a two-wheel gig/A wombat at the bit." Base provides readers with one of the best introductions to the fauna of the Australian bush. Although Base's best-selling extravaganza, *Animalia*, has won him reputation for pictorial skill, this, on the whole, is a better book. There is as much wit and humor in the rhyming text as there is mastery and opulence in the illustrations.

Block, Francesca Lia. *Weetzie Bat.* HarperCollins, 1989. $12.89 (0-06-020536-9). paper avail.
FORMAT: Novel   GRADES: 7–up.

Collapse teenage vernacular into one hip dictionary; people a glittering pink flamingo universe with a fairy godmother, homosexual boys so sweet you could hug 'em, and a wide-eyed innocent named Weetzie Bat; map it all out among the jammed highways and cement strips of L.A.'s boulevards, and you have this funny debut. A blithe, frank tale with a spirit so generous and a vision so clear that any innocents in the crowd will glide through this blue-sky-sand-and-surf scene unscathed.

Blume, Judy. *Otherwise Known as Sheila the Great.* Dutton, 1972. $11.95 (0-525-36455-2). paper avail.
FORMAT: Novel   GRADES: 4–6.

The fears and concerns of a young girl are treated with unfeathered honesty and unbridled compassion, but the story is held together by Blume's wit. She put the golden rule back into children's books, treating kids as peers and combining humor and realism in the telling.

Brancato, Robin. *Uneasy Money.* Knopf, 1986. $11.95 (0-394-96954-0). paper avail.
FORMAT: Novel   GRADES: 7–up.

Like Bill Brittain's *All the Money in the World*, this book features a fine piece of wish fulfillment when Mike Bronti wins over two million dollars in a lottery. The lessons he learns are hard ones, but Brancato puts it over in a breezily assured style that never falters, never gets weighed down. And yes, readers will come away with the feeling that if they had a million, they would do things far, far differently. Sure.

Browne, Anthony. *Willy the Wimp.* **Illus. by the author.** Knopf, 1985. LB $13.99 (0-394-97061-6). paper avail.
FORMAT: Picture book   GRADES: Preschool–Grade 3.

With neat quips and bold illustrations, Browne unravels the bully dilemma once and for all. Tidy Willy is tired of the gangly bunch of apes that pick on him. He lifts weights, becomes a muscular knight errant to Millie's damsel-in-distress, and puts those apes on permanent notice. Biting comedy, underscored by a real understanding of children's concerns.

Burkert, Nancy Ekholm. *Valentine and Orson.* **Illus. by the author.** Farrar, 1989. $16.95 (0-374-38078-3).
FORMAT: Picture book   GRADES: 1–up.

In polished rhyming couplets the author of *Snow White and the Seven Dwarfs* brings readers the story of twins separated at birth, one a wild man, the other courtly. Carried by the verse are exhilarating scenes of the theatrics of the tale, skillfully composed and full of details to be unearthed and pored over.

Busselle, Rebecca. *Bathing Ugly.* Orchard, 1989. LB $12.99 (0-531-08401-9). paper avail.
FORMAT: Novel   GRADES: 7–up.

Betsy's season at camp is far less than she bargained for, and to top it all off, there is a beauty pageant looming at summer's end. She handles it all with wit and dignity, offering herself and readers a way out of disaster that is both original and satisfying.

Byars, Betsy. *The Golly Sisters Go West.* **Illus. by Sue Truesdell.** HarperCollins, 1986. LB $12.89 (0-06-020884-8). paper avail.
FORMAT: Chapter book   GRADES: 2–4.

These energetic sisters intend to make their fortunes out West, but aren't quite certain just how they'll do that until they get there. Young readers will love the feisty blend of humor in both text and art, and—we hope—trouble themselves to find Byars's other books on the shelves. It just proves that comedy can be its own reward.

Byars, Betsy. *The Moon and I.* Messner, 1992. LB $14.98 (0-671-74165-9).
FORMAT: Autobiography   GRADES: 4–7.

Apparently unwilling to concede that her life might be entertaining enough on its own merits to warrant the interest of a mostly fiction-reading public, Byars muses over and amuses readers with stories of her up-close, nearly personal relationship with a large black snake who ensconced itself on her porch. The poetic weaving of snake tales with incidents from Byars's childhood and adult life that have contributed to her writing, as well as with her working methods, becomes a comical, mesmerizing blend.

Byars, Betsy. *Wanted . . . Mud Blossom.* **Illus. by Jacqueline Rogers.** Delacorte, 1991. $14.00 (0-385-30428-5).
FORMAT: Novel   GRADES: 4–7.

The beloved pet of the eccentric Blossom family, Mud Blossom, is accused of eating Junior's hamster. But as Pap reminds everyone, even a dog is innocent until proven guilty, and the way in which the truth unfolds is as funny as it is triumphant. Readers who have loved this clan through readings of the Blossom family quartet will devour this install-ment, as good a yarn as any Byars has spun—and that's saying a lot.

Carroll, Lewis. *Alice's Adventures in Wonderland.* **Illus. by Anthony Browne.** Knopf, 1988. LB $19.99 (0-394-90592-X).
FORMAT: Storybook   GRADES: All grades.

In the opening pages of the story, Browne hints at his presence in Car-roll's world. With a burning key, a fish swimming through space, and a green thread winding its way through icons, the artist has established that this will be no ordinary Alice. In short, the volume is so consumed by the unexpected that readers will find their eyes leaving the text to pore over the pictures, replete with jaunty details and stunning surreal images that grandly point back in the direction of the written word. Tenniel, who?

Carter, Peter. *Borderlands.* Farrar, 1990. $16.95 (0-374-30895-0).
FORMAT: Novel   GRADES: 7–up.

This is a tale of the Old American West and a feisty young survivor, Ben. Before readers leave him, he has learned to skin buffalo, faced his brother's killer, and discovered that the hardened beliefs he's grown up with regarding Indians and blacks have no meaning in the teeming, vibrant, cruel new land. A glib narration bears readers along on Ben's odyssey. Vivid and original, Carter's hefty tale upends the edifying myths of a young country without diluting the epochal images of the not-so-distant past.

Cole, Babette. *Prince Cinders.* **Illus. by the author.** Putnam, 1988. $13.95 (0-399-21502-6). paper avail.
FORMAT: Picture book   GRADES: Preschool–Grade 3.

This homely boy, in true Cinderella fashion, is at home alone on the night of the ball. But since Cole always gives her fairy tales an attitude, readers will know that Prince Cinders's fortunes are about to change—and not necessarily for the better.

Cole, Brock. *Celine.* Farrar, 1989. $15.00 (0-374-31234-6). paper avail.
FORMAT: Novel   GRADES: 7–up.

Wanted: one indomitable type, with unflagging good spirits even though the rest of the world is appallingly indifferent. Found: an extraordinary heroine trapped among mundane worries in Cole's brilliant novel. Mildly eccentric and even kooky, Celine wants to prove how mature she is so she can "be drifting over the hills of Tuscany, my box easel strapped to my back, the Mediterranean sun bronzing my brow." The obstacles in her path are daunting but Celine, vulnerable and wise, comes equipped; her strong points have been sketched out with intelligence and verve by her creator. And with her temperament and her breathless attempts at self-portraiture, she is one of the most believable budding artists in young adult fiction.

Conly, Jane Leslie. *R-T, Margaret, and the Rats of Nimh.* **Illus. by Leonard Lubin.** HarperCollins, 1990. LB $13.89 (0-06-021364-7). paper avail.
FORMAT: Novel   GRADES: 5–up.

Good old-fashioned storytelling makes this book a success on its own merits, but it also demonstrates a fine melding of the events of two previous books, *Rasco and the Rats of Nimh* and *Mrs. Frisby and the Rats of Nimh*. It is possible to enjoy this book without the context or continuity provided by the other two. But the uninitiated will surely want to seek out those next, or simply sink into all three.

Cox, David. *Bossyboots.* **Illus. by the author.** Crown, 1987. $10.95 (0-517-56491-2).
FORMAT: Picture book   GRADES: Kindergarten–Grade 4.

"Once there was a girl called Abigail, who was, so they say, the bossiest girl in New South Wales." In the first frame of this Australian import, this little miss is shown giving instructions to a very attentive dog. She even bosses a stagecoach robber into shamefully abandoning his task. A spoof of the Old West in a new setting, this is a delightfully disarming tale from beginning to end.

Dahl, Roald. *The Giraffe and the Pelly and Me.* **Illus. by Quentin Blake.** Farrar, 1985. $11.95 (0-374-32602-9). paper avail.
FORMAT: Picture book   GRADES: Preschool–Grade 3.

A boy, giraffe, pelican, and monkey each make appropriate and fabulous contributions to their not-so-ordinary window-cleaning business. Dahl's humor has been called outrageous, subversive, and satirical, and adults argue about his place in children's books. But children don't hesitate over whether to laugh out loud over his books; they just do. Longtime collaborator Quentin Blake has worked with Dahl on other books, including—for older readers—*The BFG* and *The Witches*.

Danziger, Paula. *Remember Me to Harold Square.* Delacorte, 1987. $14.95 (0-385-29610-X). paper avail.
FORMAT: Novel   GRADES: 7–up.

A hot summer in the city looks terrible to Kendra, and even worse when her parents come up with that most awful idea: A Project. But the Serendipity Scavenger Hunt takes Kendra and company around New York City's many sights, and makes for a diverting novel.

de Brunhoff, Jean. *The Story of Babar.* **Illus. by the author.** Random, 1933. LB $10.99 (0-394-90575-X). paper avail.
FORMAT: Storybook   GRADES: 2–4.

This is the book that began all the royal fun. A publishing legacy that continues today, this is the best of the Babar bunch. Is the humor distinctly French, or is it universal? Let children remain innocent of the debate, and enjoy Babar. (Caveat: after the works of father Jean have been exhausted, send readers on to those by Laurent, which are not as polished as their ancestors, but which will satisfy the need.)

Donnelly, Elfie. *A Package for Miss Marshwater.* **Illus. by Ute Krause.** Dial, 1987. $9.95 (0-8037-0453-4).
FORMAT: Chapter book   GRADES: 2–5.

A deadpan telling relates the proper habits of gray-haired Emmie Marshwater, who has been a lady in high heels and white gloves for a long time. She remembers being the wildest little girl on the block, but she was shamed into correct behavior by her mother. With the arrival of two pudgy, playful platypuses sent by an Australian relative, "ladylikeness" begins to slip away. An affectionate tale of transformation bursts with humor and good will; Krause's jovial pictures show the undoing of Miss Marshwater's carefully regulated routines as her life grows daily more chaotic, and more snug.

Drescher, Henrik. *The Yellow Umbrella.* **Illus. by the author.** Macmillan, 1987. $12.95 (0-02-733240-3).
FORMAT: Picture book   GRADES: Preschool–Grade 2.

When a zoo monkey and its child come into possession of an umbrella, they take off, Mary Poppins-style, and soar into the jungle where one of their own kind greet them. Their odyssey from civilization to their own place of contentment is simply articulated by Drescher's eccentrically wonderful two-color illustrations. The crosshatching and crabbed ink lines produce offbeat approximations of familiar forms.

du Bois, William Pène. *The Twenty-One Balloons.* **Illus. by the author.** Viking, 1947. $13.95 (0-670-73441-1). paper avail.
FORMAT: Storybook   GRADES: Kindergarten–Grade 3.

Professor William Waterman Sherman is found in the middle of the ocean with the remains of 21 balloons. How he arrived there, and what happens next, unfolds in a book that has entertained fantasy lovers for 45 years.

Dupasquier, Philippe. *Jack at Sea.* **Illus. by the author.** Prentice Hall, 1987. $12.95 (0-13-509209-4).
FORMAT: Picture book   GRADES: 2–5.

This action-adventure, a high seas romp, will lure readers away from comic books. A multitude of frames tell the story of Jack; it's a send-up of the seafaring life. Dupasquier's cinematic perspectives show realistic ships and landscapes.

Fakih, Kimberly Olson. *Grandpa Putter and Granny Hoe.* **Illus. by Tracey Campbell Pearson.** Farrar, 1992. $13.00 (0-374-32762-9).
FORMAT: Chapter book   GRADES: 1–3.

These vignettes feature two grandparents—not wed to each other—who are inflicted with what is otherwise known in family lore as a deep-rooted difference of opinion. Sharing their two grandchildren means bickering, upmanship, and debates over what the kids should wear, what they should eat, and where they should sleep. The kids wish for a united front where all four can be together in one place, in one piece, indivisible, with liberty and justice for all.

Fitzhugh, Louise. *Harriet the Spy.* **Illus. by the author.** HarperCollins, 1964. LB $14.89 (0-06-021911-4). paper avail.
FORMAT: Novel   GRADES: 4–6.

She is a spy, is Harriet, but for the right reason: she wants to know *everything.* This glimpse into the working of a preadolescent's mind perhaps is a bit too searing for many adults, but readers recognize Harriet as one of their own from the very first page. In this first book about her (the other is *The Long Secret*), her notebooks containing all her thoughts and observations are lost.

Fleischman, Paul. *Shadow Play.* **Illus. by Eric Beddows.** HarperCollins, 1990. LB $14.89 (0-06-021865-7).
FORMAT: Picture book   GRADES: Preschool–Grade 3.

A retelling of *Beauty and the Beast* is the subject of the shadow play two children witness, but the real story is the manipulation of the "actors" from behind the scenes. Pointed comedy, high-spirited fun, and one unforgettable revelation that will have readers poring over every page a second and third time.

Fleischman, Sid. *The Whipping Boy.* **Illus. by Peter Sis.** Greenwillow, 1986. $13.95 (0-688-06216-4). paper avail.
FORMAT: Novel   GRADES: 4–up.

This highly original tale, a sort of takeoff on *The Prince and the Pauper*, shows what happens when an obnoxious prince switches places with the boy who is punished for the prince's every misdeed—the whipping boy.

Splendid entertainment, and a Newbery Medal-winning book in 1987. Fleischman's earlier works, such as the 1966 *Chancy and the Grand Rascal* and *By the Great Horn Spoon!* are also sure treats, and happily still in print.

French, Fiona. *Cinderella.* **Illus. by the author.** Oxford Univ. Pr., 1988. $12.95 (0-19-279841-3).
FORMAT: Picture book   GRADES: Preschool–Grade 3.

After winning the Kate Greenaway medal for her Jazz Age *Snow White in New York*, French regresses to a Regency period of empress waistlines and ornate coiffures. Straightforward telling with short and captionlike pieces of text keep track of the action on each page. It's not nearly as novel and fresh as *Snow White*, but the saucy, irreverant look to the pictures is still welcome.

French, Fiona. *Snow White in New York.* Oxford Univ. Pr., 1987. $14.95 (0-19-279808-1). paper avail.
FORMAT: Picture book   GRADES: Kindergarten–Grade 3.

Astonishing pictures highlight this sophisticated book about a classy New York dame named Snow White whose troubles come when her father marries the Queen of the Underworld. When Snow White is left to die on the streets of New York by the Queen's henchman, our heroine stumbles into a club where seven jazzmen make her their singer. Suave and witty, this story is elevated by its dizzying art deco pictures. It may be readers' first look at a unique style of art, but they may wish for a change in the ending—Snow White's stepmom should have been given a pair of cement shoes.

Fuchshuber, Annegert. *Giant Story/Mouse Tale.* **Illus. by the author.** Carolrhoda, 1988. LB $12.95 (0-87614-319-2). paper avail.
FORMAT: Picture book   GRADES: Preschool–Grade 3.

Two "half books" compose a whole. Two stories—one about a mouse, the other about a giant—are bound back to back, and readers may begin wherever they like. The giant is a lonely forest dweller, the mouse a brave creature; both are in need of a consoling friend. They meet in the middle of the forest, and in the middle spread of the book. A good composite of 20/20 vision, a palindromelike structure and topsy-turvy fun. The plain message that differences—even opposites—can't come in the way of good friendships will capture readers' hearts.

Gannett, Ruth Stiles. *My Father's Dragon.* **Illus. by Ruth Chrisman Gannett.** Random, 1948. LB $14.99 (0-394-91438-4). paper avail.
FORMAT: Novel   GRADES: 4–6.

Elmer Elevator rescues a baby dragon, sealing a friendship that was sustained through two other volumes, *Elmer and the Dragon* and *The*

Dragons of Blueland. Funny, cherishable fantasy, and a Newbery Honor book.

Gardam, Jane. *A Long Way from Verona.* Macmillan, 1972. $13.95 (0-02-735781-3).

FORMAT: Novel   GRADES: 7–up.

Headstrong, independent Jessica, at 13, already knows she will be a writer. This early work from a fine British novelist is one of her wittiest. A treasure for sophisticated readers, who won't be shy about seeking out Gardam's adult novels as well, such as *Robinson Crusoe's Daughter.*

Gerrard, Roy. *The Favershams.* Illus. by the author. Farrar, 1983. $15.00 (0-374-32292-9). paper avail.

FORMAT: Picture book   GRADES: Preschool–Grade 3.

The squashed stature of the Favershams is but one of the satiric touches in this ornate first book by Gerrard. His intricate and expressive illustrations accompany the story of a Victorian family with an understated text rich for the images and era it evokes.

Gogol, Nikolai. *Sorotchintzy Fair.* Illus. by Gennady Spirin. Godine, 1991. $16.95 (0-87923-879-8).

FORMAT: Picture book   GRADES: Preschool–Grade 4.

A farmer arranges his daughter's marriage, and then reneges. Much of the mischief can be found rolling across Spirin's lively paintings, replete with comic figures.

Gray, Nigel. *The One and Only Robin Hood.* Illus. by Helen Craig. Little, Brown, 1987. $12.95 (0-316-32578-3).

FORMAT: Picture book   GRADES: Preschool–Grade 3.

The ever-fashionable Robin Hood creeps into the king's garden, takes his money, eats the queen's royal bread and honey, lets 4 and 20 blackbirds loose, and runs away with the maid. The money is distributed to the poor and an exuberant ring dance and the marriage of Robin and Merry Maid follows. Gray's retelling of the legend is cast appropriately in the question-and-answer format of medieval ballads sung by troubadours; Craig's Robin is true to the spirit of the prankish and heroic original. This updated version preserves and invigorates the story in rib-tickling pictures and words.

Griffith, Helen V. *Journal of a Teenage Genius.* Greenwillow, 1987. $11.75 (0-688-07226-7). paper avail.

FORMAT: Novel   GRADES: 3–7.

Griffith displayed a gentle, wry humor in *Georgia Music* and *Grandaddy's Place;* here, she pulls out the stops on a much zanier wit. Zack, a journal-keeping genius, seems to be telling the truth about the results of his experiments: a poodle becomes a boy; a growing solution makes Zack shrink; a time machine sends him back into the past. The prose has a rat-a-tat pace in this upbeat fantasy, which has a joyfully optimistic genius at its helm.

Hale, Lucretia. *The Lady Who Put Salt in Her Coffee.* **Adapted and illus. by Amy Schwartz.** Harcourt, 1989. $13.95 (0-15-243475-5).
FORMAT: Picture book   GRADES: Preschool–Grade 3.

Victoriana reigns in this illustrated excerpt from the 1867 classic, *The Peterkin Papers.* When absentminded Mrs. Peterkin puts salt, instead of sugar, into her coffee, both chemist and herbalist are called in to make the brew taste better, but of course it's that gentle lady from Philadelphia who saves the day. Raucous 19th-century-style furnishings, fabrics, and costume outfit this tale, with art that deftly expresses the comic personalities of each adult with a remarkable use of posture and form.

Heine, Helme. *Seven Wild Pigs: 11 Picture Book Fantasies.* **Illus. by the author.** Macmillan, 1988. $18.95 (0-689-50439-X).
FORMAT: Storybook   GRADES: Kindergarten–Grade 3.

Heine's watercolors in this picture book are among the finest and most exquisite to be found in children's books, while the stories seem incomplete, incoherent, crazed, nonsensical, or otherwise hallucinatory and wild. In the most representative tale, "The Crazy Farm," the mouse attacks the cat, the bee collects rocks, the cow produces beer, and the pig, sleeping late, is on strike. Some of the individual paintings are most essentially childlike, inasmuch as they are baffling. After all, the chaos of kids' bedrooms and dreams is an important part of children's territory and readers will be glad such a weirdly funny book exists.

Himmelman, John. *Montigue on the High Seas.* **Illus. by the author.** Puffin, 1990. paper $3.95 (0-14-050789-2).
FORMAT: Picture book   GRADES: Preschool–Grade 3.

Montigue is a content mole until a heavy rain floods his underground home. Needing a place to weather the storm, he climbs into a dry-looking hole. But the hole is actually a green bottle and by morning Montigue has been swept out to sea. Soon he, and a bottle-fleet of mice, head to a new home on an island. An amiable story about a mole unafraid to live by himself, but tickled by the circumstances that give him neighbors.

Holmes, Barbara Ware. *Charlotte the Starlet.* **Illus. by John Himmelman.**
HarperCollins, 1988. $12.89 (0-06-022608-0). paper avail.
FORMAT: Novel   GRADES: 4–6.

Charlotte, first discovered in *Charlotte Cheetham: Master of Disaster,* is back
with a new place to put her lies—in her new novel. It's a critical success,
at least among the lunch set at school, but Charlotte goes for the cheap
thrill and is fast becoming a hack writer. This send-up of the lure of the
big time makes for a very funny novel, perfect for middle-grade readers.

Horejs, Vít. *Pig and Bear.* **Illus. by Friso Henstra.** Macmillan, 1989. $12.95 (0-
02-744421-X).
FORMAT: Storybook   GRADES: 2–4.

Invoking characters from Czech folk tales, Horejs has composed four
witty stories about an irresistible friendship between two profoundly
funny fellows. Their quiet forest is the backdrop for a world of misunderstandings that are always amicably resolved; they squabble about squabbling, and create emergencies while trying to avoid them. Henstra's
idiosyncratic drawings of the scratchy tenderness between these two
genial souls invite readers progressing just beyond picture books into a
world of nonsense and fun.

Hurd, Thacher. *Mama Don't Allow.* **Illus. by the author.** HarperCollins,
1984. LB $14.89 (0-06-022690-0). paper avail.
FORMAT: Picture book   GRADES: Preschool–Grade 3.

A traditional song is the taking-off point for Hurd's tale of the highs and
lows of the Swamp Band's seemingly guileless fan club. Sharp and witty.
Follow it up with *The Pea Patch Jig* and *Blackberry Ramble,* where children
can meet incorrigible Baby Mouse.

Irving, Washington. *Rip Van Winkle.* **Retold and illus. by John Howe.**
Little, Brown, 1988. $14.95 (0-316-37578-0).
FORMAT: Picture book   GRADES: Preschool–Grade 3.

Howe, working in a realistic style of illustration, highlights the comic
gifts of Irving's story. Henry Hudson's crew are a wild-eyed, caricatured
bunch. Rip, upon awakening from his famous nap, has ivy and brambles
clinging to his hat and pants, and his beard sails down pass his knees. A
vivid piece of storytelling, this takes full advantage of the atmospheric
Catskill setting. Howe blithely taps the elements of the tale that make it
an American favorite.

Jacques, Brian. *Mossflower.* **Illus. by Gary Chalk.** Putnam, 1988. $16.95 (0-
399-21549-2).
FORMAT: Novel   GRADES: 5–up.

Right from the start of this rousingly old-fashioned prequel to *Redwall,*
readers will submerge themselves in the culture of the woodlanders and

their council, the Corim, against the wicked Kotir. Into the fray comes Martin the Warrior, whose heroics pale in comparison to the acts of his fellow fighters, so colorful are their escapades. *Redwall* fans will not be disappointed, but no prior knowledge of that book is necessary to thoroughly enjoy this one.

James, Mary. *Shoebag.* Scholastic, 1990. $12.95 (0-590-43029-7). paper avail.
FORMAT: Novel   GRADES: 5–7.

This is a witty near-fable about a small cockroach who becomes a boy overnight. How this former creepy-crawler adjusts to his human shape (and its accompanying problems) is the thrust of a nice piece of satire for young readers. Who cares if the rip-off of Kafka is only slight?

Joyce, William. *Dinosaur Bob and His Adventures with the Family Lazardo.* **Illus. by the author.** HarperCollins, 1988. LB $14.89 (0-06-023048-7).
FORMAT: Picture book   GRADES: Preschool–Grade 3.

When the Lazardos bring back a dinosaur from their safari, they consider him one of the family, and name him Bob. But when he becomes a nuisance—though an innocent one—and it appears that he'll have to be returned to his home, Bob saves a baseball team from defeat and ensures his place in America. The suave family, Bob's sheer mass, and the beautifully polished vistas of Pimlico Hills make for one visual delight after another, while the story is a pure, witty piece of entertainment. Some children already know it as a Reading Rainbow feature selection.

Juster, Norton. *The Phantom Tollbooth.* **Illus. by Jules Feiffer.** Knopf, 1961. $16.95 (0-394-81500-9). paper avail.
FORMAT: Novel   GRADES: 4–6.

When Milo receives a tiny turnpike tollbooth, he can't imagine what will await him on the other side of the gates. He and two companions face the Lands Beyond and events that go beyond his—and readers'—wildest expectations. Warmly humorous, surprising to the last.

Kalman, Maira. *Ooh-La-La (Max in Love).* **Illus. by the author.** Viking, 1991. $14.95 (0-670-84163-3).
FORMAT: Picture book   GRADES: All grades.

High school French students will love this book as much as their younger brothers and sisters do, for taking all the grimaces out of learning words from a foreign language. Max the beagle immerses himself in *esprit de Paris* and, as one must when one is in France, falls in love. Existentialists and surrealists wander the City of Lights; this book may be savored like a *bonbon*.

Kamen, Gloria. *Edward Lear: King of Nonsense.* **Illus. with drawings by the author and by Edward Lear.** Macmillan, 1990. $13.95 (0-689-31419-1).
FORMAT: Biography   GRADES: 4–6.

In this wonderful biography of the author of *The Owl and the Pussycat* and other small gems, Kamen will send off giggling readers to seek out the original verse on their own.

Karlin, Barbara. *Cinderella.* **Illus. by James Marshall.** Little, Brown, 1989. $12.95 (0-316-54654-2).
FORMAT: Picture book   GRADES: Preschool–Grade 3.

A send-up of the tale of the scruffy princess wannabe, only this time she forgives those crummy stepsisters. The illustrations are as full of caricature and slapstick as any found in Marshall's work; the telling is briskly funny.

Kennedy, Richard. *The Boxcar at the Center of the Universe.* **Illus. by Jeff Kronen.** HarperCollins, 1982. $11.89 (0-06-023187-4).
FORMAT: Novel   GRADES: 7–up.

This is a ripping good yarn about a teenager's ride on a railroad boxcar where he is regaled by the colorful stories of his intriguing fellow traveler. Way out and wonderful. For slightly younger readers, this author's *Amy's Eyes* is the magical, mystical, seagoing story of a girl and her doll, the Captain.

Kerr, M. E. *Little Little.* HarperCollins, 1981. LB $14.89 (0-06-023185-8). paper avail.
FORMAT: Novel   GRADES: 7–up.

"The Roach," a dwarf, loves Little Little LaBelle, another small person though perfectly formed. Kerr's fun is aimed at the systems of superiority that inflict people of all sizes. A hilarious work.

King-Smith, Dick. *Babe: The Gallant Pig.* **Illus. by Mary Rayner.** Crown, 1985. $11.95 (0-517-55556-5).
FORMAT: Novel   GRADES: 4–6.

Like another well-loved pig, Babe is just a meal-in-waiting until he, too, makes a friend who changes his life. This is fresh, funny, playful fare, and a splendid introduction to King-Smith, one of Britain's cheekiest exports.

Kitamura, Satoshi. *Lily Takes a Walk.* **Illus. by the author.** Dutton, 1987. $9.95 (0-525-44333-9). paper avail.
FORMAT: Picture book   GRADES: Preschool–Grade 3.

Lily may be talking the walk, but it is her dog Nicky who provides all the humor, as he imagines or perceives fearful occurrences around every corner and lurking in every shadow. Colorful, cartoon-bright pictures show the oblivious Lily and the wary Nicky against landscapes that may or may not be benign, but will certainly evoke giggles from observant readers.

Kitchen, Bert. *Tenrec's Twigs.* **Illus. by the author.** Putnam, 1989. $14.95 (0-399-21720-7).
FORMAT: Picture book   GRADES: Preschool–Grade 4.

Tenrec is a small creature who wakes up one morning and knows that it is a great day for building. So he happily assembles some twigs, until a grumpy warthog mutters, "Useless! A Waste of Time!" Tenrec must seek encouragement before he can begin anew. Kitchen's animals are characteristically sharp and defined on the page. The story moves well, although adults may be troubled by Tenrec's need for the approval of others. But for those who can get past the preachier aspect of Tenrec's dilemma, Kitchen provides an unusual tale with humorous flourishes.

Koertge, Ron. *The Boy in the Moon.* Little, Brown, 1990. $15.95 (0-316-50102-6). paper avail.
FORMAT: Novel   GRADES: 7–up.

The world is shifting beneath Nick's feet as he faces the return of a much-changed old friend, and the pending departure of the girl he's falling in love with. Koertge achieves a subtlety in the comic incidents not found in his previous works; those were laugh-out-loud funny while this one is informed by a quieter, more sophisticated wit. Romantic to the hilt, the book is comprised of brief, telling episodes that culminate in a realistic ending. These teens have a nice, wry dignity.

Latimer, Jim. *Fox Under First Base.* **Illus. by Lisa McCue.** Scribner, 1991. $13.95 (0-689-19053-2).
FORMAT: Picture book   GRADES: Preschool–Grade 2.

The idea sets readers off before the story is even fully under way. From his advantageously situated home under first base, Fox steals baseballs. Why would he do this? And how does Detective Porcupine find out about the scam? A very witty tale, and the kind of sports fiction that appeals to *all* readers.

Lester, Julius. *The Knee-High Man and Other Tales.* **Illus. by Ralph Pinto.** Dial, 1972. $12.95 (0-8037-4593-1). paper avail.
FORMAT: Picture book   GRADES: Preschool–Grade 3.

Six tales from African-American literature are conveyed in a conversational, spirited tone that emboldens the humor and will inspire children to go on to Lester's other fabled storytelling feats. This acclaimed title, perfect for reading aloud, features vibrant, full-color paintings by Pinto.

Lorenz, Lee. *A Weekend in the Country.* **Illus. by the author.** Prentice Hall, 1985. $11.95 (0-13-947961-9).
FORMAT: Picture book   GRADES: Kindergarten–Grade 3.

When two animals are invited to the country for a weekend, they don't realize that there is no way to get there. The picture editor of the *New Yorker* shows that he is not only a master of highbrow comedy and wit but also of childlike touches that will please every reader.

Lowry, Lois. *All about Sam.* **Illus. by Diane de Groat.** Houghton, 1988. $12.95 (0-395-48662-9). paper avail.
FORMAT: Chapter book   GRADES: 1–5.

The first funny story about Anastasia Krupnik's brilliant little brother Sam begins at his birth and ends when he has given up nightlights. Readers who love Anastasia's tales will have to pass this on to their own young siblings, but may find that Lowry's sense of humor transcends traditional age classifications. Adults laugh out loud at this book.

Lowry, Lois. *Attaboy, Sam!* **Illus. by Diane de Groat.** Houghton, 1992. $13.95 (0-395-61588-7).
FORMAT: Chapter book   GRADES: 1–5.

Anastasia's brother Sam is back, with a child's enthusiasm for investing thought and energy into homemade birthday presents for others. A stinky substitute, invented by Sam, is to take the place of his mother's favorite perfume; this is the centerpiece for a whole hysterical tangle of amusing incidents that will keep readers clamoring for more.

Macaulay, David. *Black and White.* **Illus. by the author.** Houghton, 1990. $14.95 (0-395-52151-3).
FORMAT: Picture book   GRADES: All grades.

This highly original picture book was vastly underrated and controversial until it won the Caldecott Medal. Leave readers alone with this pictorial extravaganza, full of zany tale-spinning and meticulously thought-out attempts to upend the conventional storyline. Darn good.

McCaughrean, Geraldine. *A Pack of Lies.* Oxford Univ. Press, 1989. $14.95 (0-19-271612-3). paper avail.
FORMAT: Novel   GRADES: 6–up.

Mrs. Povey's antiques business is a disaster—she talks customers out of buying objects, and undercharges them when they finally make a purchase. Then along comes MCC Berkshire, a mysterious helper who insists on working for free. Each chapter amounts to a short story about a particular object, but McCaughrean isn't content creating mere diversions. She pens each story in a different literary style (gothic, romance, folkloric) and displays an astonishing command of her powers. She leaps from genre to genre, in a writer's equivalent of sleight of hand, and swoops in at the last with an ending that both provokes and amuses.

MacGregor, Marilyn. *On Top.* **Illus. by the author.** Morrow, 1988. $7.95 (0-688-07490-1).

FORMAT: Picture book   GRADES: All grades.

In this wordless, colorless, and almost dimensionless picture book a sheep detaches itself from the herd and journeys up a steep mountain top. At the summit it views the world from five spatial directions—east, north, south, west, and down—and recognizes its own distinct identity as an individual. The value of this work lies mostly in MacGregor's daring to use such a minimal form of expression to articulate a 30-second odyssey. Readers will surely get the insight of not mistaking the forest for the tree.

MacLachlan, Patricia. *Cassie Binegar.* HarperCollins, 1982. LB $11.89 (0-06-024034-2). paper avail.

FORMAT: Novel   GRADES: 4–7.

Much has been made of this writer's Newbery Medal-winning book, *Sarah, Plain and Tall,* and of her first book, *Arthur, for the Very First Time.* In some ways, however, this is her most lyrical, undulating like a wave on the summer sand. The characters are funny and down-home, each one contributing to Cassie's ongoing quest to discover why things must change. Joy-filled.

Marshall, Edward. *Fox and His Friends.* **Illus. by James Marshall.** Dial, 1982. LB $10.89 (0-8037-2669-4). paper avail.

FORMAT: Chapter book   GRADES: 1–3.

One of the first of the enduring Fox books, ripe for beginning readers, is about a duty-bound young hero who wants to take a little time off from obligations, but can't seem to make himself do it. Young readers will want to follow-up with *Fox at School, Fox in Love,* and the other stories about this likable guy.

Marshall, Edward. *Three by the Sea.* **Illus. by James Marshall.** Dial, 1981. LB $10.89 (0-8037-8687-5). paper avail.

FORMAT: Chapter book   GRADES: 1–3.

Introducing Lolly, Sam, and Spider, Three funny storytellers who know how to wile away an afternoon. Every tale they espouse is a contribution to witty one-upmanship, but the real winners are readers, who can find out more about this trio in *Three up a Tree* and *Four on the Shore.*

Marshall, James. *Goldilocks and the Three Bears.* **Illus. by the author.** Dial, 1988. LB $12.89 (0-8037-0543-3).

FORMAT: Picture book   GRADES: Preschool–Grade 3.

This Caldecott Honor book enchanted even those who erroneously believed that readers didn't need another *Goldilocks.* For any child sick of the "classics," start here.

Marshall, James. *The Three Little Pigs.* **Illus. by the author.** Dial, 1989. LB $12.89 (0-8037-0594-8).

FORMAT: Picture book   GRADES: Preschool–Grade 3.

Readers who smile when they pick up this title can be forgiven for correctly anticipating amusing antics within, especially if they are familiar with Marshall's other fractured fairy tales. Children know this story, and in some ways the author sows a traditional path. Of course, the pig who invests in bricks has wolf stew at the end of his long labor, after a merry mass of near-misses that scathingly build suspense. There are fairy tales, and there are Marshall's tales—let readers chew on this one while they decide which they like best.

Meigs, Cornelia. *Invincible Louisa.* **Illus. with photographs.** Little, Brown, 1933. $16.95 (0-316-56590-3).

FORMAT: Biography   GRADES: 6–up.

This biography of Louisa May Alcott, written with wit and precision, earned a Newbery Medal.

Naylor, Phyllis Reynolds. *The Agony of Alice.* Macmillan, 1985. $13.95 (0-689-31143-5). paper avail.

FORMAT: Novel   GRADES: 4–7.

Motherless Alice debuts as a sixth-grader, worried about all things female and aware that her father and older brother are not the help she needs at this point in her life. Dead-on humor and bittersweet asides roundly capture Alice's dilemmas. She further blossoms in later books, such as *Alice in Rapture, Sort Of,* and *Reluctantly Alice.* A keeper, from the Newbery Medal–winning author of *Shiloh.*

Naylor, Phyllis Reynolds. *Alice in Rapture, Sort of.* Macmillan, 1989. $13.95 (0-689-31466-3).

FORMAT: Novel   GRADES: 3–7.

The course of true love runs so smoothly that Alice, increasingly worried about her motherlessness in her formative adolescent years, wonders whether she's really ready to settle down with just one boy, no matter how nice he is. The trials and tribulations of first love are sparked to tender, comic proportions thanks to this robust heroine's spunk despite her lack of worldliness.

Nelson, Peter. *Sylvia Smith-Smith.* Crosswinds, 1987. paper $2.25 (0-373-98007-8).
FORMAT: Novel   GRADES: 6–up.

Readers may have met her in short stories in *Seventeen* magazine, but this is Sylvia Smith-Smith's first full-length feature role. And she was born to it. She's hip, cool, sensible to a fault, and always getting herself in and out of hot spots that would slay other teenage heroines. For readers who demand a change of pace, Sylvia is a trip.

Nesbit, E. *Melisande.* **Illus. by P. J. Lynch.** Harcourt, 1991. $13.95 (0-15-253164-5).
FORMAT: Picture book   GRADES: 1–4.

With tongue-in-cheek humor and mischievous use of fairy tale conventions, Nesbit's classic tale of a bald princess is returned to the laps of modern readers with vibrant new illustrations.

Nordqvist, Sven. *The Hat Hunt.* **Illus. by the author.** R&S, 1988. $12.95 (91-29-59070-1).
FORMAT: Picture book   GRADES: All grades.

Nordqvist's zany tale about a search that leads to more than objects found has been called philosophical and wise by the critics, but children will simply see it as amusing. Almost any book by this author/illustrator will please in a pinch; his point of view is unique and childlike and he never fails to intrigue, whether with his musings or with the small critters that inhabit so many of his books.

Numeroff, Laura Joffe. *If You Give a Moose a Muffin.* **Illus. by Felicia Bond.** HarperCollins, 1991. LB $12.89 (0-06-024406-2).
FORMAT: Picture book   GRADES: Preschool–Grade 3.

In the same escalation of events that made *If You Give a Mouse a Cookie* such a tremendous hit, Numeroff supplies an unfolding of burgeoning demands a moose might make of anyone foolish enough to entice him with a muffin. Blithe humor, sure to hit the spot with preschoolers.

O'Neill, Catharine. *Mrs. Dunphy's Dog.* **Illus. by the author.** Puffin, 1989. paper $3.95 (0-14-050622-5).
FORMAT: Picture book   GRADES: Preschool–Grade 3.

Mrs. Dunphy's dog teaches himself to read; by the end of this tale, James has cheered for Nana in *Peter Pan* and wept through *Lassie Come Home.* Witty and intelligent, O'Neill's first solo effort is one surprise after another. She satirizes the screaming headlines with childlike literal-mindedness, adds a gentle plea for reading, and splashes the whole thing up with singing watercolors. Throngs of humor.

Pacovska, Kveta. *One, Five, Many.* **Illus. by the author.** Houghton, 1990. $16.95 (0-395-54997-3).
FORMAT: Picture book   GRADES: Preschool–Grade 3.

A Czech artist puts on a disarming display of patterns, images, color, and geometric shapes in an inventive book that incorporates concepts of counting and rhythm—much like fireworks going off overhead, these pages place demands on readers, inviting them to look here, no here, no *there.* Unlike fireworks, the book remains behind, so children may submerge themselves again and again. Dizzying, distracting, deliriously exciting.

Pinkwater, Jill. *Buffalo Brenda.* Macmillan, 1989. $14.95 (0-02-774631-3). paper avail.
FORMAT: Novel   GRADES: 7–up.

A sidesplitting saga of Brenda Tuna and India Ink Teidlebaum, determined to swim upstream against the tide of conformists that are *de rigueur* in any high school setting. The passing neuroses of teenagers have never borne such meticulous scrutiny and fared so farcically well.

Pollack, Pamela, ed. *The Random House Book of Humor for Children.* **Illus. by Paul O. Zelinsky.** Random, 1988. LB $16.99 (0-395-98049-2).
FORMAT: Anthology   GRADES: 4–6.

Delia Ephron and Garrison Keillor join such children's favorites as Betsy Byars and Beverly Cleary in this outstanding anthology for middle readers. Children have tried to browse through this, but sooner or later they all come across a selection that they can't resist delving into, and come away hours later, unaware of the time that's passed—almost the definition of good humorous reading.

Pullman, Philip. *The Ruby in the Smoke.* Knopf, 1987. LB $11.99 (0-394-98826-4). paper avail.
FORMAT: Novel   GRADES: 7–up.

This Dickensian romp began the trilogy that includes *The Shadow in the North* and *The Tiger in the Well.* Following the death of her father, intrepid Sally Lockhart is launched into a shadowy chain of events in the squalid backstreets of 19th-century London. Marvelous, brilliantly entertaining, and in many ways a send-up of a genre.

Round, Graham. *Hangdog.* **Illus. by the author.** Dial, 1987. $7.95 (0-8037-0448-8).
FORMAT: Picture book   GRADES: Preschool–Grade 2.

Readers have probably passed Hangdog often, but just never noticed him. No one ever notices the loneliest dog in the world. Sad and friendless, he goes to sea and is stranded on an island where he confronts a tiger. The End? "Not on your life!" says the tiger, who himself has been waiting for a friend like Hangdog for a good long time. Round's comic strip style of squiggles and scribbles tells readers as much about Hangdog in the droll pictures as they get from the text. A surprising and hilarious adventure.

Scieszka, Jon. *The Frog Prince, Continued.* Illus. by Steve Johnson. Viking, 1991. $14.95 (0-670-83421-1).
FORMAT: Picture book   GRADES: 1–5.

The Frog Prince, now a nice young man, and his nagging wife go their separate ways. He encounters witches from other fairy tales, and tires of his adventures, returning home for yet another happy ending with his Princess. To appreciate this send-up, children should have at least a passing acquaintance with the original. It will make them feel like insiders in the land of fractured stories.

Scieszka, Jon. *The Knights of the Kitchen Table.* Illus. by Lane Smith. Viking, 1991. $10.95 (0-670-83622-2).
FORMAT: Chapter book   GRADES: 3–7.

Give readers this rousing send-up of Arthurian lore, and they may just go on to T. H. White's wonderful works. When Joe's uncle, a magician, gives the boy a book that sends him and two friends back in time, the formal language of yore meets up with American slang for some very funny dialogue. The boys, considered enchanted because they can read, are asked to save Camelot.

Scieszka, Jon. *The Not-So-Jolly Roger.* Illus. by Lane Smith. Viking, 1991. $10.95 (0-670-83754-7).
FORMAT: Chapter book   GRADES: 3–7.

Pirate stories are always popular; here, the heroes of *The Knights of the Kitchen Table* meet up with Blackbeard. Not as smoothly humorous as the other tale, this tale will more than satisfy the craving for a sequel that *Knights* will inspire.

Scieszka, Jon. *The True Story of the Three Little Pigs.* Illus. by Lane Smith. Viking, 1989. $14.95 (0-670-82759-2).
FORMAT: Picture book   GRADES: Preschool–Grade 3.

A revisionist history of the classic tale, in which Al Wolf declares to one and all that he was framed for the whole sorry mess. Readers will believe him; adults will, too. And the lightly spiced lesson about the old adage involving "two sides to every story" has never been more comically proven.

Sharmat, Marjorie Weinman. *Nate the Great.* **Illus. by Marc Simont.** Putnam, 1973. $11.95 (0-698-20627-4). paper avail.

FORMAT: Chapter book   GRADES: 4–6.

This beginning reader, for the pre-Encyclopedia Brown set, is but one of many that stars an intrepid detective. Droll humor, pseudo "tough-guy" language, and Nate's reputation for bringing every case to a sound close make any book in the series a funny favorite with children. The illustrations by Caldecott Medalist Simont are a pleasure, with wry touches on every page.

Silsbee, Peter. *Love Among the Hiccups.* Macmillan, 1987. $14.95 (0-02-782760-7). paper avail.

FORMAT: Novel   GRADES: 7–up.

Comedy, romance, and timeless rites of initiation culminate but never clash in Silsbee's farce, as the disinherited are reinherited and the adopted find a mansion full of family skeletons. Palmer and Liana don't suspect that they are mere pawns in a power struggle between two eccentric sisters. The frenzy of action is related in a style not quite tongue in cheek.

Steig, William. *Abel's Island.* **Illus. by the author.** Farrar, 1985. $14.00 (0-374-30010-0). paper avail.

FORMAT: Picture book   GRADES: 1–up.

A very proper mouse, in the simple act of rescuing his wife's scarf, ends up stranded for a year on an island. Deceptively straightforward, the tale is replete with buried wit.

Steig, William. *Doctor De Soto.* **Illus. by the author.** Farrar, 1982. $15.95 (0-374-31803-4).

FORMAT: Picture book   GRADES: Preschool–Grade 3.

A mouse dentist faces a classic dilemma of all in the medical profession— what to do when someone threatening (in this case, a fox) is in need of aid? Compassion and wisdom rule side by side, tied together by the ribbon of humor that is woven through all Steig's work, including his Caldecott Medal-winning book, *Sylvester and the Magic Pebble.*

Talbott, Hudson. *We're Back: A Dinosaur's Story.* **Illus. by the author.** Crown, 1987. $12.95 (0-517-56599-4).

FORMAT: Picture book   GRADES: Preschool–Grade 3.

The prize for a group of dinosaurs who sample a new product, Brain Grain, is a drop into midtown Manhattan in the 20th century; destination: Dr. Bleeb's office at the Museum of Natural History. Those who think original dinosaur books are extinct are going to change their minds with this one. A very welcome bunch of monsters has landed in kids' laps; Talbott's prehistoric characters all have that certain *je ne sais quoi*, from the glints in their eyes to the way they slather over snacks.

Terris, Susan. *Author! Author!* Farrar, 1990. $14.95 (0-374-34995-9).
FORMAT: Novel   GRADES: 7–up.

A child prodigy is expected to turn out a second publishable work of writing, but also to move into her teenage years with the maturity she exhibited all through childhood. Some parental double-talk and casual allusions remain maddeningly oblique—both to the heroine, Valerie, and to readers. Yet Terris writes rivetingly of Valerie's heartfelt confusion in the face of so many changes—ordinary and extraordinary—that readers will root for her to the last.

Thurber, James. *Many Moons.* **Illus. by Marc Simont.** Harcourt, 1990. $14.95 (0-15-251872-X). paper avail.
FORMAT: Storybook   GRADES: All grades.

This is a reillustrated version of the famous tale about Princess Lenore, bedridden from the gluttony of devouring too many tarts. Simont's new pictures are witty and bright, and those who look closely may find Thurber himself among the scenes. Choose the old edition (see below) or the new one. Both are dandy.

Thurber, James. *Many Moons.* **Illus. by Louis Slobodkin.** Harcourt, 1943. $14.95 (0-15-251873-8). paper avail.
FORMAT: Storybook   GRADES: 3–7.

This tale of a princess who declares "I want the moon" has been reillustrated by Caldecott Medalist Marc Simont, but this version is still available in many collections. Thurber's humor is wonderful out loud, and may lead readers, on their own, to *The Thirteen Clocks* or his other works.

Thurber, James. *The Thirteen Clocks.* **Illus. by Marc Simont.** Donald I. Fine, 1990. $13.95 (1-55611-188-6). paper avail.
FORMAT: Storybook   GRADES: All grades.

It begins as many tales do. A prince must rescue a princess from an evil duke. Still, there is Thurber's deadpan humor and the exact pieces of plotting, which lead to a less-than-conventional fairy tale, roundly sent up and rib-ticklingly told. A facsimile edition of the book many adults will recall fondly.

Thurber, James. *The Wonderful O.* **Illus. by Marc Simont.** Donald I. Fine, 1957, 1990. $10.95 (1-55611-189-4). paper avail.

FORMAT: Storybook   GRADES: All grades.

A facsimile edition of the allegorical story of a tiny island, Ooroo, invaded by treasure-seeking pirates who ban the letter "O" for the duration. This means that walls go without doors, keys without locks—a world gone topsy turvy, in a terrific piece of fun.

Trivas, Irene. *Emma's Christmas.* **Illus. by the author.** Orchard, 1988. $14.95 (0-531-05780-1). paper avail.

FORMAT: Picture book   GRADES: Preschool–Grade 2.

If there is such a thing as a fractured fairy tale, then certainly this book qualifies as a cracked Christmas carol. Emma turns down an offer of marriage from a prince. He sends her a partridge in a pear tree, and so the barrage of gifts begins. Trivas leads readers on this merry dance, taking time to run up totals now and then—Emma makes 90 omelettes one morning, for all those blasted lords and ladies. Lyrical nonsense on every page.

Udry, Janice May. *Let's Be Enemies.* **Illus. by Maurice Sendak.** Harper-Collins, 1961. LB $12.89 (0-06-026131-5). paper avail.

FORMAT: Picture book   GRADES: Preschool–Grade 3.

Udry, author of *A Tree Is Nice* (the first true ecology book) and *Thump and Plunk*, takes on the theme of conflict in this comedy about two best friends who fight. Generous in spirit, blissfully brief, this is a classic.

White, T. H. *The Sword in the Stone.* Dell, 1978. paper $3.50 (0-440-98445-9).

FORMAT: Novel   GRADES: 7–up.

This witty and robust 1939 telling of an Arthurian boyhood leads readers effortlessly into The Once and Future King tetralogy. Don't let children proclaim they've "seen the Disney movie." No animated image competes with White's words on the page and his unique combination of slapstick and erudition.

Willard, Nancy. *East of the Sun & West of the Moon.* **Illus. by Barry Moser.** Harcourt, 1989. $14.95 (0-15-224750-5).

FORMAT: Picture book   GRADES: 3–up.

In script form, Willard retells the Norwegian folktale with verve and humor, relying entirely on witty dialogue and pared-down stage directions to conjure up the world of the Troll King and his captives. Moser provides portraits of the cast, charmingly keyed into Willard's surprisingly modern references to telephone and TV. The volume is elegant, and readers will be pleasantly surprised by the humor.

Willard, Nancy. *Simple Pictures Are Best.* **Illus. by Tomie dePaola.** Harcourt, 1977. paper $3.95 (0-15-682625-9).

FORMAT: Picture book   GRADES: Preschool–Grade 3.

The taking of a wedding anniversary photograph becomes the occasion on which the shoemaker and his wife take account of their marriage, frustrating the photographer in the process. The Newbery Medal-winning author of the whimsical *Marzipan Moon* renders a chipper story in a comic vein.

Yolen, Jane. *Piggins.* **Illus. by Jane Dyer.** Harcourt, 1987. $14.95 (0-15-261685-3). paper avail.

FORMAT: Picture book   GRADES: Preschool–Grade 3.

A sort of "Upstairs, Downstairs" for children, this tale of a porcine butler who, from the very proper household where he works, solves the occasional mystery led to two justifiable sequels: *Picnic with Piggins* and *Piggins and the Royal Wedding.*

Yorinks, Arthur. *Company's Coming.* **Illus. by David Small.** Crown, 1988. $12.95 (0-517-56751-2). paper avail.

FORMAT: Picture book   GRADES: Preschool–Grade 3.

When small cockroaches wearing helmets step out of the spaceship that lands in his backyard, Moe is hysterical, while his wife Shirley simply sets another place at the table. Lovably childlike aliens (who know the rules regarding hostess gifts) and a deadpan text make this a solid main course.

Yorinks, Arthur. *Oh, Brother.* **Illus. by Richard Egielski.** Farrar, 1989. $15.95 (0-374-35599-1). paper avail.

FORMAT: Picture book   GRADES: Preschool–Grade 3.

Milton and Morris are twins, apparently orphaned at sea (the title page reveals that they were not innocent of the act of sinking the ship), who make their way through life by posing as short adults in business for themselves. Grandly witty in its use of deadpan text and pictures which belie that tone.

Additional Titles

The following titles, annotated elsewhere in this book (see index), could also fit the "Parody, Wit, Irony . . .") category.

Aardema, Verna. *Rabbit Makes a Monkey of Lion*
Agee, Jon. *The Incredible Painting of Felix Clousseau*
Andersen, Hans Christian. *The Princess and the Pea*

Ashabranner, Brent. *I'm in the Zoo, Too!*
Block, Francesca Lia. *Witch Baby*
Bottner, Barbara. *Let Me Tell You Everything*
Bradman, Tony. *Look Out, He's Behind You!*
Brittain, Bill. *All the Money in the World*
Brittain, Bill. *The Wish Giver*
Burgess, Gelett. *The Little Father*
Byars, Betsy. *The Pinballs*
Carlson, Lori M., and Cynthia Ventura. *Where Angles Glide at Dawn*
Cassedy, Sylvia. *Behind the Attic Wall*
Cassedy, Sylvia. *Lucy Babbidge's House*
Cassedy, Sylvia. *M.E. and Morton*
Chaucer, Geoffrey. *Chanticleer and the Fox*
Cole, Brock. *The Giant's Toe*
Cole, Joanna, and Stephanie Calmenson. *The Laugh Book*
Cresswell, Helen. *Ordinary Jack*
Day, Alexandra. *Carl Goes Shopping*
Disch, Thomas M. *The Brave Little Toaster*
Disch, Thomas M. *The Brave Little Toaster Goes to Mars*
Eastman, P. D. *Are You My Mother?*
Fitzgerald, John D. *The Great Brain*
Fleischman, Paul. *Graven Images*
Graham, Bob. *Crusher Is Coming!*
Harris, Joel Chandler. *Jump!*
Haswell, Peter. *Pog*
Heide, Florence Parry. *The Problem with Pulcifer*
Hennessy, B. G. *The Missing Tarts*
Hewitt, Kathryn. *Two by Two*
Joyce, William. *George Shrinks*
Kaye, M. M. *Ordinary Princess*
Kennedy, Richard. *Richard Kennedy*
Kipling, Rudyard. *The Best Fiction of Rudyard Kipling*
Kipling, Rudyard. *The Elephant's Child*
Kirshenbaum, Binnie. *Short Subject*
Lawson, Robert. *Ben and Me*
Leroe, Ellen W. *Robot Raiders*
Lester, Julius. *How Many Spots Does a Leopard Have?*
Lobel, Arnold. *Fables*
Lopshire, Robert. *Put Me in the Zoo*
Macaulay, David. *Why the Chicken Crossed the Road*
Mahy, Margaret. *The Great White Man-Eating Shark*
Marcus, Leonard S., and Amy Schwartz. *Mother Goose's Little Misfortunes*
Marshak, Samuel. *The Pup Grew Up!*
Marshall, Edward. *Space Case*

Marshall, James. *James Marshall's Mother Goose*
Marshall, James. *Red Riding Hood*
Miller, Edward. *The Curse of Claudia*
Milne, A. A. *Winnie the Pooh; The House at Pooh Corner*
Minarik, Else Holmelund. *No Fighting! No Biting!*
Nesbit, E. *The Cockatoucan*
Nordqvist, Sven. *Porker Finds a Chair*
Nygren, Tord. *The Red Thread*
Ormerod, Jan. *The Story of Chicken Licken*
Poortvliet, Rien, and Wil Huygen. *The Book of the Sandman and the Alphabet of Sleep*
Robertson, Keith. *Henry Reed, Inc.*
Rylant, Cynthia. *Henry and Mudge*
Rylant, Cynthia. *The Relatives Came*
Salinger, J. D. *The Catcher in the Rye*
Schwartz, Amy. *Bea and Mr. Jones*
Seuss, Dr. *The 500 Hats of Bartholomew Cubbins*
Silverstein, Shel. *Where the Sidewalk Ends*
Singer, Isaac Bashevis. *The Fools of Chelm and Their History*
Steig, William. *The Amazing Bone*
Stevenson, Jocelyn. *O'Diddy*
Tennyson, Noel. *The Lady's Chair and the Ottoman*
Thompson, Kay. *Eloise*
Twain, Mark. *The Adventures of Tom Sawyer*
Ungerer, Tomi. *The Beast of Monsieur Racine*
Van Allsburg, Chris. *The Z Was Zapped*
Willey, Margaret. *The Bigger Book of Lydia*
Yorinks, Arthur. *Hey, Al*

9: "'s Not Fair!"

Humor as Rebellion

Most children have learned to sort through the rules and regulations of home and school and blithely to abide by them. The day always comes, however, when a child will break the barriers, head into Mach I with no prior flying skills, and swish over the fence to the other side; a transgression that, if not curbed, can lead to full-scale rebellion. No one seems to know the reason for these sudden flights. It could be the influence of other children, or just some inexhaustible resource of impertinence that burbles up in the face of authority. (A common defense tactic, when asked to explain the reason for transgressing, is the child's firm answer of "Because!," a non-sequitur that, like a shoe that fits all sizes, is a rationalization for every action.)

Children seem to recoil instinctively from, or at least exhibit an initial hesitancy toward, rigid structures, order, imperatives. And perhaps that's why there are plenty of characters of all ages, shapes, and sizes in children's books who reflect that itch to defy. Children have an inborn inclination to pressure systems and tumble down any laws that get in their way; they are able suddenly to transform themselves into rebels without a cause.

Babbitt, Natalie. *Phoebe's Revolt.* **Illus. by the author.** Farrar, 1968. $11.95 (0-374-34907-5). paper avail.

FORMAT: Storybook   GRADES: 1–3.

In 1904 a little girl named Phoebe Euphemia Brandon Brown resists the bows, ribbons, and hairdos that are all the rage. A snappy, upbeat rebellion sure to sound alarms with any child who has ever tolerated a stiff collar or an itchy piece of lace.

Banks, Kate. *Alphabet Soup.* **Illus. by Peter Sis.** Knopf, 1988. $12.95 (0-394-89151-1).

FORMAT: Picture book   GRADES: Preschool–Grade 3.

Banks's story begins with a typical dinnertime trauma—a boy will not eat his soup. What follows is an adventure across a tablecloth landscape of cups that sail, wise-looking salt shakers, and a house (painted on the side of a teapot) where the boy and the bear take shelter for the night. Everything that transpires is governed by what was placed on the table before the fantasy begins, so that readers can flip back to the opening shot of the boy and venture guesses as to what might happen next.

Barrie, J. M. *Peter Pan.* **Illus. by Scott Gustafson.** Viking, 1991. $19.95 (0-670-84180-3).

FORMAT: Novel   GRADES: 4–7.

The quintessential rebel, dead-set against growing up, returns in luminous, almost ethereally beautiful paintings that stop short of heavy-duty formality in their expressiveness and liveliness. No caricatures or stereotypes here; these are characters, full of life, and ready to soar through the pages of Barrie's classic journey to Neverland.

Bloom, Suzanne. *We Keep a Pig in the Parlor.* **Illus. by the author.** Crown, 1988. $13.95 (0-517-56829-2).

FORMAT: Picture book   GRADES: Preschool–Grade 1.

The narrator relates in catchy verses how a pig came to live in a farm family's parlor; he made the choice and then caused trouble until his wishes were granted: "He snorted and said,/'I detest a straw bed/Corn that's unpopped,/Supper called slop,/Mud on my face,/That ramshackle place.' " He adds that he is lonesome and that argument seems to win the day, for the next scene shows him and the narrator cozily watching TV on the settee. Bloom—in her first book—wields colored pencils and a brush full of vibrant, eye-popping paints to give this pig a blazing pink hue and to carve out the surrounding landscapes in chipper tints. The text is bouncing and lilting; the line, "We keep a pig in the parlor," is downright contagious.

Broeger, Achim. *The Santa Clauses.* **Illus. by Ute Krause.** Dial, 1986. $11.95 (0-8037-0266-3). paper avail.

FORMAT: Picture book   GRADES: Preschool–Grade 3.

Envision a bunch of chubby, white-bellied, white-bearded old men in loud bathing trunks clustered around palm trees on a Miami beach; that's what happens when all the Santa Clauses around go on strike as a reaction to the muckraking headline that there is no Santa Claus. One small believer saves Christmas. Aim young readers toward this one at holiday time or anytime for a guaranteed piece of priceless fun.

Dana, Barbara. *Necessary Parties.* HarperCollins, 1986. LB $14.89 (0-06-021409-0). paper avail.
FORMAT: Novel   GRADES: 7–up.

When Chris decides to sue his parents to prevent them from getting divorced and enlists the help of an unconventional lawyer, an alternately funny and wise story ensues.

Gauch, Patricia Lee. *Christina Katerina and the Time She Quit the Family.* **Illus. by Elise Primavera.** Putnam, 1987. $12.95 (0-399-21408-9).
FORMAT: Picture book   GRADES: Preschool–Grade 3.

The spirited heroine of *Christina Katerina and the Box* returns, ready to wage a child-size rebellion by isolating herself from the rest of her family for the better part of a week. With realistic illustrations, this witty declaration of independence always strikes a chord with children.

Heide, Florence Parry. *The Problem with Pulcifer.* **Illus. by Judy Glasser.** HarperCollins, 1982. $12.89 (0-397-32002-7). paper avail.
FORMAT: Picture book   GRADES: 3–6.

A send-up about a child so addicted to reading that he refuses to watch TV. His parents are hand-wringers, but Pulcifer wins. The illustrations are hilariously exaggerated, showing characters who are all angles and bones.

Henkes, Kevin. *Sheila Rae, the Brave.* **Illus. by the author.** Greenwillow, 1987. LB $13.88 (0-688-07156-2). paper avail.
FORMAT: Picture book   GRADES: Preschool–Grade 3.

Boastful, fearless Sheila Rae decides to go home from school by taking a new route, and promptly gets lost. Little sister Louise saves the day and steals the show, helping Sheila find her way home. Everything that happens here is completely credible, hence appealing, to kids' intuitions. Everyone, even someone as courageous as old Sheila Rae, gets carried away sometimes, and learns about limitations the hard way.

Kennedy, X. J. *Brats.* **Illus. by James Watts.** Macmillan, 1986. $12.95 (0-689-50392-X).
FORMAT: Poetry   GRADES: 3–5.

Only Edward Gorey has come as close to a celebration of bad children as Kennedy's poetry does here. Perhaps cautionary, perhaps simply chronicling, the verses ring with the fates of some of these children, and a few verses will get even the most sedentary jump rope going with their chant-inducing rhythms. This poet went on to write *Fresh Brats* and *Ghastlies, Goops, & Pincushions*, two other comic collections.

Khalsa, Dayal Kaur. *Sleepers.* **Illus. by the author.** Crown, 1988. LB $7.95 (0-517-56917-5).
FORMAT: Picture book   GRADES: Preschool–Kindergarten.

The author of *I Want a Dog* and *Tales of a Gambling Grandma* tells of the different ways people and animals sleep, through the eyes of a girl who insists she will stay awake all night. In this eye-filling, hand-sized book, floral patterns of little more than dots and lines show off the degree of control Khalsa brings to her whimsical art. Any child who argues against the value of a good night's sleep will find a determined kindred spirit within these pages.

Kirshenbaum, Binnie. *Short Subject.* Orchard, 1989. $13.95 (0-531-05836-0).
FORMAT: Novel   GRADES: 7–up.

Audrey is short, underdeveloped, and a movie fan extraordinaire. She sneaks off to a revival house every night, despite her mother's steady disapproval. With her offbeat, single-minded way of doing things, Audrey will remind readers of an M. E. Kerr heroine. Glib, likable, she narrates the story with no lack of self-consciousness that is endearing and funny. A first novel.

Knight, Joan. *The Baby Who Would Not Come Down.* **Illus. by Debrah Santini.** Picture Book, 1989. $14.95 (0-88708-107-X).
FORMAT: Picture book   GRADES: Kindergarten–Grade 4.

This book will delight younger readers, who won't delve into some of its obvious flaws. When a baby, who has had too much of the nonsensical burbling aimed its way by ridiculous adults, is tossed into the air—whoopsy-daisy style—it doesn't come down. Won't. Floats around, and eventually lands. Older readers come away wanting more from this story. Funny, appealing.

Konigsburg, E. L. *From the Mixed-Up Files of Mrs. Basil E. Frankweiler.* **Illus. by the author.** Macmillan, 1967. $13.95 (0-689-20586-4). paper avail.
FORMAT: Novel   GRADES: 3–7.

Claudia is a dreamer and planner who wants to be someone special. Her younger brother Jamie is deft with cards and money. When Claudia decides that they should run away to live in New York's Metropolitan Museum, what unfolds is a tale steeped in humor, concerns of growing up, suspense, and adventure. For reading again and again. A Newbery Medal book.

Leaf, Munro. *The Story of Ferdinand.* **Illus. by Robert Lawson.** Viking, 1936. $11.95 (0-670-67424-9).
FORMAT: Picture book   GRADES: Preschool–Grade 3.

The bull who would not fight still entertains children after all these years. The silhouette of Ferdinand beneath the cork tree is the very vision of the lonely individual. Wryly simple, with wisdom to spare.

McConnachie, Brian. *Lily of the Forest.* **Illus. by Jack Ziegler.** Crown, 1987. $11.95 (0-517-56595-1).
FORMAT: Picture book   GRADES: Preschool–Grade 2.

Lily is bored with her job of painting smiles on dog houses. She runs away to the woods where her true creative spirit is unleashed. In text and art, the dog house industry is depicted with meticulous detail and crafty attention to humor. Autumnal reds, sunny yellows, spring greens, and azures seem to burst off the page.

Marshall, James. *The Cut-Ups.* **Illus. by the author.** Viking, 1984. $12.95 (0-670-25195-X). paper avail.
FORMAT: Picture book   GRADES: Preschool–Grade 3.

The cut-ups will crack-up readers with their antics. Spud and Joe can't sit still for long, but that's all right—most children will follow them anywhere.

Marshall, James. *The Cut-Ups Carry On.* **Illus. by the author.** Viking, 1990. $12.95 (0-670-81645-0).
FORMAT: Picture book   GRADES: Preschool–Grade 3.

The cut-ups Spud and Joe have thrived through many adventures, but perhaps this is their peak—they shoehorn themselves into suits and ties and attempt to win a television dance contest. Their rebellions are always worth watching.

Modesitt, Jeanne. *The Story of Z.* **Illus. by Lonni Sue Johnson.** Picture Book, 1990. $14.95 (0-88708-105-3). paper avail.
FORMAT: Picture book   GRADES: 1–3.

Z is feeling neglected and ill-used by the rest of the alphabet, and one day just walks off the job. Suddenly, there is havoc all over town—oos are open for business, but now they have ebras in them instead of zebras. A theme also treated in James Thurber's *The Wonderful O.*

Montgomery, L. M. *Anne of Green Gables.* Bantam, 1976. paper $2.95 (0-553-24295-4).
FORMAT: Novel   GRADES: 7–up.

This first of the Anne books has been read and loved by girls for years, but the award-winning PBS television show seems to have won new, even adult, readers. Yes, it's a heartwarming tale of an orphan, but more; there are funny adventures and endless mishaps as Anne wends her way into Marilla Cuthbert's heart.

Novak, Matt. *While the Shepherd Slept.* **Illus. by the author.** Orchard, 1991. LB $13.99 (0-531-08515-5).

FORMAT: Picture book   GRADES: Preschool–Grade 2.

Beneath those placid facades, these sheep are just waiting for their master to doze off so that they can pull out all the stops in their matinee performance at a local theater. And just why is the shepherd so tired? Readers will love this funny peek into the hidden need for celebrity that seems to lurk in every ovine soul.

Salinger, J. D. *The Catcher in the Rye.* Little, Brown, 1951. $17.95 (0-316-76953-3). paper avail.

FORMAT: Novel   GRADES: 7–up.

Long passed into classic status, this book still manages to surprise readers who equate "classic" with "inaccessibility" and "stuffiness." Holden, the original young adult hero, marches on through his adolescent trials, marking the way for us all. Splendid, and dead-on funny.

Seuss, Dr. *I Am Not Going to Get Up Today!* **Illus. by James Stevenson.** Random, 1987. $6.95 (0-394-89217-8).

FORMAT: Picture book   GRADES: Kindergarten–Grade 3.

This light piece of whimsy is narrated by a boy in striped pajamas who, through closed eyes, proclaims that under no circumstances will he be getting out of bed and going anywhere. "I don't choose to be up walking. I don't choose to be up talking. The only thing I'm choosing is to lie here woozy-snoozing." In this every child's fantasy, the boy is in charge of his own destiny on this particular morning. Stevenson shows the surrounding madcap lunacy, as well as the neat, sublime smile of the narrator recounting his plans. Easygoing and funny fare, not for beginning readers only.

Simmonds, Posy. *Lulu and the Flying Babies.* **Illus. by the author.** Knopf, 1989. $9.95 (0-394-89597-5).

FORMAT: Picture book   GRADES: Kindergarten–Grade 3.

A sullen Lulu, on an outing with her father to the museum, is jollied out of her bad mood by two cherubs who have flown out of the artworks. The museum she sees from that point on is markedly different from her father's more conventional tour. Brisk.

Steig, William. *Spinky Sulks.* **Illus. by the author.** Farrar, 1988. $15.00 (0-374-38321-9). paper avail.

FORMAT: Picture book   GRADES: Preschool–Grade 3.

The sulk of the century has Spinky's family attempting every trick in the book to shake him from it. Steig restores his hero to good spirits, but boy, can this kid wring the most from his moment out of the sun. Young readers will relate, and wait for the right time to start sulks of their own.

Stevenson, James. *Monty.* **Illus. by the author.** Greenwillow, 1992. $14.00 (0-688-11241-2).

FORMAT: Picture book   GRADES: Preschool–Grade 2.

What do you do when your ferry service is disrupted because the main vehicle—an alligator who feels he's being taken for granted—goes on strike? This funny piece of work was followed up a few years later by *No Need for Monty*, another childhood classic of comedy. With Stevenson's hallmark cartoons, complex as always but displaying only a deceptive ease.

Stevenson, Suçie. *Do I Have to Take Violet?* **Illus. by the author.** Dell, 1987. paper $3.99 (0-440-40682-X).

FORMAT: Picture book   GRADES: Preschool–Grade 3.

This buoyant, appealing book is full of adorable, toddler-sized observations about siblings and friendship. Elly, the older sister who wants to take a bike ride "BY MYSELF," gets roped into taking little Violet for a walk. First it's a chore; then it's a celebration in which both the girls— and readers—can partake.

Wood, Audrey. *King Bidgood's in the Bathtub.* **Illus. by Don Wood.** Harcourt, 1985. $14.95 (0-15-242730-9).

FORMAT: Picture book   GRADES: Preschool–Grade 3.

This Caldecott Honor book tells of a king's stubborn streak and the sort of rebellion any child will understand: His Royal Highness refuses to leave his tub and get on to the business of kingly rule. Charming and funny, with opulent pictures. These collaborators' other delightful books include *Heckedy Peg*.

Zinnemann-Hope, Pam. *Time for Bed, Ned; Let's Go Shopping, Ned.* **Illus. by Kady MacDonald Denton.** Macmillan, 1986. $6.95 each (0-689-50415-2; 0-689-50416-0).

FORMAT: Picture book   GRADES: Preschool–Grade 2.

Parents of toddlers who have outgrown their board books might pounce on this sunny pair. The author's minimalist dialogue is reminiscent of Dick and Jane but much livelier. "I don't like shopping. I like hopping. Come on Fred. Hop, hop, hop!" Denton's cheeky watercolors give these books a pell-mell pace and turn Ned's mayhem into good-natured mischief.

Zion, Gene. *Harry the Dirty Dog.* **Illus. by Margaret Bloy Graham.**
HarperCollins, 1956. LB $14.89 (0-06-026866-2). paper avail.
FORMAT: Picture book   GRADES: Preschool–Grade 3.

Any child who has ever tried to get out of a bath will endorse Harry's rebellion with gusto. He buries his bath brush and lives for the pursuit of dirtiness for the rest of the day. Ebullient in both words and pictures.

Additional Titles

The following titles, annotated elsewhere in this book (see index), could also fit the "Humor as Rebellion" category.

Anholt, Catherine. *Chaos at Cold Custard Farm*
Bellows, Cathy. *Four Fat Rats*
Collodi, Carlo. *Pinocchio*
Mills, Claudia. *After Fifth Grade, the World!*
Oppenheim, Joanne. *The Story Book Prince*
Pinkwater, Jill. *Buffalo Brenda*
Shepperson, Rob. *The Sandman*
Van Allsburg, Chris. *Two Bad Ants*

10: Fool's Play

Impostors, Rascals, Buffoons, and Tricksters

*B*rer Rabbit is the first trickster many children meet; as they grow older they become acquainted with Anansi, or Iktomi, or any of the other profusion of rascals and tricksters whose goal in literature, if a goal can be attributed to these ne'er-do-wells, is to confuse everyone while innocently cooking up laughter. If lofty heroic figures in dramatic stories put things to right, then surely the lowly impostors, impersonators, and imps can be accused of putting things to wrong. With relish.

Humor can result, as we know from Shakespeare, from confusion over false identity. Thus the work of jesters, fools, and pranksters and their misinformation; good-hearted folk with misguided or sometimes slyly guided intentions; clowns in full mask with hearts full of misdirection and divergence; and children with naughty ideas prancing through their heads, all star in this chapter. They are accorded the one-day April 1 holiday, but seem in fact to populate the real and fictional worlds the year round. Readers are pleased and amused.

Aardema, Verna. *Rabbit Makes a Monkey of Lion.* Illus. by Jerry Pinkney.
Dial, 1989. $11.95 (0-8037-0297-3).
FORMAT: Picture book   GRAᴅES: Preschool–Grade 3.

The author of the majestic *Bringing the Rain to Kapiti Plain* journeys here into the land of funny folktales with a pungent story of two longtime foes. Rabbit craves the taste of honey, but Lion, who prizes the honey tree, craves a taste of rabbit. This comic tale of give-and-take on the African plains offers up classic trickster themes in a biting text and sun-drenched paintings. A Swahili tale, this will remind some of Brer Rabbit's pranks on Brer Fox, and other rascal tales. Folksy antics, grand fun.

Bellows, Cathy. *Four Fat Rats.* **Illus. by the author.** Macmillan, 1987. $12.95 (0-02-708830-8).
FORMAT: Picture book   GRADES: Preschool–Grade 3.

Four fat rats leave their parents' nest and eat their way out into the world. By nightfall they try to find shelter in other animals' houses. In this surprisingly odd but funny story of blunt social climbers, Bellows leaves little room for sympathy for how the other half lives. The artist's lodging places are warm and hospitable, with decorous interiors and urbane dwellers. An eccentric find.

Brink, Carol Ryrie. *Caddie Woodlawn.* **Illus. by Trina Schart Hyman.** Macmillan, 1935. $14.95 (0-02-713670-1). paper avail.
FORMAT: Novel   GRADES: 4–6.

Revised in 1973, this illustrated version of the favorite old frontier tale is full of mischievous vignettes featuring indomitable, "unladylike" Caddie and her family. Readers can try these tales one chapter at a time, although most will be snagged into reading straight through. A Newbery Medal winner.

Fitzgerald, John D. *The Great Brain.* **Illus. by Mercer Mayer.** Dial, 1967. LB $11.89 (0-8037-3076-4). paper avail.
FORMAT: Novel   GRADES: 4–6.

The first of the series about the fabulous money-maker from 1896 Utah, the Great Brain. Tom's skills at manipulating situations to his own advantage have not been matched, and readers who stumble onto his adventures in this book will find there are plenty more volumes to curl up with later. Ingenious fun.

Goble, Paul. *Iktomi and the Berries.* **Illus. by the author.** Orchard, 1989. $14.95 (0-531-05819-0). paper avail.
FORMAT: Picture book   GRADES: Preschool–Grade 2.

Iktomi, the Plains Indian mischief-maker, was last spotted wrestling successfully with a vengeful boulder. Now the havoc Iktomi wreaks in his confrontation with a bunch of berries also bears telling. In his last scene, Iktomi is humbled once more and temporarily outfitted not in traditional garb, but in the attire of a jogger. This is but one way in which Goble reminds readers of the story's contemporary value; of course, humor is always timely.

Hamilton, Virginia. *The Dark Way: Stories from the Spirit World.* **Illus. by Lambert Davis.** Harcourt, 1990. $19.95 (0-15-222340-1).
FORMAT: Short stories   GRADES: 4–7.

There is no child who won't want to curl up with these parables, fables, ghost stories, witch tales, and folk fictions. They dwell on aspects of the non-physical world, those elements just beyond human understanding around which various cultures have imagined and constructed careful truths. Yes, there is humor in these pages, whether found in the tricks of Baba Yaga or in the transformation of a prankster into a teakettle. The diversity and scholarship evident in the work is worth celebrating as well.

Harris, Joel Chandler. *Jump! The Adventures of Brer Rabbit.* **Adapt. by Parks Van Dyke and Malcolm Jones. Illus. by Barry Moser.** Harcourt, 1986. $15.95 (0-15-241350-2).
FORMAT: Storybook   GRADES: 4–6.

Sparkling, vigorous retellings of the Uncle Remus stories of the 1800s combine with ironic character studies by Moser to create a comedic, sophisticated piece of Americana. Serve up more adaptations of Harris's familiar stories in the sequel, *Jump Again!*, by these same collaborators. Great for reading aloud.

Lindgren, Astrid. *Pippi Longstocking.* Puffin, 1977. paper $3.95 (0-14-030957-8).
FORMAT: Chapter book   GRADES: 4–6.

Self-reliance is Pippi's strength, and what she can't do doesn't need to be taken on. This red-haired, freckle-faced child has given readers adventure after adventure for years, and always with the exuberant high spirits that characterize all this author's books. Readers will love not only Pippi's other books, but *Ronia, the Robber's Daughter* as well.

Marshall, James. *Fox Outfoxed.* **Illus. by the author.** Dial, 1992. LB $10.89 (0-8037-1037-2).
FORMAT: Storybook   GRADES: Preschool–Grade 3.

The ultimate trickster is back, trying to line up the planets in his favor through a series of devious attempts. Of course, the best laid plans of naughty foxes go more than simply awry, and it makes for a funny book for beginning readers. As usual, droll as they come.

Marshall, James. *Red Riding Hood.* **Illus. by the author.** Dial, 1987. LB $10.89 (0-8037-0345-7).
FORMAT: Picture book   GRADES: Preschool–Grade 3.

The well-mannered wolf of this treat has a charming straw hat; he takes the trusting Red by the hand, and with all the gusto of an uninvited guest he gobbles her up. This retelling invigorates the spirit of the classic tale without doing violence to its fundamental structure. Red is irresistably vulnerable and good-looking, too. As part of this utterly funny version she is shown to have learned her lesson, and declines the kind offer of another friendly carnivore.

Nones, Eric Jon. *Wendell.* **Illus. by the author.** Farrar, 1989. $13.95 (0-374-38266-2).

FORMAT: Picture book   GRADES: Preschool–Grade 3.

Only Wendell, a family's cat, can see the tiny creatures that perform much mischief in the household. Splendid paintings of a 1950s home. Nostalgic for adults, fun for children.

Paterson, Katherine. *The Great Gilly Hopkins.* HarperCollins, 1978. LB $13.89 (0-690-03838-0). paper avail.

FORMAT: Novel   GRADES: 5–up.

This Newbery Honor book by the two-time Newbery Medalist is the story of Gilly, an embittered victim of the foster care system and a little too knowing about her chances of survival. It's every-girl-for-herself, until Gilly arrives in the last foster home she's ever going to need and finds herself scratching out a little piece of family. On the surface, blithe, but the feelings run deep, and so do the lessons.

Pryor, Bonnie. *The Porcupine Mouse.* **Illus. by Maryjane Begin.** Morrow, 1988. $13.95 (0-688-07153-8).

FORMAT: Picture book   GRADES: Preschool–Grade 2.

Two mouse brothers, Louie and Dan, leave their overcrowded house in search of a home of their own. Disaster is averted when Louie persuades a black cat not to eat Dan, convincing the feline that a "porcupine" is a terrible meal. The plot is slight and uncomplicated, but Begin's pictures make up for the shortcomings. A snug miniature world is created as much by an illusionist as by a skillful artist. The disparity in size between cat and mouse when they encounter each other in the dark generates real dramatic surprise, in contrast to some blissfully cheerful interior shots.

Reuter, Bjarne. *Buster's World.* Dutton, 1989. $12.95 (0-525-44475-0). paper avail.

FORMAT: Novel   GRADES: 4–up.

Buster's world is almost too grim, and so his escapes are extra fanciful. For example, when there is no money for new pants, he settles for long, colorful socks to bridge the gap between pantleg and sandletop. The novel, with its Danish backdrop, is a source of many surprising pieces of plotting; one of the funniest involves Buster and his third (artificial) arm, which falls off in a confrontation with a bully. Buster is a funny, utterly childlike hero of the underdog, and while many of his exploits will not be comfortably digested by American readers, the bulk of this book is comically exuberant.

Salassi, Otto R. *Jimmy D., Sidewinder, and Me.* Greenwillow, 1987. $11.75 (0-688-05237-1).
FORMAT: Novel   GRADES: 5–up.

"Me" is Dumas Monk, an orphan who is cast from one odd situation to the next in 1948, leading to a shoot-out that he now must explain to a judge in a series of letters, and hope for a lighter sentence. But what a story! This account is that of a true innocent getting an unbridled initiation into life, at the hands of scamps and no-accounts—which is not to say they don't have their good points. A daring, sometimes screwball view of life off the beaten track.

Slobodkina, Esphyr. *Caps for Sale.* **Illus. by the author.** HarperCollins, 1947. LB $12.89 (0-06-025778-4). paper avail.
FORMAT: Picture book   GRADES: Preschool–Grade 3.

Under a tree, where the pedlar sleeps, he is unaware of the rascally bunch of thieves stealing away with his wares. Every hat is gone, and only a bunch of grinning monkeys can change such misfortune into a madcap adventure for every lover of *les chapeaux.*

Thompson, Kay. *Eloise.* **Illus. by Hilary Knight.** Simon & Schuster, 1955. $15.95 (0-671-22350-X).
FORMAT: Storybook   GRADES: 3–5.

This romp through New York City's famous Plaza Hotel is led by its youngest and most precocious resident, the dauntless Eloise. No child yet has been able to resist her proprietary guide to the hotel's many perks.

Twain, Mark. *The Adventures of Tom Sawyer.* Puffin, 1983. paper $2.95 (0-14-035003-9).
FORMAT: Novel   GRADES: 3–7.

There are many hardcover editions of this available, and illustrated versions may suit a younger child, but this is a good portable edition for carrying in the back pocket, just in case someone else can be persuaded to take over some chores. Of course, you can send more sophisticated readers to *The Adventures of Huckleberry Finn,* but it is probably best to wait a few years.

Ungerer, Tomi. *The Beast of Monsieur Racine.* **Illus. by the author.** Farrar, 1971. $15.95 (0-374-30640-0). paper avail.
FORMAT: Picture book   GRADES: Preschool–Grade 3.

Not until the end of the story does Monsieur Racine discover the dual nature of the odd-looking creature that wandered through his garden and devoured the fruit of his trees. But tricksters more endearing than those beastly ones found here are hard to imagine. Other books by Ungerer are eccentrically funny, but this one blissfully mixes humor and the sentimental. Enchantè!

Van Laan, Nancy. *Possum Come A-Knocking.* **Illus. by George Booth.** Knopf, 1990. LB $14.99 (0-394-92206-9). paper avail.
FORMAT: Picture book   GRADES: Preschool–Grade 3.

In lilting language with the swinging, comforting creak of a rocking chair, the narrator relates that the possum came a-knocking but no one in the family would believe it. This rascal, hiding every time the door is opened, is a hit with children at story hours, and the laughter is contagious.

Young, Ed. *Lon Po Po: A Red Riding Hood Tale from China.* **Illus. by the author.** Putnam, 1989. $14.95 (0-399-21619-7).
FORMAT: Picture book   GRADES: Preschool–Grade 3.

The trickster tale is turned around in the hands of a reliably gifted illustrator. Three Chinese children convince the wolf at their door to climb the gingko tree, where he'll find a nut of eternal life. No one will mistake this wolf for any but a malevolent presence, but the stalwart girls of the story reassure all readers that addressing the enemy head-on is the beginning of vanquishing all fears.

Additional Titles

The following titles, annotated elsewhere in this book (see index), could also fit the "Fool's Play" category.

Babbitt, Natalie. *The Devil's Other Storybook*
Bang, Betsy. *The Old Woman and the Rice Thief*
Banks, Lynne Reid. *I, Houdini*
Carey, Valerie Scho. *The Devil and Mother Crump*
Collodi, Carlo. *Pinocchio*
Dupasquier, Philippe. *The Great Escape*
Goble, Paul. *Iktomi and the Boulder*
McCaughrean, Geraldine. *A Pack of Lies*
Marshall, James. *Goldilocks*
Wood, Audrey. *Heckedy Peg*

11: Nothing Is Sacred

Irreverent Humor

The free spirit of humor and the awesome world of children's books are hardly accommodating toward sacred cows and other venerable creatures of the high-and-mighty. They, too, will be prodded and pulled and pushed until they are mere shadows of their formerly sanctified selves. More often than not, children themselves are never the high-principled idealized creatures adults hope for. Their territories are neither noble nor consecrated. Their concerns are less than lofty; in fact, children are possessed by an interest in the mundane, and even the profane—natural outposts for humor.

The curse of young children—and even teenagers—is that their pragmatic temperaments unwittingly serve to *deflate* grandiose issues, serious intent, high-mindedness, sobriety, and prudish morality. The vulgar rolling-in-the-mud clown is of more interest to them than the head-in-the-cloud aristocratic hero. The emperor may be exalted, but he is also stark naked. Leave it to a child to cut everything down to size with a little clear-eyed honesty (and perhaps down-to-earth realism); it's not that they *believe* "nothing is sacred," but that, just maybe, nothing *is*. And so their attitudes reflect a time-honored conclusion that laughter is mostly for the irreverent masses. Humor muscles in to oppose elitism. After all, humor is a baser form, a lowly art, aimed at the populace, as were Mozart's operas with such unholy characters and themes as barbers, chambermaids, and magic flutes. Does all this imply that mundane, lowbrow, "realistic," play-loving Americans are funnier than those who came before? Kids would sum up: "Who cares!"

Anno, Mitsumasa. *Anno's Aesop: A Book of Fables by Aesop and Mr. Fox.*
Illus. by the author. Orchard, 1989. $18.95 (0-531-05774-7).
FORMAT: Picture book   GRADES: Preschool–Grade 2.

Anno frames the celebrated fables by employing a storyteller, a Mr. Fox, in a read-aloud setting involving his son Freddy Fox as a listener. This elaborate restructuring allows the fox to unite the many varied tales into one large storyline. Some of the stories are radical interpretations of familiar ones, others are straight commentaries on or parallel versions to the original intent of the fables (whatever that may be), and still others are merely parodies or metafables that build on what is already there. Such an original approach breathes new life into an old and fossilized form of wisdom.

Bible, King James Version. *The Nativity.* **Illus. by Julie Vivas.** Harcourt,
1988. $13.95 (0-15-200535-8).
FORMAT: Picture book   GRADES: Preschool–Grade 3.

The excerpts from the New Testament story of Jesus's birth are delivered with absolute sobriety, but the pictures bend all previous images readers may have had of this tale; Gabriel wears unlaced, clumsy work boots and delivers his message over coffee or soup at Mary's kitchen table, and when there is no room at the inn, the rest of the town's visitors deck out a tree and snooze in stairwells. Vivas irreverently unravels the mystique of the famous birth, showing a bulging Mary and first peeks at the child barely out of the womb. A part of this mad charm is elegance; wispy, glimmering watercolors show comic characters in the midst of grand events.

Chaucer, Geoffrey. *Chanticleer and the Fox.* **Retold and illus. by Barbara**
Cooney. HarperCollins, 1958. LB $13.89 (0-690-18562-6). paper avail.
FORMAT: Picture book   GRADES: All grades.

The Caldecott Medal-winning fable is taken from *Chaucer's Tales* and beautifully brought to life in Cooney's period art. Let children look forward to wrestling with the original in a couple of decades; this version preserves the humor of that first one, and yet remains wonderfully accessible to youngsters.

Gellman, Marc. *Does God Have a Big Toe? Stories about Stories in the*
Bible. **Illus. by Oscar de Mejo.** HarperCollins, 1989. LB 15.89 (0-06-022433-9).
FORMAT: Short stories   GRADES: 4–up.

If humor is the antidote to the heavy business of real life, further relief is in sight. You want fun? Here's fun. If God were a vaudevillian delivering religious instruction accompanied by rim shots, he could cull material from here. Gellman's grating, lively style engages even nonbelievers with stories about Adam, Eve, Noah, and others. This is a book adults steal to share among themselves.

Goble, Paul. *Iktomi and the Boulder.* **Illus. by the author.** Orchard, 1988. $14.95 (0-531-05760-7). paper avail.

FORMAT: Picture book   GRADES: Preschool–Grade 2.

Iktomi, a genuine mischief-maker from the Plains Indian tales, is a grandiose departure from Goble's other, more somber tellings. Comic asides abound, and the typeface cues readers to the places where improvisation is allowed. With all the "ennobled" myths and legends around, Iktomi will elicit belly laughs; for this troublemaker, getting laughed at is just the fate he deserves. Readers will also like *Iktomi and the Berries* and *Iktomi and the Buffalo Skull.*

Hewitt, Kathryn. *Two by Two: The Untold Story.* **Illus. by the author.** Harcourt, 1984. $12.95 (0-15-291801-9). paper avail.

FORMAT: Picture book   GRADES: Preschool–Grade 3.

Readers will pore over the pages searching for signs, large and small, of Hewitt's mirth in her goofy upending of the story of Noah's Ark . . . and how those 40 days and nights slipped speedily away.

Kaye, M. M. *Ordinary Princess.* **Illus. by the author.** Pocket, 1989. paper $2.95 (0-671-69013-2).

FORMAT: Chapter book   GRADES: 4–6.

Princess Amethyst receives the gift of "ordinariness" from a curmudgeonly fairy godmother. Tongue-in-cheek, witty storytelling, certain to please fans of the form and those a little weary of extraordinary royalty.

Lattimore, Deborah Nourse. *Why There Is No Arguing in Heaven: A Mayan Myth.* **Illus. by the author.** HarperCollins, 1989. LB $13.89 (0-06-023718-X).

FORMAT: Picture book   GRADES: 1–4.

Hunab Ku, the Creator God of the Mayas, is tired of the squabbling between the Moon Goddess and Lizard House as to which of them should be the second most important god. When Hunab Ku declares that whomever creates a being that will worship all the gods will win a place next to him, the Maize God watches the other two fight it out. Throughout, the storytelling and the illustrations dazzle with details. Humor abounds; how refreshing to see a creation myth in which mistakes are made before the gods get it right!

Marshall, James. *James Marshall's Mother Goose.* **Illus. by the author.**
Farrar, 1979. $14.95 (0-374-33653-9). paper avail.
FORMAT: Picture book   GRADES: Preschool–Grade 3.

Marshall is destined to dominate any book with both "best" and "humorous" in the title. He is a master of the form, enlisting sly irony and sheer slapstick, with a simplicity that stuns. In this book he courts Ms. Goose with the timing of an experienced suitor and makes familiar territory fresh and funny again.

Peet, Bill. *Bill Peet: An Autobiography.* **Illus. by the author.** Houghton, 1989. $16.95 (0-395-50832-7).
FORMAT: Autobiography   GRADES: 4–6.

An illustrated autobiography of a former Disney cartoonist who left corporate life at the Magic Kingdom for the joys of picture-book creation, and only looked back once (in this book). Is there any other work like this? Readers will, perhaps for the first time, see an adult's rise in his career in cartoons. An openhearted invitation to survey aspects of a life, this is the sort of dip into an inkpot of facts that those without illustrative talents could never attempt.

Seuss, Dr. *The 500 Hats of Bartholomew Cubbins.* **Illus. by the author.**
Random, 1938. LB $10.99 (0-394-94484-4).
FORMAT: Picture book   GRADES: Preschool–Grade 3.

No matter how many times Bartholomew doffs his hat before the king, more hats show up. Utter nonsense, the kind that has delighted children for over half a century.

Additional Titles

The following titles, annotated elsewhere in this book (see index), could also fit the "Irreverent Humor" category.

Broeger, Achim. *The Santa Clauses*
Lattimore, Deborah Nourse. *The Prince and the Golden Axe*
Opie, Iona, and Peter Opie. *Tail Feathers from Mother Goose*
Seuss, Dr. *How the Grinch Stole Christmas*
Stolz, Mary. *Bartholomew Fair*
Wood, Audrey. *King Bidgood's in the Bathtub*

12: Goose Bumps and Chills

Gothic Humor

*F*rom the fabula of Hieronymus Bosch to the gargoyles that haunt the rooftops of high and holy architecture, to the full-of-shivery-promise covenants of Halloween, signs of the grotesque and rapturous tremors surround children most of the year, providing them with the dark glimpses of humor that in the adult world can be clearly frightening, but in children's books have been entombed in nothing more injurious than some wicked fun or gooseflesh-raising thrill. Children have been touched by gothic humor and relished its pungency in the baroque, eccentric tang of Edward Gorey's illustrations for the jackets of John Bellairs's best works, the ghoulish upending of monster mythology in Edward Miller's *The Curse of Claudia* and Delessert's *A Long Long Song*, the ghastly fates of innocents walking through the black forests of the Brothers Grimm, and the mischievous, paroxysmal deeds attributed to Old Scratch in *The Devil's Storybook*. Even the youngest have seen it, in Max's Wild Things, and have been reassured that as long as what's scary is also funny, it may do no harm.

Babbitt, Natalie. *The Devil's Other Storybook*. Illus. by the author. Farrar, 1987. $13.00 (0-374-31767-4). paper avail.
FORMAT: Storybook GRADES: 3–6.

Are young readers' minds going to the Devil? Most will agree that this is not the case in this logical follow-up to the little red volume of *The Devil's Storybook*. Ten more tales are told by a very dexterous fiddlemaster. There are familiar diabolical incarnations, the instances of mistaken identity usually associated with tales of devilry, and even stories about "justice" and Christmas. The author's travels to the very gates of Hell brings to this children's book a spacious dimension of unadulterated maturity. These stories are simply some of the funniest available. The Devil in Babbitt is more than a subject for amusement and less than an article of belief; the writer, however, for good or for bad, is still well within the orbit of the religious. As in the "Simple Sentences" story, Babbitt can rightly be placed in the middle ground between the two very eloquent and hilarious protagonists, the rascal and the writer.

Babbitt, Natalie. *The Something.* **Illus. by the author.** Farrar, 1970. $11.00 (0-374-37137-7). paper avail.
FORMAT: Storybook   GRADES: Preschool–Grade 3.

Milo fears the unnameable presence that comes through his window at night until he creates The Something out of modeling clay; this story goes for the core of children's apprehension of the unknown, unseen, unfathomable. Purely excellent, one of Babbitt's best.

Bellairs, John. *The Chessmen of Doom.* Dial, 1989. $13.95 (0-8037-0729-0).
FORMAT: Novel   GRADES: 4–6.

In a book for fans of stories involving Johnny Dixon and the ever-cranky Professor Roderick Childermass, a British villain conjures up dark forces to advance his plans to take over the world. Bellairs began this series in 1973 with *The House with a Clock in Its Walls,* and each novel since has carried the tried and true formula of good versus evil to its predictable end, via speed-laden, clue-dropping humor, and large doses of suspense.

Brewton, Sarah, and John E. Brewton. *Shrieks at Midnight: Macabre Poems, Eerie and Humorous.* **Illus. by Ellen Raskin.** HarperCollins, 1969. $13.95 (0-690-73518-9).
FORMAT: Poetry   GRADES: 5–up.

Puns, epitaphs, and old ballads are just some of the weirdly wonderful poems gathered in these pages. Children love laughing at the macabre, and will delight in Raskin's spooky drawings.

Brittain, Bill. *Devil's Donkey.* **Illus. by Andrew Glass.** HarperCollins, 1981. LB $13.89 (0-06-020683-7). paper avail.
FORMAT: Novel   GRADES: 3–7.

Sophisticated wits will find plenty to whet their appetites here; Dan'l is changed into a donkey by a witch, and goes to the devil himself to negotiate a better deal for himself.

Brittain, Bill. *The Wish Giver*. Illus. by Andrew Glass. HarperCollins, 1983.
$13.89 (0-06-020687-X). paper avail.
FORMAT: Novel GRADES: 3–7.

Stew Meat relates three tales of people in Coven Tree who were given
wishes, and saw them fulfilled—much to their regrets. By turns humorous and sinister, Brittain's story entertains thoroughly, and perhaps
teaches a lesson or two?

Carey, Valerie Scho. *The Devil and Mother Crump*. Illus. by Arnold Lobel.
HarperCollins, 1987. $11.95 (0-06-020982-8). paper avail.
FORMAT: Storybook GRADES: 2–5.

Meet Mother Crump, meaner than the devil himself. When he comes
sniffing around her bake shop, she uses her bread paddle on him! Imagine a book in which the Devil locks someone out of his base of opera-
tions, yelling "You're mean enough to go start a Hell of your own." The
story is ornery and somewhat awkwardly told, but Lobel's illustrious
craft provides the necessary supplement, in characters with angular features whose antics provide slapstick relief.

Christian, Mary Blount. *Swamp Monsters*. Illus. by Marc Brown. Dial,
1983. LB $9.89 (0-8037-7616-0). paper avail.
FORMAT: Chapter book GRADES: 2–4.

This "easy-to-read" book is about monstrous Crag and Fenny, who dis-
guise themselves as children about whom they have heard so much (and
whom they fear), then join a class of students. Brown's sunny pictures
take the BOO! out of these two boggy boys and introduce beginning
readers to humor based on expectations turned upside down. Blissful
slapstick.

Coombs, Patricia. *Dorrie and the Wizard's Spell*. Illus. by the author.
Lothrop, 1968. LB $12.88 (0-688-51083-3).
FORMAT: Storybook GRADES: Preschool–Grade 3.

This early adventure about Dorrie foreshadowed a delightful relationship between this stumbling young witch and readers that has lasted 25
years. Here she makes an appearance at a witches' bazaar and tea, with
horribly humorous results for her dear mother. Since tales about Dorrie
are good all year 'round, don't be afraid to lead readers to *Dorrie and the
Halloween Plot* and *Dorrie and the Museum Case*, as well.

de Mejo, Oscar. *Journey to Boc Boc: The Kidnapping of a Rock Star.* Illus. by the author. HarperCollins, 1987. $12.95 (0-06-021579-8).
FORMAT: Picture book   GRADES: 1–3.

While de Mejo's view of the world is idiosyncratic, this story of true love has very traditional roots. Jack Michaels loves Noona, but is kidnapped by the alien, Lysidra. The tone of this is entirely tongue-in-cheek, as quirky for adults as for children. Blocky figures and weird landscapes make both planet Boc Boc and Earth very strange lands indeed.

de Regniers, Beatrice Schenk. *Red Riding Hood.* Illus. by Edward Gorey. Aladdin, 1990. paper $4.95 (0-689-71373-8).
FORMAT: Storybook   GRADES: Preschool–Grade 3.

This droll retelling of a familiar tale is illustrated with verve by the incomparable Gorey. First published in hardcover by Atheneum, this inexpensive version is worth seeking out. Another of this author's worthwhile versions of fairy tales is *Jack the Giant Killer.*

DeFelice, Cynthia C. *The Dancing Skeleton.* Illus. by Robert Andrew Parker.* Macmillan, 1989. $13.95 (0-02-726452-1).
FORMAT: Picture book   GRADES: Preschool–Grade 3.

Aaron's widow attempts to go down the path to remarriage, but finds it hard with the skeleton of her former husband sitting in his chair, refusing to budge. Parker's pictures show the devastation some good old-fashioned music wreaks on this bony fellow.

Delessert, Etienne. *A Long Long Song.* Illus. by the author. Farrar, 1988. $13.95 (0-374-34638-0).
FORMAT: Picture book   GRADES: Preschool–Grade 3.

"As I was going along, long, long/A-singing a comical song, song, song." The landscape of this pictorial expansion on a nursery rhyme is that of the pure imagination. Delessert dips his brush in the open-ended paint pot of a Hieronymous Bosch or a surrealist artist to produce a dimension where mythical creatures roam and where the line is blurred between the real and the unreal, the human and the animal-like, the credible and the impossible. Clearly, the most interesting aspect of this is that such a free-floating world is precisely one that children find most appealing. This extraordinary interpretation is radically personal. The astonishing vistas may inspire readers to do a little interpreting on their own.

Fleischman, Paul. *Graven Images: Three Stories.* **Illus. by Andrew Glass.**
HarperCollins, 1982. LB $13.89 (0-06-021907-6). paper avail.
FORMAT: Short stories   GRADES: 7–up.

A wooden figurehead holds the secrets to the death of sailors; a copper
weathervane points the way to romance; a statue commissioned by a
ghost offers a message of murder. Fleischman's brazenly witty, pithy
stories are wonderful for reading aloud to younger children, but are
chilling enough to elicit sighs from older ones. Twisty, humorous, and
better on each rereading.

Fuchshuber, Annegert. *The Cuckoo-Clock Cuckoo.* **Illus. by the author.**
Carolrhoda, 1988. $12.95 (0-87614-320-6). paper avail.
FORMAT: Picture book   GRADES: Kindergarten–Grade 4.

Not only will children learn how to read time from this story (there is
almost hour-by-hour reportage of a cuckoo's adventure beyond time) but
they will readily perceive the natural link between clock time and real
events in the ever-changing, everyday worlds. Ghosts, dreams, and fantasies belong only in a world where time stops. In the book's 12 illustrations, Fuchshuber retains a fixed perspective on a dollhouse-like structure where the family Zeitler lives. Undoubtedly, this book will survive
the passage of time and readers of all ages will rediscover the inherent
magic of the midnight hour. Comedy by the clockface, this one's timing
is impeccable.

Graves, Robert. *The Big Green Book.* **Illus. by Maurice Sendak.** Macmillan,
1962. $14.95 (0-02-736810-6). paper avail.
FORMAT: Storybook   GRADES: Preschool–Grade 3.

Jack's big green book is full of spells just waiting to be tried on the
tiresome adults who surround him. Delicious good fun, from a master
wordsmith and not-bad illustrator who went on to have quite a career in
children's books. For more fun, send children to Sendak's *Nutshell Library,* or on to any of his classics.

Grimm, Jacob, and Wilhelm Grimm. *The Complete Grimm's Fairy Tales.*
Illus. by Josef Scharl. Random, 1944. paper $16.00 (0-394-70930-6).
FORMAT: Anthology   GRADES: 5–up.

Translated by Margaret Hunt. Published for adults, many older children
will nab this one from the shelves. The power of the original tellings is
fully retained, and there is additional commentary by Joseph Campbell.
Compared to this one, many other editions will seem watered-down to
readers.

Grimm, Jacob, and Wilhelm Grimm. *Hansel and Gretel.* **Illus. by Anthony Browne.** Knopf, 1988. paper $3.95 (0-394-89859-1).
FORMAT: Picture book   GRADES: All grades.

This moody, intense version is infused with modern references that heighten the uncanny aspects of an already frightening story. Famine has struck and the father is persuaded by frowsy stepmother to ditch the kids. She dies by the time Hansel and Gretel find their way out of the woods. Browne provides jarring touches through his surrealist's eye— Gretel's knees are dirty, the oily-looking wallpaper in their home is cracked and peeling. If the peasant poverty of other versions has an aura of romance, this book shows a grimy, terrible hunger—for food first, and then for happiness. A radically different, moving vision.

Haseley, Dennis. *The Cave of Snores.* **Illus. by Eric Beddows.** HarperCollins, 1987. $11.95 (0-06-022214-X).
FORMAT: Picture book   GRADES: 1–3.

This shrewd and diverting story of foolery and mystery is about a shepherd boy who finds danger at his campsite. The moon is down and wolves are circling; Kabul the wizard and his band of robbers are closing in. What does the boy do to save his camp? He goes to sleep. His "snores," like his father's before him, drive the wolves away and bewitch the bandits. Throughout these antics readers are smoothly hoodwinked into following the path of the narrator in his nightmare. Beddows's nocturnal world of bogeys, wolves, and night watchers is breathlessly captivating. Black-and-white pictures depict the dark abyss of the dream world.

Hoban, Russell. *Monsters.* **Illus. by Quentin Blake.** Scholastic, 1990. $13.95 (0-590-43422-5).
FORMAT: Picture book   GRADES: 1–4.

Hoban scores again with an exceedingly dry telling of a well-behaved boy who loves drawing monsters all the time. The illustrations show his childlike, utterly hideous creations, reason enough (his parents believe) to cart him off to therapy. The child may or may not be dysfunctional, but the monster the therapist meets shortly before his demise is certainly not. A bang-up story, to be relished and reread.

Howe, Deborah, and James Howe. *Bunnicula: A Rabbit Tale of Mystery.* **Illus. by Alan Daniel.** Macmillan, 1979. $12.95 (0-689-30700-4). paper avail.
FORMAT: Chapter book   GRADES: 4–6.

A witty upending of vampire legends begins when the Monroe family— whose lives are chronicled by their pet dog/author, Harold—bring home a rabbit from a movie theater that was showing "Dracula."

Hutchins, Pat. *The Very Worst Monster.* **Illus. by the author.** Greenwillow,
1985. LB $11.88 (0-688-04011-X). paper avail.
FORMAT: Picture book   GRADES: Preschool–Grade 3.

Not to be usurped by her father's claim that a new baby brother Billy will
be the worst monster in the world, just-as-monstrous Hazel plans to
secure her spot as defender of the title. A glee-filled story and a good
introduction to Hutchins's offbeat work.

Ivimey, John W. *Three Blind Mice.* **Illus. by Paul Galdone.** Clarion, 1987.
$13.95 (0-89919-481-8).
FORMAT: Picture book   GRADES: Kindergarten–Grade 3.

Galdone's last work is an expected delight. In the course of this longer
version of the familiar rhyme, the mice go from bold to scared, and grow
hungry, sad, and sick. A narrow escape from cat sends them into the
bramble hedge that scratches their eyes and makes them blind. Then
their tails are cut off by the farmer's wife. Now, "they could not see and
they had no end." But this story doesn't end unhappily. It's a joy, lit by a
large orange sun disk and colored with a variety of flowers, insects, and
birds, where things good and bad can happen and where adventure,
experience, and learning are fully possible.

Jeschke, Susan. *Lucky's Choice.* **Illus. by the author.** Scholastic, 1987. $13.95
(0-590-40520-9).
FORMAT: Picture book   GRADES: Preschool–Grade 2.

Lucky is a house cat, sheltered, fed, and safe until the day comes when
his mistress orders him to kill a mouse he has befriended. A comical,
straightforward story—the dilemma of choosing the life of earthbound
safety or airborne adventure is a perennial theme that confronts all ages.
Jeschke's all-too-human animals are remarkably sane and sensible; her
art, parsimonious and tart.

Johnston, Norma Tadlock. *Bats on the Bedstead.* Houghton, 1987. $12.95 (0-
395-43022-4). paper avail.
FORMAT: Novel   GRADES: 3–7.

A funny thriller that gives the old "new kid on the block" story a horrify-
ing twist. Ricky wakes up in the middle of the first night in their new
home to face a murderous bat named Voro. More bats arrive, and they
are seriously evil; nevertheless, readers will happily sweat through the
nights with Ricky until he finally fights back.

Johnston, Tony. *The Witch's Hat.* **Illus. by Margot Tomes.** Putnam, 1984. $10.99 (0-399-61223-8). paper avail.
FORMAT: Picture book   GRADES: Preschool–Grade 3.

A witch without a hat is almost no witch at all—and this one, who loses her headpiece in a pot she's trying to stir, has more than her share of troubles in simply trying to get it back. Wonderful to read aloud, the book features innovative pictures by well-loved Tomes.

Jones, Diana Wynne. *Witch Week.* Greenwillow, 1982. $11.75 (0-688-01534-4). paper avail.
FORMAT: Novel   GRADES: 7–up.

A thrilling, humorous tale by a masterful writer of fantasies, this focuses on one week following the revelation that someone in class is a witch. And witches must be rooted out and burned. Deliberate, well-paced excitement. Don't miss this author's highly original *Howl's Moving Castle, A Tale of Time City,* or for that matter, any of her other works.

Kimmel, Eric. *Hershel and the Hanukkah Goblins.* **Illus. by Trina Schart Hyman.** Holiday, 1989. $14.95 (0-8234-0769-1).
FORMAT: Picture book   GRADES: Preschool–Grade 4.

When goblins take over the synagogue on the hill, Hershel knows how to outwit—and outwait—them. Hyman's spooky illustrations bring this tale glimmering ghoulishly to life.

Klein, Robin. *Tearaways: Stories to Make You Think Twice.* Viking, 1991. $12.95 (0-670-83212-X).
FORMAT: Short stories   GRADES: 7–up.

The talented novelist (*Hating Alison Ashley*) turns in ten compact, briskly varied short tales. Readers can partake of the gleeful "Little Beast," in which the besieged outcast at boarding school wreaks heady revenge on her tormentors, or the guilt-laden "Octopi," about a young girl who uses pathos to insinuate herself into the lives of others, or "We'll Look After You," which artfully twists Good Samaritanship into a nightmare, a la Stephen King's *Misery.* Pithy, provocative, and plenty of fun.

Mahy, Margaret. *The Boy with Two Shadows.* **Illus. by Jenny Williams.** HarperCollins, 1988. LB $12.89 (0-397-32271-2).
FORMAT: Picture book   GRADES: Preschool–Grade 3.

This is an odd, funny tale about a boy who is acting as caretaker to a witch's shadow while she goes for a ride on her broomstick. Of course, there are complications; of course, Mahy delivers marvelous and satisfying solutions.

Marshall, Edward. *Space Case.* **Illus. by James Marshall.** Dial, 1980. LB $12.89 (0-8037-8007-9). paper avail.
FORMAT: Picture book   GRADES: Preschool–Grade 3.

The earth has been invaded, this time by the Marshall version of an alien critter. Buddy is delighted by the eccentric visitor who arrives for Halloween, so much so that he invites him back in this book's sequel, *Merry Christmas, Space Case.* Both are deadpan and zany, no small feat.

Merriam, Eve. *Halloween ABC.* **Illus. by Lane Smith.** Macmillan, 1987. $14.95 (0-02-766870-3).
FORMAT: Picture book   GRADES: Preschool–Grade 3.

Playful poems for each letter of the alphabet trumpet the enchantments of the holiday, from the downright spooky to the laugh-out-loud pleasing. Smith's paintings, like other-worldy etchings, bring their own kind of shiver to the work.

Miller, Edward. *The Curse of Claudia.* **Illus. by the author.** Crown, 1989. $12.95 (0-517-57408-X).
FORMAT: Picture book   GRADES: Preschool–Grade 3.

Take every campy horror film that was ever made and serve it up in a deadpan tone, then pose an old school chum of a zombie's on the doorstep of a gloomy, rotting paradise, ready to drop in for a visit. Chipper Claudia, in a sunny yellow dress and bursting with *joie de vivre*, makes life a cheerful living hell for the inhabitants of a monster mansion. Miller takes a clever idea and delivers a good old-fashioned thriller, a humor-filled nightmare about a truly wacky universe.

Nesbit, E. *The Ice Dragon.* **Illus. by Carole Grey.** Dial, 1988. $10.95 (0-8037-0475-5).
FORMAT: Picture book   GRADES: 1–4.

This journey of two children in search of the aurora borealis becomes a literal-minded morality tale in the illustrator's hands. The look is decidedly old-fashioned, but the tale is as imaginative and witty as any reader could expect of Nesbit.

O'Connor, Jane. *Lulu Goes to Witch School.* **Illus. by Emily Arnold McCully.** HarperCollins, 1987. LB $12.89 (0-06-024629-4). paper avail.
FORMAT: Picture book   GRADES: Preschool–Grade 3.

In this sequel to *Lulu and the Witch Baby,* Lulu is off to witch school with her broom and Dracula lunch box. Miss Slime, the teacher, is pretty, with a long nose and wart on her chin. This story is funny and full of the "gross" details kids love—like snake flakes and lizard tarts. Simple, free-hand illustrations add a good dose of silliness to an already absurd and funny idea.

Paige, Rob. *Some of My Best Friends Are Monsters.* **Illus. by Paul Yalowitz.** Bradbury, 1988. $12.95 (0-02-769640-5).
FORMAT: Picture book   GRADES: Preschool–Grade 2.

A boy gives a first-person account of his unusual circle of friends. They are monsters, and good buddies to have around. He is pretty convincing. Pencil drawings show a boy almost as eccentric-looking as his pals. While the telling is deliberately dry, the pictures deliver a pack of harmless, whimsical monsters who will find favor with readers.

Peck, Richard. *The Dreadful Future of Blossom Culp.* Delacorte, 1983. $15.00 (0-385-29300-3). paper avail.
FORMAT: Novel   GRADES: 7–up.

When a 14-year-old psychic time-travels from 1914 to the middle of the 1980s, there are bound to be difficulties in adjusting. This book and two others—*The Ghost Belonged to Me* and *Ghosts I Have Been*—are among the funniest of Peck's works, although many readers are fans of his more serious books—*Are You in the House Alone?* and *Princess Ashley,* among them.

Perl, Lila. *Don't Sing Before Breakfast, Don't Sleep in the Moonlight: Everyday Superstitions and How They Began.* **Illus. by Erika Weihs.** Houghton, 1988. $13.95 (0-89919-504-0).
FORMAT: Nonfiction   GRADES: 3–6.

Perl and Weihs, whose *Blue Monday and Friday the Thirteenth* was an excellent assembly of the facts and fictions surrounding the days of the week, have put similar care into this book. They begin at sunup and conclude at bedtime, listing almost everything that can go wrong or right, depending on certain foreshadowing actions. The writing is smooth, the tone humorous, and Weihs's graceful pictures show some of the quirkier aspects of superstition and self-induced fear. To be enjoyed with a grain of garlic salt and a brisk *Gesundheit*.

Schertle, Alice. *Bill and the Google-Eyed Goblins.* **Illus. by Patricia Coombs.** Lothrop, 1987. $11.75 (0-688-06701-8).
FORMAT: Picture book   GRADES: Preschool–Grade 3.

Schertle's Bill is an autonomous character with a cheerful disposition, who dances to his own tune and wins the respect and recognition of those who once tried to change him. Coombs's foreboding goblins and subterranean dance numbers evoke all the fun and fright of a Halloween night, with a pebbly, crayon effect in various intensities of light and shadow.

Scullard, Sue. *Miss Fanshawe and the Great Dragon Adventure.* **Illus. by the author.** St. Martin's, 1987. $9.95 (0-312-00510-5).
FORMAT: Picture book   GRADES: Kindergarten–Grade 4.

Miss Harriet Fanshawe is an intrepid explorer who goes on an odyssey to the center of the earth. Scullard successfully transfigures her grand vision of this journey into an illustrated book for children—readers will believe that they, too, were aboard.

Seuss, Dr. *How the Grinch Stole Christmas.* **Illus. by the author.** Random, 1957. LB $9.99 (0-394-90079-0).
FORMAT: Picture book   GRADES: Preschool–Grade 3.

The happy residents of Who-ville have always gotten under the Grinch's skin, but at Christmas he finds their cheer inexcusable. He does his best to thwart the holiday—and the ending is one children relish no matter how many times they've read this book. Many adults can't read this out loud without attempting to imitate Boris Karloff's notable inflections. Ah, well.

Small, David. *Paper John.* **Illus. by the author.** Farrar, 1987. $15.00 (0-374-35738-2). paper avail.
FORMAT: Picture book   GRADES: Preschool–Grade 3.

Paper John comes to the town at the edge of the sea, wearing a paper hat. He makes paper roses for ladies and paper boats for children, and consequently, builds a paper house to live in. But he also does battle with a poor thieving devil. Small's fabulously imagined story is inventive and likable. His pictures show angular homes hit by the unflincing light of seaside sun, long shadows, and a gawky, capable Paper John.

Willard, Nancy. *Pish, Posh, Said Hieronymous Bosch.* **Illus. by Leo Dillon and Diane Dillon.** Harcourt, 1991. $18.95 (0-15-262210-1).
FORMAT: Picture book   GRADES: Preschool–Grade 5.

Ornately framed paintings make a gallery for the Dillons' fantastical depiction of Hieronymous Bosch's difficulties with his maid. Slyly witty, this is not (nor is it meant to be) a literal translation of a life, but perhaps a partial paean to the bizarre forms and figures for which the 15th-century Dutch painter was known. For small-fry sophisticates.

Willis, Val. *The Surprise in the Wardrobe.* **Illus. by John Shelley.** Farrar, 1991. $15.00 (0-374-37309-4).

FORMAT: Picture book   GRADES: Preschool–Grade 3.

An unusual show-and-tell idea: Bobby finds a witch in his wardrobe and takes her to school. She misbehaves in a beautifully witchlike fashion; all the highjinks are conveyed in Shelley's darkly funny classroom scenes. See this pair's *The Secret in the Matchbox* for another gothic treat.

Wood, Audrey. *Heckedy Peg.* **Illus. by Don Wood.** Harcourt, 1987. $14.95 (0-15-233678-8).

FORMAT: Picture book   GRADES: Preschool–Grade 3.

Although text and art in this picture book match as hand and glove, it is really the elaborate illustrations that carry it aloft to the dimension of classic fairy tale. How a mother of seven children, named Monday through Sunday, outwits the witch Heckedy Peg provides a playful, eerie matching game. There are wonderful contrasts in scenes of the happy cottage full of children and the shadowy, ghastly hideout of Heckedy Peg.

Zemach, Harve. *Duffy and the Devil.* **Illus. by Margot Zemach.** Farrar, 1973. $16.95 (0-374-31887-5). paper avail.

FORMAT: Picture book   GRADES: Preschool–Grade 3.

Hailed as an animated, lively version of the Rumpelstiltskin story, the Zemachs' book is but one of several lively collaborations—some retellings, some original, all delightful: *Awake and Dreaming, The Judge,* and *Mommy, Buy Me a China Doll,* among others. Also root out the solo efforts of Margot Zemach: the hilarious Yiddish folktale, *It Could Always Be Worse,* the ferociously funny *To Hilda for Helping,* and many more.

Zirkel, Lynn. *Amazing Maisy's Family Tree.* **Illus. by Peter Bowman.** Oxford Univ. Pr., 1987. $9.95 (0-19-279830-8).

FORMAT: Picture book   GRADES: 1–3.

At a first glance this British import might look to American readers like the "Invasion of the Body Snatchers." But when they "look beside things and behind things" as the book suggests, things will appear less grim. Maisy's single seed in a worn-out pot grows to a plant that takes over the house and all its inhabitants. The glory of this vortex of procreation lies in Bowman's art, with its maze of tantalizing visual puns, puzzles, and paradoxes. Pages are progressively filled out from the simple to the manifold, in one splendid spread after another.

Additional Titles

The following titles, annotated elsewhere in this book (see index), could also fit the "Gothic Humor" category.

Bright, Robert. *Georgie*
dePaola, Tomie. *Bill and Pete Go Down the Nile*
Hamilton, Virginia. *The Dark Way*
Irving, Washington. *Rip Van Winkle*
Kitamura, Satoshi. *Lily Takes a Walk*
Pendergraft, Patricia. *Brushy Mountain*
Sendak, Maurice. *Where the Wild Things Are*

13: Crude Humor

Mockery, Cruelty, Vulgarity

Gross humor and its closely related extremes—scatology, cruelty, vulgarity, perversity, malevolence, invective, abjectness, obscenity, etc.— are human realities that touch children as well; witness their fondness for dead cat and Helen Keller jokes, and for toy trends such as the Garbage Pail Kids. Adults recognize gross humor as part of kids' worlds, but the generally good taste of writers, editors, publishers, and the buying public has already screened or weeded out most of the truly awful, hurtful excesses.

Beyond the gothic, beyond the healthy prodding of the oppressive authoritarian clutch, there is a brand of humor that can be radically destructive (Baudelaire called it "evil"). No teenager who has ever witnessed a peer demoralized by the teasing of others would disagree. Mockery, cruelty, and the most extreme cases of making sport of someone do yield laughs, but require delicate handling. Some authors have achieved this balance in children's eyes, but have lost support among adults. Surely laughing *at* people, as opposed to laughing *with* them, creates the bitterest moments in real life and is hard to replicate authentically without resorting to morals, cautionary tales, or despair-laden conclusions about the meaning of existence.

Allard, Harry. *The Stupids Die*. Illus. by James Marshall. Houghton, 1981. $13.95 (0-395-30347-8). paper avail.
FORMAT: Picture book   GRADES: Preschool–Grade 3.
This book follows up the now-classic *The Stupids Have a Ball* and *The Stupids Step Out*. These three books are so goofy and *stupid* that children can't help but laugh themselves silly, and remember this family forever.

Aylesworth, Jim. *Old Black Fly.* **Illus. by Stephen Gammell.** Holt, 1992. $15.95 (0-8050-1401-2).
FORMAT: Picture book   GRADES: Preschool–Grade 3.

A big bad fly wreaks alphabetical havoc on a household in lilting rhyme that brings readers to a resounding "Swat!" on the very last page. A solid refrain invites partial participation, but the whole sordid story, accompanied by Gammell's energetic vision of this watercolor pest, is easy to remember and chant.

Bishop, Claire Huchet. *The Five Chinese Brothers.* **Illus. by Kurt Wiese.** Putnam, 1938. $11.95 (0-698-20044-6). paper avail.
FORMAT: Storybook   GRADES: Preschool–Grade 3.

Children love this story of the five siblings with vastly different talents who triumph only because they work together. It's a spirited tale, and although the book is considered controversial, it can still be shared with an adult who will dispel any misunderstandings about stereotype.

Cole, Babette. *The Smelly Book.* Simon & Schuster, 1988. $10.95 (0-671-65670-8).
FORMAT: Picture book   GRADES: Preschool–Grade 5.

Following odoriferously on the heels of *The Slimy Book* and *The Hairy Book*, Cole's book bestows upon readers light poems about some of the more fragrant objects in life: "Smelly socks that go quite stiff . . . have the most disgusting whiff," and "Our dog likes to roll around/in smelly things left on the ground." A subject with an almost magnetic attraction for children, smelliness in Cole's book is downright tangy.

Cole, Brock. *The Goats.* Farrar, 1987. $15.00 (0-374-32678-9). paper avail.
FORMAT: Novel   GRADES: 7–up.

Two children are stripped of their clothes and marooned on an island by their fellow campers. They escape and learn, in addition to survival-on-the-run skills such as petty thievery and grand theft/auto, cooperation, intimacy, and loyalty. Quietly witty, this remarkable book yields new depths with each reading.

Cooney, Caroline B. *Among Friends.* Bantam, 1987. $13.95 (0-553-05446-5). paper avail.
FORMAT: Novel   GRADES: 6–up.

Count on Cooney for good, humorous stories set within the high school milieu. Count on her also to occasionally suprise, as she does in this darkly funny story of Jennie, a brilliant overachiever. Told in the diary entries of Jennie and five other juniors, the story peaks when Jennie walks out of a contest that would guarantee her a place in Connecticut history. While the various voices are not always distinct, they do advance the plot. Cruelty reigns at Cooney's high school, but only until students and adults come to their senses. Not a pretty sight, but it seems real.

Corbett, Scott. *Jokes to Tell Your Worst Enemy.* **Illus. by Annie Gusman.** Dutton, 1984. $10.95 (0-525-44082-8).
FORMAT: Storybook GRADES: 4–6.

Generous illustrations and jokes to groan over have made this a favorite with young readers; it is the work of a humorous novelist whose books include *Down with Wimps* and *The Trouble with Diamonds.*

Cresswell, Helen. *Ordinary Jack: Being the First Part of the Bagthorpe Saga.* Macmillan, 1977. $14.95 (0-02-725540-9). paper avail.
FORMAT: Novel GRADES: 7–up.

This book, with its ordinary title, launched a series of adventures starring the family Bagthorpe, an eccentric bunch of madcappers. Their actions are slapstick, the humor arch, the characters—well, they've been called obnoxious. But only in the best of spirits, because once readers latch on to this group, they'll have to read all the books, straight through. Look also to *Bagthorpes Unlimited, Bagthorpes Abroad, Absolute Zero,* and several other titles.

Dahl, Roald. *James and the Giant Peach.* **Illus. by Nancy Ekholm Burkert.** Knopf, 1961. LB $18.99 (0-394-91282-9). paper avail.
FORMAT: Storybook GRADES: 4–6.

Cruel Aunt Sponge and Aunt Spiker are the most hideous guardians an orphan could ever get. When magical events put a giant peach in his path, James goes inside and discovers a whole other world, inhabited by charming, erudite, oversized insects. Delectable fantasy, but the emotions are childlike and real. Also send readers to *Matilda,* and for older readers, *Boy.*

Dahl, Roald. *The Twits.* **Illus. by Quentin Blake.** Knopf, 1981. LB $12.99 (0-394-94599-9). paper avail.
FORMAT: Storybook GRADES: 4–6.

Mr. and Mrs. Twit, as villainous as they come, love catching birds with glue and incarcerating monkeys. They meet their match, their long overdue comeuppance, and face a disgusting demise when the Roly-Poly Bird intervenes. Hello, readers, and bye-bye Twits.

Estes, Eleanor. *The Hundred Dresses.* **Illus. by Louis Slobodkin.** Harcourt, 1944. $14.95 (0-15-237374-8). paper avail.
FORMAT: Storybook GRADES: 3–7.

No one believes that Wanda, a Polish girl in an American school, has 100 dresses at home, and they continue to treat her horribly for wearing the same faded blue dress day in and day out. Only when she moves away do they realize that she had never lied to them, and the poignancy of her truthfulness is almost unbearable. The humor gets nasty in the terrible teasing of the children and becomes wonderful in the spirited Wanda's imaginative wardrobe—drawings of beautifully dressed girls who look very much like her former classmates.

Gantos, Jack. *Rotten Ralph.* **Illus. by Nicole Rubel.** Houghton, 1976. $13.95 (0-395-24276-2). paper avail.

FORMAT: Picture book   GRADES: Preschool–Grade 3.

Sarah, a very nice girl who loves a very bad cat, can never quite fathom just how awful he truly is. He's really rude, and she's really forgiving. It's a rueful, but winning combination, and the two have gone on to appear in *Rotten Ralph's Rotten Christmas* and *Worse Than Rotten Ralph.*

I Know an Old Lady Who Swallowed a Fly. **Illus. by Glen Rounds.** Holiday, 1990. $14.95 (0-8234-0814-0). paper avail.

FORMAT: Picture book   GRADES: Preschool–Grade 1.

Right down to "I know an old lady who swallowed a horse" (who died, of course), Rounds makes this exaggerated tale of an explosive demise all his own. Readers will join in the refrain—and will face the eternal "Why?" that acccompanies this song.

Keller, Charles. *Waiter, There's a Fly in My Soup.* **Illus. by Lee Lorenz.** Prentice Hall, 1986. $10.95 (0-13-944182-4). paper avail.

FORMAT: Anthology   GRADES: 3–7.

Adults will wince at this collection of restaurant jokes. Children, who go wild at anything disgusting, may make this their bible.

Kennedy, Richard. *Richard Kennedy: Collected Stories.* **Illus. by Marcia Sewall.** HarperCollins, 1987. LB $14.89 (0-06-023256-0).

FORMAT: Short stories   GRADES: 3–6.

A collection in the best sense, running from the ribald to the righteous with plenty of kid-pleasing vulgarity in between, Kennedy's witty tales show such a mastery of form that children will be champing after these short bits and will head for *The Boxcar at the Center of the Universe* and *Amy's Eyes.*

Kennedy, X. J. *Ghastlies, Goops & Pincushions.* **Illus. by Ron Barrett.** Macmillan, 1989. $12.95 (0-689-50477-2).

FORMAT: Poetry   GRADES: 3–up.

These short and funny poems, by the author of *Brats* and *Fresh Brats,* explore subjects that are of endless fascination to young readers.

Kerr, M. E. *Dinky Hocker Shoots Smack!* HarperCollins, 1972. LB $12.89 (0-06-023151-3). paper avail.
FORMAT: Novel   GRADES: 7–up.

This is early Kerr, certain to reel readers into her other books. In order to get the attention of her parents—who are too concerned with problems of strangers to spend much time on her—overweight Dinky posts signs about her (completely false) drug use around town. A riot, but thoughtful as well.

Marcus, Leonard S., and Amy Schwartz, selectors. *Mother Goose's Little Misfortunes.* **Illus. by Amy Schwartz.** Macmillan, 1990. $15.95 (0-02-781431-9).
FORMAT: Picture book   GRADES: All grades.

Dr. Fell is here, as are other unfortunates whose lives are altered for the worse in 18 familiar Mother Goose rhymes. Schwartz's work, so loved in *OMA and Bobo* and *Annabelle Swift, Kindergartner* (among many others), loosens up here and delivers wonderfully free swoops of line, color, and shape.

Opie, Iona, and Peter Opie. *I Saw Esau: The School Child's Pocket Book.* **Illus. by Maurice Sendak.** Candlewick, 1992. $19.95 (1-56402-046-0).
FORMAT: Anthology   GRADES: Kindergarten–up.

In this new, revised edition of one of the Opies' early works, children's sayings, chants, taunts, riddles, rhymes, games, and more have been astutely assembled in one collection. Chronicled in these pages is the love of children for vulgar humor and their natural rebellion; complementing the words are illustrations by one who understands and reflects, in his comic strokes, the underground world of children's fascination for things gross, violent, and otherwise taboo to adults.

Park, Barbara. *Maxie, Rosie, and Earl: Partners in Grime.* **Illus. by Alexander Strogart.** Knopf, 1990. LB $13.99 (0-679-90212-0). paper avail.
FORMAT: Novel   GRADES: 4–6.

A well-known comic writer for the middle grades, Park brings her skewed perspective to the tale of a three-way friendship among the most eccentric of schoolmates. Maxie, Rosie, and Earl can't really live with each other, but they can't get along without each other, either. Brisk pacing, funny dialogue, and antic misadventures will keep readers smiling.

Pendergraft, Patricia. *Brushy Mountain.* Putnam, 1989. $14.95 (0-399-21610-3).
FORMAT: Novel   GRADES: 5–up.

The meanest man alive is surely Tice Hooker, an old man who lives among the folk of Brushy Mountain, and Arny sets out to kill him. But every time Arny goes off to murder Hooker, he ends up saving the old coot's life. It sounds morbid, but Pendergraft paints this earthy love-hate relationship with the scrappiest of brushes, delivering a townful of eccentrics and kindly folk who discover that they can do the most harm by being falsely helpful, and the most good by living by their deepest instincts and impulses. Dandy doings.

Pilling, Ann. *The Big Pink.* Viking, 1988. $11.95 (-0-670-81156-4).
FORMAT: Novel   GRADES: 3–7.

Angela thinks she has several strikes against her when she enters an exclusive girls' school: her aunt is the owner and headmistress, she doesn't have to pay tuition, she is self-conscious about her religious upbringing, she has a North Country accent, and she is quite overweight. The girls find her an easy target for their amusement and mean jokes. Through her determination not to let them best her, she gains self-esteem and ends her first term heavier but far happier. Pilling's book dares to break the mold of certain social predispositions; Angela proves that she is no fat doormat for anyone's dumping. A gossipy, chatty feeling of boarding school pervades this thoughtful drama, with some well-chosen surprises.

Provensen, Alice. *Punch in New York.* Illus. by the author. Viking, 1991. $14.95 (0-670-82790-8).
FORMAT: Picture book   GRADES: Preschool–Grade 3.

Punch has left Judy behind, it appears, and faces down some of the most villainous types ever to haunt the streets of New York City. Of course, Punch is no angel, either, so one way or the other, the bad guys win. But why not? It's all in good fun, lightened up considerably by the vibrant pictures by well-known, well-respected Provensen.

Robinette, René. *The Robin Family.* Illus. by the author. Houghton, 1989. $10.95 (0-395-49214-9).
FORMAT: Picture book   GRADES: Preschool–Grade 3.

The Robin family is nuts. Mrs. Robin's tongue sticks out and she can't get it back in her mouth until she lubricates it with jelly. Mr. Robin "had a runny nose on both sides," but successfully blocks the flow with a bandage. Daughter Chelsea hangs upside down on the couch to take care of her messy hair. It takes a certain sense of humor to go along with the antics in this book; one should be easily amused by nonsense, willing to follow absurd lines of logic, and capable of dropping, in a second, any storyline that is in danger of becoming cumbersome. One should also be prepared for the cartooniest of illustrations to come down the pike in a long while. Most children will qualify, gladly, and demand another dose of this wacky bunch.

Robinson, Barbara. *The Best Christmas Pageant Ever.* **Illus. by Judith Gwyn Brown.** HarperCollins, 1972. LB $13.89 (0-06-025044-5). paper avail.
FORMAT: Novel   GRADES: 3–6.

The Herdman children are part of the most hated family in town, and they're taking over the annual holiday pageant. With pell-mell pacing and guffaw-producing dialogue, this is sure to be a perennial favorite with readers.

Rockwell, Thomas. *How to Eat Fried Worms.* **Illus. by Emily Arnold McCully.** Franklin Watts, 1973. LB $13.90 (0-531-02631-0). paper avail.
FORMAT: Novel   GRADES: 4–6.

Billy Forester takes a dare, and fulfills it beautifully. There is no last-minute reprieve, no phone call from the governor's office—he really does eat worms. Even children who have never read a novel will dare to read this one. Gross and engrossing.

Schwartz, Alvin. *And the Green Grass Grew All Around.* **Illus. by Sue Truesdell.** HarperCollins, 1992. LB $14.89 (0-06-022758-3).
FORMAT: Anthology   GRADES: 3–up.

Saucy, rude, funny, scary, and somewhat naughty songs and playground rhymes have miraculously found their way to one child-minded compendium, possibly the *Steal This Book* of the under-12 set. There are tidbits straight from the folklore and culture of children; that they delight is an all but foregone conclusion.

Schwartz, Mary Ada. *Spiffen: A Tale of a Tidy Pig.* **Illus. by Lynn Munsinger.** Whitman, 1988. LB $13.95 (0-8075-7580-1).
FORMAT: Picture book   GRADES: Preschool–Grade 3.

Imagine being a fastidious pig in a town called Slobbyville, where King Hog's visit means preparations that include the scattering of trash and the dumping of pungent garbage. Spiffen is a pig who sweeps and cleans and tidies to the beat of a different drummer. The illustrations give this silly tale extra zip. And Spiffen is no goof, he is just being true to himself.

Silverstein, Shel. *Where the Sidewalk Ends: Poems and Drawings.* **Illus. by the author.** HarperCollins, 1974. LB $14.89 (0-06-025668-0). paper avail.
FORMAT: Poetry   GRADES: 3–up.

This zany collection of masterfully comic poems is the forerunner to *A Light in the Attic*. Adults enjoy reading both books out loud, because they provide a childlike, child-size scrutiny of the world that leads to side-splitting revelations. The drawings back up the humor. Enough said.

Steig, William. *Shrek!* **Illus. by the author.** Farrar, 1990. $10.95 (0-374-36877-5).
FORMAT: Picture book   GRADES: Preschool–Grade 4.

The quest tale is turned asunder when Shrek, a hideous monster, must leave the home of his ugly parents in search of his ideal bride. He finds his vision of repulsiveness, and they live "horribly ever after." The running gag is one to which children will respond immediately, but there are also depths to be plumbed on repeat readings.

Van Allsburg, Chris. *Two Bad Ants.* **Illus. by the author.** Houghton, 1988. $16.95 (0-395-48668-8).
FORMAT: Picture book   GRADES: Preschool–Grade 5.

Even older readers will relish, with the odd sense of humor children exhibit, what happens to these two rebels; this is no homage to Beatrix Potter's *The Tale of Two Bad Mice.* The ants get boiled in coffee, toasted by a familiar household appliance, and even shocked by an electric outlet. Were the sugar crystals worth it? Readers will have to decide for themselves.

Van Allsburg, Chris. *The Z Was Zapped.* **Illus. by the author.** Houghton, 1987. $16.95 (0-395-44612-0).
FORMAT: Picture book   GRADES: All grades.

The Caslon Players perform this theatrical piece about an alphabet, which in Gorey-esque style is done in, letter by letter. "K" is kidnapped, "N" is nailed, "F" is flattened. Readers are not meant to sympathize with these letters—obviously they deserve such treatment or this book would not be so hysterically funny to the children who have encountered it thus far.

Wood, Audrey. *The Horrible Holidays.* **Illus. by Rosekrans Hoffman.** Dial, 1988. LB $9.89 (0-8037-0546-8). paper avail.
FORMAT: Chapter book   GRADES: Preschool–Grade 3.

The focus is cousins. Poor Alf has to put up with loud-mouth, perfect, snotty Mert, who arrives like clockwork with the holidays: Thanksgiving, Christmas, and New Year's. These two are funny rivals; their tricks and their insults are pitch-perfect. Hoffman's idiosyncratic relatives, with their oddly expressive faces and postures, carry out Wood's nasty piece of plotting with aplomb.

Additional Titles

The following titles, annotated elsewhere in this book (see index), could also fit the "Crude Humor" category.

Browne, Anthony. *Piggybook*
Carter, Alden. *Wart, Son of Toad*
Field, Eugene. *The Gingham Dog and the Calico Cat*
Graves, Robert. *The Big Green Book*
Grimm, Jacob, and Wilhelm Grimm. *Hansel and Gretel*
Grossman, Bill. *Tommy at the Grocery Store*
Hall, Katy, and Lisa Eisenberg. *Buggy Riddles*
Ivimey, John W. *Three Blind Mice*
Kerr, M. E. *Little Little*
Klein, Robin. *Tearaways*
Miller, Edward. *The Curse of Claudia*
O'Connor, Jane. *Lulu Goes to Witch School*
Viorst, Judith. *Alexander and the Terrible, Horrible, No Good, Very Bad Day*

14: Saturnalia

A Madcap World

*T*he comparative familiarity and stability children and teenagers seek in their lives results in high comedy when violation of expectation reaches the apex of the carnivalesque. Differences are exaggerated and overstated in caricatures, in mistaken identity within comedies of errors, in role reversals (such as the mother and daughter who find themselves inside each other's bodies in Rodgers's *Freaky Friday*), gender switches, distortions, deformities, revelry, masks, excesses, and disparities not only of size but also between appearance and reality.

Carnivalesque humor means a holiday from order, a journey to the pandemonium of a topsy-turvy circus world. Servants become queens, kings become laborers, children show up in their parents' clothing (as in Schwartz's *Bea and Mr. Jones*), and a man becomes a quadruped (in Brittain's *Devil's Donkey*).

The notion of size, cherished by those who watched Paul Bunyan make lakes wherever he stepped, becomes unreliable and relative (Gulliver finds himself first a giant among Lilliputians, and then a man-in-miniature himself, woefully among giants). Uncertainty, chance, weirdness, contradiction, and coincidence seize the reins from coherence and invariant order. Anything goes, and chaos rules. If there is a lesson, beyond simple entertainment (of one grand shaggy dog story that goes nowhere), it may be that from an abiding fondness for this kind of humor can come a sort of tolerance. A marginal upending of the status quo can be invigorating and revitalizing.

Ahlberg, Janet, and Allan Ahlberg. *The Cinderella Show.* **Illus. by the authors.** Viking, 1987. paper $4.95 (0-670-81037-1).
FORMAT: Picture book   GRADES: Preschool–Grade 3.

The Town End Primary School presents a play based on Cinderella, and readers are invited to watch the onstage, backstage, and audience in action. The funniest scenes are of the stepsisters bossing poor Cindy around, but the entire comic strip-like production, in black-and-white miniature drawings, is as informative as it is fun.

Andersen, Hans Christian. *The Princess and the Pea.* **Illus. by Eve Tharlet.** Picture Book, 1987. $13.95 (0-88708-052-9).
FORMAT: Picture book   GRADES: Preschool–Grade 3.

Long before there were lie detectors, there was the great pea test—the real princess's genteel character is not numbed by 20 mattresses and 20 eiderdown quilts. Tharlet's narrative scenes are portrayed from a high-ground perspective. Readers look down at castles, their majestic interiors, and the people that inhabit them, from a vantage point that reveals the artist's acute awareness of size and dimension as language for humor. All royal folk look alike, with their stiff upper lips, twisted noses, and surprised looks.

Anno, Mitsumasa. *Topsy-Turvies: More Pictures to Stretch the Imagination.* **Illus. by the author.** Putnam, 1989. $13.95 (0-399-21557-3).
FORMAT: Picture book   GRADES: All grades.

This is another product of Anno's poetic imagination to challenge the preconceived notions of the possibilities of space. A children's playground is the ideal place to explore new horizons and to skim over such hurdles as boundaries, dead-ends, and infinite regressions. Children will welcome wholeheartedly Anno's elfin, dancing-on-the-ceiling troops, and will do well to treasure this book as an endless source of entertainment.

Atwater, Richard, and Florence Atwater. *Mr. Popper's Penguins.* **Illus. by Robert Lawson.** Little, Brown, 1938. $14.95 (0-316-05842-4). paper avail.
FORMAT: Novel   GRADES: 3–6.

This perennial favorite needs no introduction; it has been roundly acclaimed for more than half a century and the title very nearly tells readers all they need to know before they simply begin to enjoy those penguins. A humorous classic, installed in its own hall of fame.

Beisner, Monica. *Topsy Turvy: The World of Upside Down.* **Illus. by the author.** Farrar, 1988. $15.00 (0-374-37679-4).
FORMAT: Picture book   GRADES: All grades.

A revealing work that asks children, as do the books of Mitsumasa Anno, to consider the world from other perspectives. This collection of verses about incongruities features beautifully textured, witty illustrations and a narrative guaranteed to entrance.

Birdseye, Tom. *Air Mail to the Moon.* **Illus. by Stephen Gammell.** Holiday, 1988. $14.95 (0-8234-0683-0). paper avail.
FORMAT: Picture book   GRADES: Preschool–Grade 3.

Ora Mae Cotton narrates the story of losing her first tooth in tangy, colorful language, full of phrases that readers will find themselves repeating. When it looks as if someone has stolen her tooth, Ora Mae vows to "open up a can of gotcha" and send the tooth-thief "air mail to the moon." The ending is weak, but Ora Mae, in Gammell's picture, is a messy, rowdy heroine in overalls and a baseball cap. The exaggeration in the illustrations, like that in the text, either mocks or pays homage to a downhome, earthy lifestyle.

Bradman, Tony. *Not Like This, Like That.* **Illus. by Joanna Burroughes.** Oxford Univ. Pr., 1988. $13.95 (0-19-520712-2).
FORMAT: Picture book   GRADES: Preschool–Grade 1.

This funny book should please all those who, with the best intentions in the world, have suddenly found themselves in foolish-looking positions. Dad cautions Thomas not to put his head through the wrought iron railings that line the park. He demonstrates. He's stuck. What follows is a counting book collection of helpful passersby, up to ten firemen. The turnaround of having the adult—not the child—in trouble will appeal to readers who need to know that everyone makes mistakes.

Brett, Jan. *The Mitten.* **Illus. by the author.** Putnam, 1989. $14.95 (0-399-21920-X).
FORMAT: Picture book   GRADES: Preschool–Grade 3.

This is a very funny version of a Ukrainian folktale about a boy's lost mitten. That small knitted object takes on gigantic proportions as more animals crowd into its warm comfort—and the ending always brings laughter. Brett, best known for the minute ornamental detail she crowds into every corner of every page, has other delightful books to her credit, including *The Twelve Days of Christmas* and *Goldilocks and the Three Bears.*

Brittain, Bill. *All the Money in the World.* **Illus. by Charles Robinson.** HarperCollins, 1979. LB $14.89 (O-06-020676-4). paper avail.
FORMAT: Novel   GRADES: 4–6.

It's every child's wish to have all that dough but Brittain's young hero not only feels his wish has been fulfilled, but overkilled, when literally *all* the money in the world is at his disposal. An exaggerated stomp through fantasyland, to be sure, but brightly funny.

Burgess, Gelett. *The Little Father.* **Illus. by Richard Egielski.** Farrar, 1985. $14.00 (0-374-34596-1). paper avail.
FORMAT: Picture book   GRADES: Preschool–Grade 3.

First published in 1899, Burgess's charmer about a father who is diminishing because of imbibing India ink has been solidly illustrated by the award-winning Egielski. A nonsense poem of the most enduring kind, set against a turn-of-the-century backdrop, full of inventive touches that have a reined-in power all their own.

Butterworth, Oliver. *The Enormous Egg.* **Illus. by Louis Darling.** Little, Brown, 1956. $14.95 (0-316-11904-0). paper avail.
FORMAT: Novel   GRADES: 4–6.

Butterworth's story was a groundbreaker when it first came out; even though dinosaur tales are now old hat, this remains one of the most comic. Good for story hours; also good for newly independent readers to attempt and succeed with.

Caple, Kathy. *Harry's Smile.* **Illus. by the author.** Houghton, 1987. $12.95 (0-395-43417-3). paper avail.
FORMAT: Picture book   GRADES: Preschool–Grade 3.

Fans of *The Biggest Nose* and *The Purse* admire the slightly goofy but lovable expressions of Caple's characters. Funny watercolor scenes of Harry and his good friend Sam will not disappoint readers, although a weak plot about Harry being too embarrassed to send a pen pal a photo of himself certainly takes some of the shine off. Still, a tidy lesson of friendship is well served by good intentions.

Casey, Patricia. *Quack Quack.* **Illus. by the author.** Lothrop, 1988. $12.95 (0-688-07765-X).
FORMAT: Picture book   GRADES: Preschool–Grade 1.

There are eggs in the farm shed, but are they Hen's eggs or Duck's? By dinner time, they are hatched, but while Hen "clucks" and Duck "quacks" their chicks all "cheep." A charming, minimal approach to a well-known, little-stated case: the younger generation speaks a common language, despite the differences. The view is chick-high—Casey's illustrations will draw readers right into the conflict and the happy hatching.

Cole, Babette. *King Change-a-Lot.* **Illus. by the author.** Putnam, 1989. $13.95 (0-399-21670-7).
FORMAT: Picture book   GRADES: Preschool–Grade 3.

A royal baby has some pretty big ideas about how to run his kingdom, which his parents have allowed to go out of control. It all begins when still-Prince Change-a-Lot rubs his potty and unleashes a baby genie. A witty spoof of any fairy tale or fantasy children have ever read.

Cole, Brock. *The Giant's Toe.* **Illus. by the author.** Farrar, 1986. $15.00 (0-374-32559-6). paper avail.
FORMAT: Picture book   GRADES: Preschool–Grade 3.

This upended version of "Jack the Giant Killer" features eccentric watercolors and even more eccentric perspectives.

Cole, Joanna, and Philip Cole. *Big Goof and Little Goof.* **Illus. by M. K. Brown.** Scholastic, 1989. $12.95 (0-590-41591-3). paper avail.
FORMAT: Picture book   GRADES: Preschool–Grade 3.

In three short stories, the Coles reveal the sweet, goofy existences of two guys, who may be brothers, daffy uncle and nephew, father and son—it doesn't matter. In one segment, when they mix up their clothes, Big Goof thinks he's getting woefully bigger, and Little Goof, drowning in Big Goof's clothes, thinks he is getting smaller. Brown's pictures are almost as silly as those she did for her own book, *Let's Go Swimming with Mr. Sillypants,* and the Coles' heroes are two nerdy originals.

Conover, Chris. *The Adventures of Simple Simon.* **Illus. by the author.** Farrar, 1987. $13.95 (0-374-36921-6). paper avail.
FORMAT: Picture book   GRADES: Preschool–Grade 2.

Conover embellishes the story of Simple Simon, who met a pieman going to the fair, with a festival of distractions. It is almost impossible to follow the rhyming story from beginning to end, as a caravan of animals—storybook characters—descends on the fair by foot, camel, and ship. Many small subplots are hatched, and readers can spend time happily flipping back and forth to see what's happening to whom.

Corbalis, Judy. *Porcellus, the Flying Pig.* **Illus. by Helen Craig.** Dial, 1988. $12.95 (0-8037-0486-0).
FORMAT: Storybook   GRADES: 1–5.

Among his litter, Porcellus alone has two ugly bumps on his shoulder pads. He sees how disappointed his father is with him, until the bumps become wings and Porcellus becomes a superhero. This has some initially disquieting signals, like Porcellus's father rejecting him for being different. However, Corbalis's porcine wordplay and Craig's spirited illustrations instill humor and goodwill throughout these pages, and readers will be left, ultimately, with a happy ending.

Cutler, Ivor. *Herbert: Five Stories.* **Illus. by Patrick Benson.** Lothrop, 1988. $13.00 (0-688-08147-9).
FORMAT: Storybook   GRADES: Preschool–Grade 2.

A friendly format might prevent readers from guessing that this story is chapter-book length. Each funny tale about Herbert Clockfoote, a boy in the habit of waking up every morning as a different animal, builds on the last one. The tales gallop along at a brisk pace, giving readers the impression that Herbert is not at all odd. In comic pictures, Benson's bespectacled Herbert is matter-of-fact, but even more cool is his mother, who goes to the library to look up the food type that Herbert—in animal form—will need for dinner.

Dahl, Roald. *Charlie and the Chocolate Factory.* **Illus. by Joseph Schindelman.** Knopf, 1964. LB $15.99 (0-394-91011-7). paper avail.
FORMAT: Novel   GRADES: 4–up.

The subject is irresistible—what happens when five children have the chance to tour an extraordinary industrial site owned by a master confectioner? Most of them meet horrible ends, to the delight of generations of readers, except for good-hearted Charlie Bucket, who triumphs over all. Don't let children get away on the excuse that they've seen the movie. Part cautionary tale, part fantasy, all grand.

Delessert, Etienne. *Ashes, Ashes.* **Illus. by the author.** Stewart, Tabori & Chang, 1990. $14.95 (1-55670-137-3).
FORMAT: Picture book   GRADES: 1–up.

Another magical tour of discovery, starring an odd-looking fellow who takes on the look of a rabbit, and so disguised, sets out.

Eastman, P. D. *Are You My Mother?* **Illus. by the author.** Random, 1960. LB $7.99 (0-394-90018-9).
FORMAT: Storybook   GRADES: 2–4.

For this baby bird philosopher, this is no Tolkeinian quest. But perhaps far more importantly after he falls from his nest, he queries each creature he meets with the question of the title. Use this as a fictional lead-in to a factual discussion of imprinting, and young readers will appreciate the humor even more. Later, give them *Go, Dog, Go!* by the same author.

Elish, Dan. *The Worldwide Dessert Contest.* **Illus. by John Steven Gurney.**
Orchard, 1988. $13.95 (0-531-05752-6). paper avail.
FORMAT: Novel   GRADES: 4–6.

A little bit of *Charlie and the Chocolate Factory,* a dash of *Homer Price,* this book cashes in on the longstanding rapport between children and sweets. John Apple longs to win The Worldwide Dessert Contest, but all his delicious desserts have a penchant for changing into something else at the last minute. Elish writes with a sure hand of this sugary world, his tongue squarely in the area of his sweet tooth. For his ability to praise desserts in an endlessly original fashion, he deserves a blue ribbon.

Grossman, Bill. *Tommy at the Grocery Store.* **Illus. by Victoria Chess.**
HarperCollins, 1989. LB $12.89 (0-06-022409-6). paper avail.
FORMAT: Picture book   GRADES: Preschool–Grade 2.

A small ingenuous pig is repeatedly mistaken for somthing he is not when his mother leaves him at the store. This from the grocer: "He thought that Tommy was salami/And set him on the deli shelf./And Tommy sat among salamis,/Softly sobbing to himself." A frantic do-si-do of mistaken identity includes several punnish incidents while Tommy is nearly "prepared" for dinner; it would be cruel were it not so deliciously funny and yes—to reassure youngsters—entirely absurd.

Heide, Florence Parry. *The Shrinking of Treehorn.* **Illus. by Edward Gorey.**
Holiday, 1971. $12.95 (0-8234-0189-8). paper avail.
FORMAT: Storybook   GRADES: 3–6.

Any child who has ever felt overlooked will identify with Treehorn. He is shrinking, literally, yet no one is taking notice of his ever-diminishing form. Droll illustrations—wouldn't you know it?—round out this wry tale.

Himmelman, John. *Amanda and the Magic Garden.* **Illus. by the author.**
Viking, 1987. $10.95 (0-670-80823-7).
FORMAT: Picture book   GRADES: Preschool–Grade 3.

Amanda of *Amanda and the Witch Switch* is back with more spells that spell trouble, especially when she accepts some magic vegetable seeds from a prankish troll. Those carrots come up six feet tall, and have an adverse effect on the surrounding animal population. Reliably funny Himmelman has a child's insight into the realm of the possible: if one eats large things, one grows large; if one eats small things, one gets smaller. Using playful illustrations, Himmelman and his witch have a wonderful sense of justice.

Jenkin-Pearce, Susie. *Bad Boris and the New Kitten.* **Illus. by the author.**
Macmillan, 1987. $10.95 (0-02-747620-0).
FORMAT: Picture book   GRADES: Kindergarten–Grade 3.

Boris, a smallish elephant, is jealous of the kitten that wanders through
his owner Maisie's door and quickly becomes the center of Maisie's
affections. To win back favor, Boris imitates the kitten—which does
dainty things like running along the piano keys and curling up in
Maisie's lap. His size creates disasters, but sprightly watercolors show
naught but good-natured chaos. Maisie, the befuddled parent who
doesn't realize that her family needs reassuring, is a lively old dear.

Jeschke, Susan. *Perfect the Pig.* **Illus. by the author.** Holt, 1981. $14.95 (0-
8050-0704-0). paper avail.
FORMAT: Storybook   GRADES: 1–3.

Pigs *might* fly in this Reading Rainbow feature selection. A sunny tale of
a flying pig and his humble mistress, who, after several misadventures
and chances for ill-got fame, retire quietly to the country. Cherishable.

Joyce, William. *Bently & Egg.* **Illus. by the author.** HarperCollins, 1992. LB
$14.89 (0-06-020386-2).
FORMAT: Picture book   GRADES: Preschool–Grade 3.

A musical frog with artistic skills to boot is put in charge of his dear
friend Kack Kack's egg. But if Bently is ambivalent about the egg—who
has displaced him, he thinks, in Kack Kack's affections—he grows to
love it in the course of a zany chase where its very survival is at stake.
Easter egg pastels make Joyce's book a distinct departure from his other
solo efforts, and make this tale of the hatching of the heart as whimsical
and generous as they come.

Joyce, William. *A Day with Wilbur Robinson.* **Illus. by the author.**
HarperCollins, 1990. LB $14.89 (0-06-022968-3).
FORMAT: Picture book   GRADES: Preschool–Grade 3.

This wacked-out family story is the product of a fertile, but eccentric,
imagination. Joyce's narrator encounters an antigravity machine, dancing frogs, concern over a missing set of false teeth, etc. By the end of the
day, the only question left for readers will be, "When can we come
back?" The answer is anytime—the door to the hospitable Robinsons'
home is always open. An insane world, made zany and welcoming.

Joyce, William. *George Shrinks.* **Illus. by the author.** HarperCollins, 1985. LB
$13.89 (0-06-023071-1). paper avail.
FORMAT: Picture book   GRADES: Preschool–Grade 3.

A deadpan text underscores the events following George's discovery
that he has shrunk. There is an entire list of chores for him to complete

before his mother gets home, and with childlike derring-do (and some Errol Flynn-style bravery), George proves himself up to the tasks.

Kasza, Keiko. *The Wolf's Chicken Stew.* **Illus. by the author.** Putnam, 1987. $13.95 (0-399-21400-3). paper avail.
FORMAT: Picture book   GRADES: Preschool–Grade 3.

Kasza pens a gracefully funny story of situations reversed: the wolf feeds Mrs. Chicken and her family, hoping to fatten her up for some nice meaty stew but instead becomes the family's benefactor and friend. Chortles guaranteed; equally whimsical is Kasza's *The Pig's Picnic*.

Lear, Edward. *The Quangle Wangle's Hat.* **Illus. by Janet Stevens.** Harcourt, 1988. $12.95 (0-15-264450-4).
FORMAT: Picture book   GRADES: Preschool–Grade 3.

The Quangle Wangle may be mysterious, but its hat is a stage set of ribbons and the perfect nest not only for Mr. and Mrs. Canary but also the eccentric characters that follow them there. Blissful nonsense, skillfully depicted.

Lobel, Arnold. *The Turnaround Wind.* **Illus. by the author.** HarperCollins, 1988. LB $12.89 (0-06-023988-3).
FORMAT: Picture book   GRADES: Preschool–Grade 3.

In a game of hidden faces, each stroller in a countryside scene is transformed by the wind; readers turn the book upside down to see that the strokes that created the hunter now comprise his prey, the fox. Children, ready fans of optical illusions of any sort, will find this well-executed gimmick first rate.

Lopshire, Robert. *Put Me in the Zoo.* **Illus. by the author.** Random, 1960. LB $7.99 (0-394-90017-0).
FORMAT: Storybook   GRADES: 2–4.

Everyone wants to be special, and Spot is no exception. This is one leopard who *can* change his spots—and juggle them, too—all in an effort to convince two young listeners that he is cut out for the big time, the zoo. Simple humor, from a simpler time, with clean clear lines.

McCully, Emily Arnold. *The Show Must Go On.* **Illus. by the author.** Western, 1987. paper $2.95 (0-307-11970-X).
FORMAT: Picture book   GRADES: Preschool–Grade 2.

McCully's bear family are traveling actors; Bruno and Sophie met on stage, and their children Edwin, Sarah, and Zaza were born to it—they sleep in steamer trunks and stage props. This surely is the "Seven Little Foys" of the picture-book set. McCully shows her family doing vaudeville, Shakespeare, and juggling acts. Ebullient fun.

Mathers, Petra. *Theodor and Mr. Balbini.* **Illus. by the author.** Harper-Collins, 1988. LB $11.89 (0-06-024144-6).
FORMAT: Picture book   GRADES: Preschool–Grade 3.

When Mr. Balbini's dog Theodor begins to speak, one of his first requests is for French lessons. In fact, now Theodor finds that his master is not really refined enough for his tastes and seeks out a new home. Companionship gone awry? Not really, in the hands of Mathers, whose quirky illustrations add humor to the deliberately dry telling.

Nesbit, E. *The Cockatoucan.* **Illus. by Elroy Hughes.** Dial, 1988. $10.95 (0-8037-0474-7).
FORMAT: Picture book   GRADES: 1–4.

Matilda ends up in an eccentric kingdom ruled by a cockatoucan; its laugh is terrible and transforming. The pictures make this brilliant work of Nesbit's somewhat stiff and formal; still, some children will find this a good introduction to the endlessly entertaining author.

Nordqvist, Sven. *Porker Finds a Chair.* Carolrhoda, 1989. $9.95 (0-87614-367-2).
FORMAT: Picture book   GRADES: Preschool–Grade 3.

A bearlike creature named Porker comes across a strange object; readers will recognize it right away as a tipped-over chair, and will delight in Porker's blithe ignorance. Passersby are no help in enlightening him, but little by little, Porker discovers the mysterious process of sitting on a chair. A hoot from beginning to end, with a philosophical edge cutting through the plot: that what some people take for granted as truth, others do not know at all—and isn't blind faith a blessing? Appearances *aren't* everything in this book, where birds fly upside down and houses rest on their sides.

Norton, Mary. *The Borrowers.* **Illus. by Beth Krush and Joe Krush.** Harcourt, 1953. $13.95 (0-15-209987-5). paper avail.
FORMAT: Novel   GRADES: 4–6.

Father Pod, Mother Homily, and daughter Arrietty star in this first tale of the famous miniaturized family. Their adventures begin under the kitchen floor of an old house, but in the other Borrower stories, readers can find them perfectly at home in a boot, a teakettle, and a rectory. Wholehearted fun, inventive fantasy, zanily realized.

Nunes, Susan. *Tiddalick the Frog.* **Illus. by Ju-Hong Chen.** Macmillan, 1989. $13.95 (0-689-31502-3).
FORMAT: Picture book   GRADES: Kindergarten–Grade 3.

In this ebullient tale from the Australian Aborigines' dreamtime, Tiddalick wakes up with great thirst and in a few slurps takes in all the water on the earth. Despite the pleas and antics of the other animals to try to get Tiddalick to open his mouth, the engorged hopper is unmoved. Only when an eel ties himself up in the knots of a frenetic dance does Tiddalick give a great, wet guffaw. That mad jig will itch any child's funny bone.

Osborne, Mary Pope. *American Tall Tales.* **Illus. by Michael McCurdy.**
Knopf, 1991. LB $18.99 (0-679-90089-6).
FORMAT: Storybook   GRADES: 1–up.

A devoted storyteller and handsome woodcut illustrations serve these nine tales well, rendering characters from Paul Bunyan to Davy Crocket as bold as britches.

Paxton, Tom. *Engelbert the Elephant.* **Illus. by Steven Kellogg.** Morrow,
1991. LB $14.88 (0-688-08936-4).
FORMAT: Picture book   GRADES: Preschool–Grade 3.

When an elephant is accidentally invited to a royal ball, the results are gleeful fun. Kellogg's pictures make the most of the contrast between Engelbert's size and that of the other guests.

Pryor, Bonnie. *Mr. Munday and the Space Creatures.* **Illus. by Lee Lorenz.**
Simon & Schuster, 1989. $13.95 (0-671-67114-6).
FORMAT: Picture book   GRADES: Preschool–Grade 3.

Last seen in *Mr. Munday and the Rustlers,* the fumbling mailman is back, ready to take on life on another planet—at least temporarily. All the action is brought zanily to life by the funniest of cartoonists, Lee Lorenz. Look for his own book, *A Sunday in the Country,* for some fast and frenzied watercolors

Rodgers, Mary. *Freaky Friday.* HarperCollins, 1972. LB $13.89 (0-06-025049-6).
paper avail.
FORMAT: Novel   GRADES: 5–8.

Mrs. Andrews and her daughter get up one morning to find that they are each occupying the other's body. Weird, well explained and fluid, the story of their day unfolds in a nearly logical fashion.

Rodgers, Mary. *Summer Switch.* HarperCollins, 1982. LB $12.89 (0-06-025059-3).
paper avail.
FORMAT: Novel   GRADES: 5–8.

Ten years after the publication of *Freaky Friday,* readers are treated to another visit with the Andrews family. This time Ben and his father trade bodies, just as one is headed off to summer camp and the other to a crucial business meeting in Hollywood. The plot may be familiar, but the resulting antics are as novel as those found in the first book. Thoroughly riveting.

Rylant, Cynthia. *The Relatives Came.* **Illus. by Stephen Gammell.** Bradbury, 1985. $14.95 (0-02-777220-9).
FORMAT: Picture book   GRADES: Preschool–Grade 3.

The text is humorous, as relatives descend on a small house and fill it to maximum capacity. Gammell's illustrations were rewarded with a Caldecott Honor citation, for their homespun good fun and increasingly merry rendering of a loving family gone nearly out of control, if not off the page. Vibrant.

Sachar, Louis. *There's a Boy in the Girls' Bathroom.* Knopf, 1987. LB $13.99 (0-394-98570-2). paper avail.
FORMAT: Novel   GRADES: 4–6.

With the catchy title, this one can't fail; it tells the story of a bully, from the bully's perspective. Bradley is a liar, and understandably has no friends, but at least two people have not yet written him off. With wit, and often painful insight, Sachar presents the tale of a boy who must learn to appreciate himself before asking others to like him. This, Sachar's first book, made a splash with kids all over the country. He must have hit a nerve.

Sandburg, Carl. *Rootabaga Stories: Parts One & Two.* **Illus. by Michael Hague.** Harcourt, 1988, 1989. $19.95 each (0-15-269061-1; 0-15-269062-X). paper avail.
FORMAT: Short stories   GRADES: 4–6.

These volumes of nonsense stories are based on the poet's 1922 remembrances of the Midwest. Readers will meet the Huckabuck Family, Jason Squiff, and others, caricatures and characters all, in lyrical language that makes for some unforgettable reading.

Sanfield, Steve. *A Natural Man: The True Story of John Henry.* **Illus. by Peter J. Thornton.** Godine, 1990. paper $9.95 (0-87923-844-5).
FORMAT: Storybook   GRADES: 2–7.

The ballad of John Henry is as much a part of American folklore as Paul Bunyan and Pecos Bill. The battle of man versus machine—for which the victorious John Henry gives his life—is one most schoolchildren know. Sanfield tells the legend anew, incorporating familiar tidbits with splendid poetic images. Thornton's diffused black-and-white pictures capture the spirit of the tale—moody and ominous in places, full of humor in others. A triumphant book about a genuine hero.

Schwartz, Amy. *Bea and Mr. Jones.* **Illus. by the author.** Macmillan, 1982. $12.95 (0-02-781430-0).

FORMAT: Picture book   GRADES: Preschool–Grade 3.

Bea goes to the office; her father takes her place at school. This satire is carried out in beautifully amusing, polished illustrations and in a wise, understated text.

Sendak, Maurice. *In the Night Kitchen.* **Illus. by the author.** HarperCollins, 1970. LB $14.89 (0-06-025490-4). paper avail.

FORMAT: Picture book   GRADES: Preschool–Grade 3.

When Mickey falls out of his clothes and into the night, he enters a world of chubby-cheeked bakers and a deceptive cityscape of household objects. Children endorse it; parents don't mind reading it aloud again, and again, and again.

Sendak, Maurice. *Where the Wild Things Are.* **Illus. by the author.** HarperCollins, 1963. LB $14.89 (0-06-025493-9). paper avail.

FORMAT: Picture book   GRADES: Preschool–Grade 3.

When his mother declares him a "Wild Thing," Max sails away without his supper to the land of all Wild Things, where he is ruler. There is a reason this story has fascinated children for 30 years, but why analyze it? Darkly humorous entertainment that, with the appearance of supper, is ultimately reassuring.

Smith, Lane. *The Big Pets.* **Illus. by the author.** Viking, 1991. $14.95 (0-670-83378-9).

FORMAT: Picture book   GRADES: Preschool–Grade 3.

By "big," Smith means "humongous." The large bug that cozies up to his boy-sized owner on the banks of Cricket Creek could be mistaken for a Volkswagen Beetle without windshield. This exaggerated look at the role of beloved pets in children's lives will elicit none-too-graceful guffaws.

Smith, Lane. *Flying Jake.* **Illus. by the author.** Macmillan, 1988. $14.95 (0-02-785830-8).

FORMAT: Picture book   GRADES: Preschool–Grade 3.

He went on to illustrate the witty, fractured tales by Jon Scieszka, but Smith's career began *here*, with a crazy story of a boy who suddenly discovers he can fly. High entertainment, accompanied by soaring pictures full of detail, wit, and warmth.

Smith, Lane. *Glasses: Who Needs 'Em?* **Illus. by the author.** Viking, 1991.
$13.95 (0-670-84160-9).
FORMAT: Picture book   GRADES: Preschool–Grade 3.

The question readers may have by the end of this trippingly good time is who *doesn't* need glasses? Smith's ideal world of those known as "four eyes" includes objects that don't even have vision, let alone eyes. Okay, okay, spuds *do* have eyes. Whether readers have foresight, hindsight, or simple 20/20 vision, this book is the site of some pretty grand views.

Stolz, Mary. *Bartholomew Fair.* Greenwillow, 1990. $12.95 (0-688-09522-4). paper avail.
FORMAT: Novel   GRADES: 7–up.

From a well-known teller of contemporary tales, this is a marvelous 16th-century confection of society's lowborns and highbrows meeting at the fair. Starving Will Shaw, Elizabeth I, one of her filthiest kitchen maids, two schoolboys, and *nouveau rich* Mr. Kempton are among the hundreds of splendid folk who make their ways to the fair; by day's end, Will has eaten his fill and found a new life while all the others have also not been untouched by the hours. A fabric of both humble and ornate origin, Stolz's book is a cacophony of sounds, period details, and frisky human foibles. Like any good day at the fair, it is over—satisfyingly so—but all too soon.

Swift, Jonathan. *Gulliver's Travels.* **Illus. by Aldren Watson.** Putnam, 1947.
$13.95 (0-448-05461-2).
FORMAT: Novel   GRADES: 7–up.

This is a beautifully accessible volume, unabridged and ready for ambitious readers. They will descend into Lilliput and see the rest of the journey through as well. An inviting typeface and design, too.

Testa, Fulvio. *Never Satisfied.* **Illus. by the author.** North-South, 1988. $12.95
(3-85539-009-6). paper avail.
FORMAT: Picture book   GRADES: Preschool–Grade 3.

Testa's odd humor creates a perfect nest for itself among the platitudes uttered by two bored children; they say that nothing ever happens, that it's always the same old faces. Testa takes off on these comments, depicting bizarre circumstances just outside the the realm of the boys' attentions. Readers will find these behind-the-boys antics amusing, especially when they hear the echoes of their own words in the text.

Thomson, Peggy. *The King Has Horse's Ears.* **Illus. by David Small.** Simon & Schuster, 1988. $12.95 (0-671-64953-1). paper avail.
FORMAT: Picture book   GRADES: Preschool–Grade 5.

Only the barber knows this royal secret; not even the queen suspects. But when the king is found out, he is relieved and even charmed to discover that no one minds, and the queen finds his ears delightful. Small creates some of the most imaginative illustrations since his *Imogene's Antlers.*

Ungerer, Tomi. *Moon Man.* **Illus. by the author.** Delacorte, 1991. $16.00 (0-385-30429-3).
FORMAT: Picture book   GRADES: Preschool–Grade 2.

Yes, *that* man in the moon comes to earth, and revels in its many warm and dainty pleasures. Readers who come to Ungerer through this title should also seek out the impeccably funny *The Beast of Monsieur Racine.*

Voake, Charlotte. *Mrs. Goose's Baby.* **Illus. by the author.** Little,Brown, 1989. $12.95 (0-316-90511-9). paper avail.
FORMAT: Picture book   GRADES: Preschool–Grade 3.

One day, Mrs. Goose finds an egg. She keeps it warm and when it hatches, loves her little gosling on sight. But as readers might suspect, it's going to grow up to be a hen. Does Mrs. Goose care? Voake's spirited tale of blind, biased mother love is as reassuring as it is dear (although it goes on exactly one page too long). Nevertheless, readers will giggle, and if there is a lesson about the love between adoptive parents and children to be found, why quibble about anything else?

Additional Titles

The following titles, annotated elsewhere in this book (see index), could also fit the "Madcap World" category.

Base, Graeme. *Animalia*
Bishop, Claire Huchet. *The Five Chinese Brothers*
Brittain, Bill. *Devil's Donkey*
Brown, Jeff. *Flat Stanley*
Carroll, Lewis. *Alice's Adventures in Wonderland*
Chetwin, Grace. *Box and Cox*
Christian, Mary Blount. *Swamp Monsters*
Cleary, Beverly. *The Mouse and the Motorcycle*
Cole, Babette. *Prince Cinders*
Dahl, Roald. *James and the Giant Peach*
Dubanevich, Arlene. *The Piggest Show on Earth*

Duke, Kate. *What Would a Guinea Pig Do?*
Fuchshuber, Annegert. *Giant Story/Mouse Tale*
Gerrard, Roy. *The Favershams*
Handford, Martin. *Where's Waldo?*
Heine, Helme. *Seven Wild Pigs*
Horejs, Vít. *Pig and Bear*
James, Mary. *Shoebag*
Kellogg, Steven. *Paul Bunyan*
Kellogg, Steven. *Pecos Bill*
Kitamura, Satoshi. *Lily Takes a Walk*
Lear, Edward, with Ogden Nash. *The Scroobious Pip*
Leedy, Loreen. *Big, Small, Short, Tall*
Lopshire, Robert. *I Want to Be Somebody New!*
MacDonald, Betty. *Hello, Mrs. Piggle-Wiggle*
Pendergraft, Patricia. *The Legend of Daisy Flowerdew*
Rodda, Emily. *The Pigs Are Flying!*
Seuss, Dr. *Green Eggs and Ham*
Voake, Charlotte. *The Ridiculous Story of Gammer Gurton's Needle*
Zavos, Judy. *Murgatroyd's Garden*

15: Hodgepodge

Just Plain Silly

This is about humor that is not elevated to the lofty realm of purpose or intention. The anomalous species of behavior called silliness, goofiness, zaniness—otherwise explained as surplus energy, emotive release or sappy adrenalin—ushers in humor with no assigned meanings, no deep satirical "beefs" about the woes of the world, no ennobled institutions to wit or parody.

Babies learn silliness very early. First they giggle at the burbled nonsense and coos flung at them by doting parents, then they innocently elicit smiles from said parents by behavior that generates laughs only because it has no place in common sense or logic.

Silly books—literature that hasn't yet lost its fresh-faced innocence—abound for children. After a book has been weighed against every other category of humor, plundered for meaning that just isn't there and ravaged for stratifications and dimensions it simply doesn't have, it is stamped "silly." And when that book is joined by others like it (and perhaps with only that in common), readers find themselves with an eclectic, entertaining jumble of the most purely delightful literature there is. Impossible to explain, too gossamer to hold up for scrutiny—a silly book tickles, therefore it is good, harmless fun.

Aylesworth, Jim. *Hanna's Hog.* **Illus. by Glen Rounds.** Macmillan, 1988. $13.95 (0-689-31367-5).

FORMAT: Picture book   GRADES: Kindergarten–Grade 3.

Backwoodswoman Hanna is pleased with her chickens and her hog—none of them ever give her any trouble. When her hog disappears, Hanna suspects her neighbor Kenny has stolen it. Aylesworth's story is more of a joke that goes on a little too long, but Rounds's pictures give it punch; his crotchety black lines are scratched around surprising colors like the mustard yellow of the hog, and the olive green of an old slop bucket.

Aylesworth, Jim. *Mother Halverson's New Cat.* **Illus. by Toni Goffe.** Macmillan, 1989. $13.95 (0-689-31465-5).
FORMAT: Picture book   GRADES: Preschool–Grade 3.

How could Farmer Halverson have known that of all his cats, only the shy yellow tabby can rid his wife's pantry of unwanted mice? The illustrations add fun to the already rhythmic, read-aloud text.

Bang, Molly. *Delphine.* **Illus. by the author.** Morrow, 1988. LB $12.88 (0-688-05637-7).
FORMAT: Picture book   GRADES: Preschool–Grade 3.

An extraordinary girl, Delphine proves herself astonishingly adept at mighty feats of skill and daring, but she has to master one of childhood's biggest accomplishments just like anyone else when her grandmother sends her a bike. There are good times on the mountain where Delphine lives, and readers will like her friends.

Barasch, Marc Ian. *No Plain Pets!* **Illus. by Henrik Drescher.** HarperCollins, 1991. LB $14.89 (0-06-022473-8).
FORMAT: Picture book   GRADES: Preschool–Grade 3.

The title is precise. The young narrator wants a pet so unusual that it will bring him fame—if not fortune—and it wouldn't hurt if it is a decent conversationalist, to boot. Drescher's wittily conceived illustrations chime in with the text to create a daydream from any child's list of wishes.

Berenstain, Stan, and Jan Berenstain. *The Big Honey Hunt.* **Illus. by the authors.** Random, 1962. LB $7.99 (0-394-90028-6).
FORMAT: Storybook   GRADES: 2–4.

One of the earliest adventures starring the Berenstain Bears, this is still the best. It is liltingly rhythmic, and the illustrations are bountifully funny. There are so many books, for many different age groups, about this family of bears that readers may become—for a time—addicted.

Blume, Judy. *Freckle Juice.* **Illus. by Sonia Lisker.** Macmillan, 1971. $12.95 (0-02-711690-5). paper avail.
FORMAT: Storybook   GRADES: Preschool–Grade 2.

Older readers have Blume's novels, but the picture-book audience doesn't get short shrift, especially when this one is read out loud in group story times. Andrew wants freckles so much that he is willing to shell out hard cash for a secret concoction. The experiment fails, but the book is a success. Try it, or *The One in the Middle Is the Green Kangaroo*, the 1967 book that was recently reillustrated for a new generation of readers.

Bright, Robert. *Georgie.* **Illus. by the author.** Doubleday, 1944. $8.95 (0-385-07307-0). paper avail.

FORMAT: Picture book   GRADES: Kindergarten–Grade 1.

This first book about the genial ghost who inhabits an attic in New England was quickly followed up by *Georgie's Christmas Carol*. Both are fast-paced and lively, and readers who meet Georgie in one book are sure to want the other.

Brown, M. K. *Let's Go Swimming with Mr. Sillypants.* **Illus. by the author.** Crown, 1986. paper $4.99 (0-517-59030-1).

FORMAT: Picture book   GRADES: Preschool–Grade 3.

As goofy as they come is Mr. Sillypants, who signs up for swimming lessons and then dreams he has become a fish (and another fish's idea of supper). Children love this story—and Mr. Sillypants's swim outfit—because the joy is all in the effort, and not in the size of the achievement. Unabashedly childlike; readers will want to look up Brown's illustrations for the Coles' *Big Goof and Little Goof.*

Bunting, Eve. *Jane Martin, Dog Detective.* **Illus. by Amy Schwartz.** Harcourt, 1984. paper $3.95 (0-15-239586-5).

FORMAT: Chapter book   GRADES: 3–5.

The popular, prolific author provides three lighthearted, easy-to-read mysteries, with genial illustrations, about an enterprising girl detective and her canine specialty.

Burningham, John. *Mr. Gumpy's Motor Car.* **Illus. by the author.** HarperCollins, 1976. LB $14.89 (0-690-00799-X). paper avail.

FORMAT: Storybook   GRADES: Preschool–Grade 3.

Almost any of Burningham's baubles shine bright with comic glitter, but this one, featuring an overcrowded touring car complete with menagerie, brings laughs out loud. The scenery is lovely, the adventure goofy, and readers will love the combination.

Cerf, Bennett. *Bennett Cerf's Book of Laughs.* **Illus. by Carl Rose.** Random, 1959. LB $7.99 (0-394-90011-1).

FORMAT: Storybook   GRADES: 2–4.

A childhood classic, this is chock-full of funny lines that will keep the laughter coming. Although the book is long, beginning readers will tackle it with relish, and then seek out Cerf's other titles.

Cohen, Peter. *Olson's Meat Pies.* **Illus. by Olof Landstrom.** R&S, 1989. $12.95 (9-12-959180-5).
FORMAT: Picture book   GRADES: Kindergarten–Grade 4.

For over 30 years, Olson has been making meat pies of only the finest ingredients, but when his accountant runs off with the money box, the baker is forced to use substitutes—watches, toys, you name it. Sophisticated cartoons and an eccentric sense of humor bring out this story's zanier moments.

Conford, Ellen. *Dear Lovey Hart, I Am Desperate.* Little, Brown, 1975. $14.95 (0-316-15306-0). paper avail.
FORMAT: Novel   GRADES: 7–up.

Ann Landers, watch out! Here comes Carrie Wasserman, with unknown intentions of turning her school upside down by starting an advice column in the paper. Conford's hand is sure as she spells out the funny disasters that ensue. This author can be relied upon for providing young adults with readable contemporary yarns.

Cousins, Lucy. *Portly's Hat.* **Illus. by the author.** Dutton, 1989. $6.95 (0-525-44457-2).
FORMAT: Picture book   GRADES: Preschool–Grade 1.

This is an idiosyncratic tale of a penguin named Portly and his red-striped hat. Stuart, the stinky seagull, steals it. Portly's friend, Little Bert, gets it back. This simple story, hardly more than a scrawl, is loaded with a sneaky sort of charm. Cousins includes comic asides, the kind of comments children mutter: "Come back Stinky Stuart," a bare-headed Portly calls out. "Stinky Stuart called me fish face and he's got my hat," the penguin sobs to his friend. Thoroughly engaging.

Delaney, Ned. *Cosmic Chickens.* **Illus. by the author.** HarperCollins, 1988. $12.95 (0-06-021583-6).
FORMAT: Picture book   GRADES: Preschool–Grade 3.

A flying saucer lands in Hank's coop; the extraterrestrials have a brilliant plan for turning his bad luck around. A goofily daring tale.

Denton, Kady MacDonald. *Granny Is a Darling.* **Illus. by the author.** Macmillan, 1988. $13.95 (0-689-50452-7). paper avail.
FORMAT: Picture book   GRADES: Preschool–Grade 3.

A visit from Granny is something Billy eagerly anticipates because she will sleep in his room. It is just as well that he doesn't tell her about the dark things that come into his room at night, for Granny snores, and that makes the scary ones back off for good. A smooth narrative style complements softly colored pictures. Swirls of shadow and light delineate the scenes of Billy's fears, and Granny truly is a dear.

dePaola, Tomie. *Big Anthony and the Magic Ring*. Harcourt, 1979. $12.95 (0-15-207124-5). paper avail.
FORMAT: Picture book   GRADES: Preschool–Grade 3.

Big Anthony snatches a magic ring and nurses a case of spring fever; this is the uproarious sequel to dePaola's Caldecott Honor winner *Strega Nona*.

Dumbleton, Mike. *Dial-a-Croc*. Illus. by Ann James. Orchard, 1991. $14.95 (0-531-05945-6).
FORMAT: Picture book   GRADES: Preschool–Grade 3.

As with Marc Ian Barasch's *No Plain Pets* and Lane Smith's *The Big Pets*, this piece of whimsy shows the unexpected bliss of having a one-of-a-kind pet. Vanessa ingeniously puts hers—a crocodile—to work.

Eager, Edward. *Half Magic*. Illus. by N. M. Bodecker. Harcourt, 1954. $14.95 (0-15-233078-X). paper avail.
FORMAT: Novel   GRADES: 4–6.

Children who haven't discovered the excitement of an Eager book can start with this one about four children who turn a boring summer around by making double-wishes on an ancient coin—full of surprises, full of fun. The same children appear in *Magic by the Lake*, but any of this author's stories will invoke similar reactions.

Edens, Cooper. *Santa Cows*. Illus. by Daniel Lane. Simon & Schuster, 1991. $14.00 (0-671-74863-7).
FORMAT: Picture book   GRADES: 2–up.

Cows replace the eight tiny reindeer in this hilarious homage to Clement C. Moore's poem, "The Night Before Christmas."

Gelman, Jan. *Marci's Secret Book of Dating*. Knopf, 1991. LB $7.99 (0-679-91106-5). paper avail.
FORMAT: Novel   GRADES: 5–up.

Marci and best friend Pam are mystified by the number of kids who have "paired off" since they entered seventh grade and they make a pact to find boyfriends fast. Frivolous fare, this light, familiar romance will suit those readers who have not yet overdosed on similar plots. Smooth.

Geringer, Laura. *A Three Hat Day*. Illus. by Arnold Lobel. HarperCollins, 1985. LB $14.89 (0-06-021989-0). paper avail.
FORMAT: Picture book   GRADES: Preschool–Grade 3.

Roundly acclaimed for its bright humor and underlying affection, this tale of love between kindred souls (and hat hobbyists) features the genial illustrations of Lobel. Jolly.

Grindley, Sally. *Knock-Knock! Who's There?* **Illus. by Anthony Browne.** Knopf, 1992. LB $8.99 (0-394-98400-5). paper avail.

FORMAT: Picture book   GRADES: Preschool–Grade 1.

The bedtime war zone may become neutral territory when children have this read-aloud book of jokes to soothe them to sleep.

Hadithy, Mwenye. *Hot Hippo.* **Illus. by Adrienne Kennaway.** Little, Brown, 1986. $14.95 (0-316-33722-6).

FORMAT: Picture book   GRADES: Preschool–Grade 3.

A hippo nearing heatstroke longs for the cool river waters. Readers have come to anticipate each Hadithy/Kennaway collaboration, for their tellings and illustrations are equally vibrant, making each work a rare treat for the ears and the eyes. This one fairly dances along, but *Crafty Chameleon* and *Greedy Zebra* are just as much fun.

Hall, Amanda. *The Foolish Husbands.* **Illus. by the author.** Bedrick, 1987. $12.95 (0-87266-154-9).

FORMAT: Picture book   GRADES: Kindergarten–Grade 3.

Humor and wisdom abound in this Norwegian folktale about two friends, Gunhild and Margit, who love a good argument. This time, each tries to make good her claim about her husband's imbecility. In the end, the two ladies wonder at their own stupidity for marrying such unsuitable husbands. This is one of the more credible of all old wives' tales, and Hall's adaptation is terse and to the point. Her patterned illustrations perfectly reflect the mood of ridicule and triviality.

Handford, Martin. *Where's Waldo?* **Illus. by the author.** Little, Brown, 1987. $12.95 (0-316-34293-9).

FORMAT: Picture book   GRADES: All grades.

A national best-seller began with this first book—an amusing game of concentration in a sea of distractions. Waldo goes through a maze of people and activities but he, unlike readers, seems to know where he is going, despite the fact that he loses his equipment along the way. The pictures are astonishing in variety, detail, and humor. The pages are filled to the rim with a simply sprawling mass of humanity.

Hoff, Syd. *Danny and the Dinosaur.* **Illus. by the author.** HarperCollins, 1958. LB $12.89 (0-06-022466-5). paper avail.

FORMAT: Storybook   GRADES: 1–3.

One of the first dinosaur books, and one of the best, entails a brief friendship that children have loved reading for more than 30 years.

Horvath, Polly. *No More Cornflakes.* Farrar, 1990. $12.95 (0-374-35530-4).
FORMAT: Novel   GRADES: 5–up.

With a new baby coming, Hortense's parents have a lot on their minds, but their outrageous behavior proves humiliating for this fifth-grader and her 14-year-old sister Letitia. Delightfully silly adults don't help Hortense muddle through this confusing period, but they do bring humor to this breezy, unbelievable tale. If readers don't mind sudden shifts—Hortense's first-person narration seems more appropriate to an eighth-grader than a fifth-grader, and her child's perspective often gives way to Horvath's own adult observations—they will discover an entertaining whole.

Knudson, R. R. *Rinehart Shouts.* Farrar, 1987. $13.00 (0-374-36296-3).
FORMAT: Novel   GRADES: 4–up.

This latest installment of the adventures of Zan Hagen and Arthur Rinehart skims toward a resolution like a racing skiff toward the finish line, with a clean, crisp use of language and no wasted motion. Zan is away but her presence is felt through postcards. This is Arthur's story; he is part of a mismatched threesome who finish in first place in the President's Cup Regatta on the Potomac.

Lindgren, Barbro. *A Worm's Tale.* **Illus. by Cecilia Torudd.** R&S, 1988. $12.95 (9-12-959068-X).
FORMAT: Picture book   GRADES: Preschool–Grade 2.

In a goofy little story with big impact, elderly Arthur meets a talking worm in the park and the two become best buddies forever. Guaranteed to launch any sobersides into giggles with a droll text and splendid, loose wash drawings.

Lorenz, Lee. *Dinah's Egg.* **Illus. by the author.** Simon & Schuster, 1990. $13.95 (0-685-35589-6).
FORMAT: Picture book   GRADES: Preschool–Grade 3.

A pretty blue egg rolls out of its nest and into a series of adventures. These are drolly penned in Lorenz's sprightly, exaggerated cartoons—a funny, precarious journey that, readers will be glad to know, ends well.

Luttrell, Ida. *Mattie and the Chicken Thief.* **Illus. by Thacher Hurd.** Putnam, 1988. $12.95 (0-396-09126-1).
FORMAT: Picture book   GRADES: Preschool–Grade 3.

Thieves be warned, that if you take Mattie's chickens, not only will she come after the loot, she'll get you as well. This exercise is told with irrepressible good humor, and accompanied by exuberant watercolors by second-generation artist Hurd. Plain fun.

Mazer, Norma Fox. *B, My Name Is Bunny.* Scholastic, 1987. $12.95 (0-590-40930-1).

FORMAT: Novel   GRADES: 6–8.

Bunny hates her name. So she introduces herself to a boy she meets at a rock concert as Emily—and Emily is the name of Bunny's very best friend. Now, all of this may sound insane, but Mazer pulls it off. She takes the silliness of being 13 and gives it a fresh, lively appeal. Funny and fun.

Modell, Frank. *Ice Cream Soup.* Illus. by the author. Greenwillow, 1988. $11.95 (0-688-07770-6).

FORMAT: Picture book   GRADES: Preschool–Grade 2.

In this further tale of the adventures of Marvin and Milton, the boys decide they want to have a birthday party, even though their mothers have both nixed the idea. The boys work hard; in zany pictures, scenes of the party and scenes of a failed baking attempt have the same air of festivity. Good-hearted humor and real zing.

Modell, Frank. *One Zillion Valentines.* Illus. by the author. Greenwillow, 1981. LB $11.88 (0-688-00569-1). paper avail.

FORMAT: Picture book   GRADES: Preschool–Grade 3.

New Yorker illustrator/cartoonist Modell could make a new career out of telling funny stories about this pair—Milton and Marvin. These good buddies, broke but full of Valentine spirit, decide that no less than one card for every person in the neighborhood will be right for their celebration. And then they set out to make them. Robust good humor for all.

Most, Bernard. *Dinosaur Cousins?* Harcourt, 1987. $13.95 (0-15-223497-7). paper avail.

FORMAT: Picture book   GRADES: Preschool–Grade 2.

Most has a funny idea about dinosaurs, one that kids will love. By pairing animals (triceratops and rhinoceros, brachiosaurus and giraffes, among others) and noting their similarities, he wonders how they might be related. The pictures are cartoony and bright. With enough facts to satisfy nonfiction fans, this will charm all readers—and get them wondering, too.

Murphy, Jill. *All in One Piece.* Illus. by the author. Putnam, 1987. $10.95 (0-399-21433-X).

FORMAT: Picture book   GRADES: Preschool–Grade 1.

Five Minutes' Peace delivered into the hands of readers a near-perfect reflection of a family's typically calamitous morning; now the adult elephants are dressing for an evening out, and their well-meaning but high-spirited children won't leave them alone. Though not as strong as its predecessor, this book, with its resemblance to real life, is still a delight.

Nash, Ogden. *Custard the Dragon.* **Illus. by Linell Nash.** Little, Brown, 1936. LB $14.95 (0-316-59841-0).
FORMAT: Picture book   GRADES: Preschool–Grade 3.

A pet dragon named Custard and his owner, Belinda, are the charming duo who star in Nash's poem. A grand pace and amusing details throughout will keep readers engaged, and perhaps send them on to this verse-maker's other works including *The Adventures of Isabel.*

Park, Barbara. *Rosie Swanson: Fourth-Grade Geek for President.* Knopf, 1991. LB $14.99 (0-679-92094-3). paper avail.
FORMAT: Novel   GRADES: 3–5.

Rosie is in the running for class president, and if she can't win, she'll at least take the other candidates down with her. The stars of Park's previous book about Rosie Swanson return, as odd a trio as readers are likely to find in middle-grade fiction. Rosie's tale is as bright and funny as they come, especially when plumpish Earl and too-smart Maxie are on the scene as reasonably loyal allies. She loses the election, and doesn't even win the day. Somehow, though, readers will want to cheer her on to further adventures.

Pinkwater, Daniel. *Guys from Space.* **Illus. by the author.** Macmillan, 1989. $13.95 (0-02-774672-0). paper avail.
FORMAT: Picture book   GRADES: Preschool–Grade 3.

The boy of this story clears it with his mother first and is soon soaring through space with the guys. Pinkwater's idiosyncratic humor shines through in words and pictures.

Pinkwater, Daniel. *The Snarkout Boys and the Avocado of Death.* **Illus. by the author.** Lothrop, 1982. $12.95 (0-688-00871-2). paper avail.
FORMAT: Novel   GRADES: 4–6.

The search for inventor/avocado expert Flipping Hades Terwilliger sends the Snarkout Boys and Rat on one farfetched adventure after another. Some children just don't "get" Pinkwater, and others practically inhale every word he writes. Everyone should read at least one, and this is as good a place to begin as any. Nonstop nonsense, indeed.

Porte, Barbara Ann. *Ruthann and Her Pig.* **Illus. by Suçie Stevenson.** Orchard, 1989. $14.95 (0-531-05825-5).
FORMAT: Chapter book   GRADES: 2–5.

Ruthann has a pig, Henry Thomas, whom her cousin Frank wants to borrow. How Ruthann deals with this is the source of a comic story, illustrated in full color, that will have many readers giggling. If some just don't get the humor herein, there are other books for them. Most readers, however, find that Porte is a perfect pick.

Rockwell, Thomas. *How to Get Fabulously Rich.* **Illus. by Anne Canevari Green.** Franklin Watts, 1990. LB $13.90 (0-531-10877-5). paper avail.
FORMAT: Novel   GRADES: 4–6.

Billy, fresh from his longstanding success in *How to Eat Fried Worms,* returns, wealthy beyond his wildest imaginings when he wins the lottery. Such vast sums do not inspire calm in his family, however, and once readers have digested this humorous work, they'll be ready for Billy's first adventure.

Rodda, Emily. *The Pigs Are Flying!* **Illus. by Noela Young.** Greenwillow, 1988. $13.95 (0-688-08130-4). paper avail.
FORMAT: Novel   GRADES: 4–6.

Rodda takes a funny idea—pigs might fly—and expands it to an entertaining novel for middle readers. On a rainy day, Rachel is tired of being cooped up with a cold and wishes for something to happen. She winds up in a very odd place where certain weather systems make pigs fly and people just a little bit crazy in storms known as grunters. The premise is lighthearted and funny, and its promise is fulfilled.

Samuels, Barbara. *Happy Birthday, Dolores.* **Illus. by the author.** Orchard, 1989. $13.95 (0-531-05701-7).
FORMAT: Picture book   GRADES: Preschool–Grade 3.

After big plans, willful designs, and nearly unbridled enthusiasm, Dolores finds that her party isn't going quite as she hoped. Such pluck comes along only once in a while; sit back and allow readers to revel in Dolores's unique *joie de vivre.*

Samuels, Barbara. *What's So Great about Cindy Snappleby?* **Illus. by the author.** Orchard, 1992. $13.95 (0-531-05979-0).
FORMAT: Picture book   GRADES: Preschool–Grade 3.

Fans of previous stories about siblings Faye and Dolores will be glad for this latest visit. Cindy is so cool that Faye, easily impressed, wants to emulate her. Little sister Dolores absolutely savages Cindy's poise and manages to flatten Faye's adoration of Cindy as well. Would that there were always little sisters around to de-puff the pompous in life!

Smith, William Jay. *Laughing Time: Collected Nonsense.* **Illus. by Fernando Krahn.** Farrar, 1990. $14.00 (0-374-34366-7). paper avail.
FORMAT: Anthology   GRADES: 1–5.

Tidy illustrations make droll work of this collection of funny verse about animals.

Tusa, Tricia. *Sherman and Pearl.* **Illus. by the author.** Macmillan, 1989. $13.95 (0-02-789542-4).

FORMAT: Picture book   GRADES: Preschool–Grade 3.

This is but one of the most recent of Tusa's eccentric outings, about two car-watchers who sit by the side of the road and wave at *everyone*. When a freeway is built, it looks as if our two heroes will have to buy a television set—but if Tusa can draw this comic pair into a corner, she also knows how to get them out. Fine fun, preceded by *Chicken, Maebelle's Suitcase*, among others, as well as the recent *Camilla's New Hairdo*.

Waddell, Martin. *Farmer Duck.* **Illus. by Helen Oxenbury.** Candlewick, 1992. $15.95 (1-56402-009-6).

FORMAT: Picture book   GRADES: Preschool–Grade 4.

The small quacker of this tale drags through dawn-to-dusk chores, hardly stopping to answer the lazy farmer's queries about how the work is going. Luckily, the other animals are sympathetic, and have enough vengeance in their hearts to right the terrible injustice daily inflicted on one lone duck. A nimble-witted tale with a point.

Wade, Alan. *I'm Flying!* **Illus. by Petra Mathers.** Knopf, 1990. LB $14.99 (0-394-94510-7).

FORMAT: Picture book   GRADES: Preschool–Grade 3.

Readers too old to reread *Where the Wild Things Are* will relish the adventures of a young, self-styled fantasist. When the narrator starts tying helium-filled balloons to various household objects and deserving people (a teacher, for one), the heavens become filled with his launchings. He satisfies his own wanderlust as well. Ably-penned drollery would be enough to give this book a proper send-off, but Mathers's idiosyncratic paintings of the far-flung corners of the world further elevate it. Plenty of good times are in store for those who thoroughly eyeball the pages. A simple idea takes flight in a kaleidoscope of technicolor.

Weatherill, Stephen. *The Very First Lucy Goose Book.* **Illus. by the author.** Prentice Hall, 1987. $9.95 (0-13-941410-X).

FORMAT: Picture book   GRADES: 1–4.

Lucy Goose's heart is certainly in the right place when she allows a mother frog and her 2001 tadpoles to stay in her birdbath. That's only the beginning of one of five stories, all of which start out as funny muddles, but Lucy always lands on those webbed feet. Weatherill's comic-strip format appeals to those readers just beyond picture-book age; there are hundreds of kid-pleasing details.

Wiesner, David. *Tuesday.* **Illus. by the author.** Houghton, 1991. $15.95 (0-395-55113-7).

FORMAT: Picture book   GRADES: Preschool–Grade 3.

In a wordless book, an ordinary neighborhood is transformed by the events one Tuesday evening; rather pleased-looking frogs levitate with their lily pads out of the pond and into the skies for the night. The following week, pigs float. Wiesner's *Free Fall* and *Hurricane* showed his artistic skill and wonderful imagination; this one presents an eccentric sense of humor that readers will share. A Caldecott Medal-winning book.

Williams, Suzanne. *Mommy Doesn't Know My Name.* **Illus. by Andrew Shachat.** Houghton, 1990. $13.95 (0-395-54228-6).

FORMAT: Picture book   GRADES: Preschool–Kindergarten.

"Little devil," "monster," and "pumpkin" are just a few of the names Hannah's mother calls her—and the pictures show these transformations. But finally Hannah has had enough, and demands the use of her real name. More than one child has questioned such terms of endearment, and this one nattily brings the point home.

Young, Frederica, and Marguerite Kohl. *More Jokes for Children.* **Illus. by Bob Patterson.** Farrar, 1966. paper $4.95 (0-374-45360-8).

FORMAT: Joke book   GRADES: 3–6.

With 650 riddles, jokes, and rhymes, this is a suitable sequel to the acclaimed and popular *Jokes for Children.*

Additional Titles

The following titles, annotated elsewhere in this book (see index), could also fit the "Hodgepodge" category.

Birdseye, Tom. *Air Mail to the Moon*
Brewton, Sarah, John E. Brewton, and George Meredith Blackburn, III. *My Tang's Tungled and Other Ridiculous Situations*
Butterworth, Oliver. *The Enormous Egg*
Cameron, Polly. *"I Can't," Said the Ant*
Cecil, Laura. *Stuff and Nonsense*
Cole, Babette. *King Change-a-Lot*
Cole, Joanna, and Stephanie Calmenson. *The Laugh Book*
Cole, Joanna, and Philip Cole. *Big Goof and Little Goof*
Cole, William. *Oh, Such Foolishness!*
Coombs, Patricia. *Dorrie and the Wizard's Spell*
Cooney, Caroline B. *The Girl Who Invented Romance*

Dahl, Roald. *The Giraffe and the Pelly and Me*
Denton, Terry. *At the Café Splendid*
Dubanevich, Arlene. *The Piggest Show on Earth*
Fleming, Ian. *Chitty-Chitty-Bang-Bang*
Goffstein, M. B. *Laughing Latkes*
Haas, Dorothy. *Burton's Zoom Zoom Va-Rooom Machine*
Hale, Lucretia. *The Lady Who Put Salt in Her Coffee*
Hoban, Lillian. *Silly Tilly and the Easter Bunny*
Hoban, Russell. *Bread and Jam for Frances*
Horvath, Polly. *An Occasional Cow*
Jeschke, Susan. *Perfect the Pig*
Kalman, Maira. *Hey Willy, See the Pyramids*
Kalman, Maira. *Sayonara, Mrs. Kackleman*
Keller, Charles. *Tongue Twisters*
Kellogg, Steven. *Pinkerton, Behave!*
Kline, Suzy. *Herbie Jones and the Class Gift*
Korman, Gordon. *Macdonald Hall Goes Hollywood*
Krause, Ute. *Pig Surprise*
Lear, Edward, with Ogden Nash. *The Scroobious Pip*
Leedy, Loreen. *The Bunny Play*
Levine, Caroline Anne. *Knockout Knock Knocks*
Mahy, Margaret. *Nonstop Nonsense*
Marshall, Edward. *Space Case*
Martin, Bill, Jr. *Brown Bear, Brown Bear, What Do You See?*
Norton, Mary. *The Borrowers*
Paige, Rob. *Some of My Best Friends Are Monsters*
Patz, Nancy. *Moses Supposes His Toeses Are Roses*
Pryor, Bonnie. *Mr. Munday and the Space Creatures*
Robinette, René. *The Robin Family*
Rosen, Michael. *We're Going on a Bear Hunt*
Rosenbloom, Joseph. *The Funniest Dinosaur Book Ever!*
Schmidt, Julie Madeline. *The Apartment House*
Schneider, Howie, and Susan Seligson. *The Amazing Amos and the Greatest Couch on Earth*
Schneider, Howie, and Susan Seligson. *Amos*
Schwartz, Alvin. *The Cat's Elbow*
Schwartz, Mary Ada. *Spiffen*
Seuss, Dr. *The Cat in the Hat*
Stevenson, James. *Monty*
Stevenson, Suçie. *Christmas Eve*
Tabott, Hudson. *We're Back*
Wolf, Janet. *Adelaide to Zeke*
Wood, Audrey. *Three Sisters*

16: Whirlwind Fun

Giddy Uproar and Joyous Energy

*T*he expression of this state in children's books comes in the depiction of small busy babies and toddlers in states of seemingly perpetual motion and vitality, and in the form of catalogues, primers, and picture books that touch on and celebrate the raw experience, the activities, and the joyous—and formless—bursts of spontaneous energy attributed to children. The truth is that comic fancy may be regarded as nothing more than a *sensibility* kids can call their own, which exists for its own sake, and is not meant to be directed, channeled, or controlled. Every moment of a child's day is a flexing of imagination, as if he/she is happily swimming within puddles of images, colors, and mists, a seemingly fluid condition of the world long before it solidifies into shape and sense. A wellspring of inner incitement and a roller-coaster of external stimuli fuse in this spirited world of charmed animation.

Ahlberg, Janet, and Allan Ahlberg. *Starting School.* **Illus. by the author.**
Viking, 1988. $11.95 (0-670-82175-6). paper avail.
FORMAT: Picture book   GRADES: Preschool–Grade 1.

In this catalog of a schoolchild's "firsts," the Ahlbergs have combined a pleasing design with salient bits of information, driven home by a band of roly-poly children. Each day and week of the semester is packed with activities and realities; the children are not always happy, and the teachers are not always serene. Children will respond to the honest, generous approach.

Anholt, Catherine. *When I Was a Baby.* **Illus. by the author.** Little, Brown, 1989. $11.95 (0-316-04262-5).
FORMAT: Picture book   GRADES: Preschool–Grade 1.

A girl, now three, asks her mother all manner of questions—"What did I eat when I was a baby?" and "Was I a noisy baby?"—in order to understand just what she was like when she was young. Her mother answers every question with loving enthusiasm, and those memories contrast with the girl's achievements as a toddler. This is a very buoyant, untroubled view of life—smiles never leave the parents' faces, and baby herself is mostly serene. An open-hearted, user-friendly view of parenting and childhood.

Bond, Felicia. *Poinsettia and Her Family.* **Illus. by the author.** Harper-Collins, 1981. LB $13.89 (0-690-04145-4). paper avail.
FORMAT: Picture book   GRADES: Preschool–Grade 3.

This Reading Rainbow selection focuses on a common sibling wish—that all those pesty brothers and sisters would somehow just disappear. Poinsettia, a pretty porcine heroine, gets her way, if temporarily. It is long enough to prove to her, however, that she loves her family just the way they are. Broad humor and quiet moments, but most of all, utterly endearing.

Carlstrom, Nancy. *Baby-O.* **Illus. by Suçie Stevenson.** Little, Brown, 1992. $14.95 (0-316-12851-1).
FORMAT: Picture book   GRADES: Preschool–Grade 3.

A West Indian family comes together ("Brother-O," "Granny-O," and all the rest) to bring their goods to market. The outburst of good feelings and the family's happy murmurs seem to rise from the pages in a rhythmic beat that is totally joyous. A celebration.

Cleary, Beverly. *Beezus and Ramona.* **Illus. by Louis Darling.** Morrow, 1955. LB $12.88 (0-688-31076-1). paper avail.
FORMAT: Novel   GRADES: 3–6.

This annotation could have almost any Cleary's Beezus or Ramona titles as its heading. They are all wonderful, proven entertainment for children interested in school, family, friendship—and what child isn't? Later books include *Ramona the Pest* and *Ramona and Her Father.* In this one, Beezus's more conventional ways come against Ramona's natural exuberance, and the clashes are glorious. Later on, send readers to the Newbery Medal-winning *Dear Mr. Henshaw* which, in quieter style, packs the same wallop.

Cleary, Beverly. *Henry Huggins.* **Illus. by Louis Darling.** Morrow, 1950. LB $13.88 (0-688-31385-X). paper avail.
FORMAT: Novel   GRADES: 3–6.

There are several books about Henry—among them, *Henry and Ribsy* and *Henry and Beezus*—and of course he shows up in the Beezus and Ramona tales. But his funny adventures begin right here, and his appeal is contagious.

Dorros, Arthur. *Abuela.* **Illus. by Elisa Kleven.** Dutton, 1991. $13.95 (0-525-44750-4).
FORMAT: Picture book   GRADES: Preschool–Grade 3.

Rosalba goes with her *abuela*, or grandmother, to New York's Central Park, where they feed the birds. All this small child has to ask is "what if I could" and suddenly she is taking the beloved old woman for a fanciful tour—by air—of their city. The ecstasy of flight is often evoked in books for children, but this one is especially affectionate and imaginative.

Dorros, Arthur. *Tonight Is Carnaval.* **Illus. with** *arpilleras* **sewn by the Club de Madres Virgenes del Carmen of Lima, Peru.** Dutton, 1991. $13.95 (0-525-44641-9).
FORMAT: Picture book   GRADES: Preschool–Grade 3.

Carnaval is the night for joyous celebration, a coming together of the community in the name of forgetting all cares and joining in the festivities. Photographs of three-dimensional fabric scenes display both the skill of the creators and their affection for the event.

Duke, Kate. *What Would a Guinea Pig Do?* **Illus. by the author.** Dutton, 1988. $12.95 (0-525-44378-9).
FORMAT: Picture book   GRADES: Preschool–Grade 2.

The *Guinea Pig ABC* was first, then came some board books and *Guinea Pigs Far and Near.* Now these little furballs face three problems: how to clean a house, how to bake a cake, and how to be somebody else. Face it, Duke's pigs make disasters look like terrific fun, and the only foreseeable problem with this book is making sure that small guinea pig fans don't take some of these situations to heart and start baking and cleaning in similar fashion. With its crazy quilt of pastels on a bright white background and small funny dialogue balloons, the entire book is a joyful offering.

Erlich, Amy. *Bunnies All Day Long.* Illus. by Marie H. Henry. Dial, 1989. $7.95 (0-8037-0226-4).

FORMAT: Picture book   GRADES: Preschool–Grade 3.

This was the first in a series of books about these winsome bunnies, mischief-makers all and just as adorably forgivable. Children will recognize themselves in the bunnies' chatter and play, and laugh out loud in recognition of their own stunts and arguments. Happily, there are more books about this family, such as *Bunnies on Their Own* and *Bunnies and Their Grandma.* Fun on a small, realistic scale.

Erlich, Amy. *Bunnies and Their Grandma.* Illus. by Marie H. Henry. Dial, 1985. $7.95 (0-8037-0186-1). paper avail.

FORMAT: Picture book   GRADES: Preschool–Grade 2.

Energetic tales show color-filled scenes of the bunnies' antics and the ups and downs of everyday living.

Geisert, Arthur. *Oink.* Illus. by the author. Houghton, 1991. $13.95 (0-395-55329-6).

FORMAT: Picture book   GRADES: All grades.

Young readers will try to give voice to the inventive uses of the word "Oink," the only dialogue in this book. When its piglet siblings perform leaps from haystack to apple tree, one holds back. With delicate, scratched-out etchings.

Gomi, Taro. *First Comes Harry.* Illus. by the author. Morrow, 1987. $11.75 (0-688-06731-X).

FORMAT: Picture book   GRADES: Preschool–Kindergarten.

Harry is first up, first to breakfast, first to leap over the garbage can, first to tumble down the slide—and the first to get hurt. He's also first in the bath, and he's the very first to get sleepy. Fun and surprising, the book has clear colors, blocky figures, and crisp design that keeps it bouncing along, from that first "first" to the last.

Gomi, Taro. *Seeing, Saying, Doing, Playing.* Illus. by the author. Chronicle, 1991. $13.95 (0-87701-859-6).

FORMAT: Picture book   GRADES: Preschool–Grade 3.

Perhaps no book yet rings out like a three o'clock bell, but this one offers an action-crammed pandemonium created from a tumult of energetic "-ing" participles that convey continuity and the ongoing hurly-burly usually reserved for recess. Gomi, treating motion like a child's sixth sense, thrusts upon onlookers scenes showing—Brueghel-like—hundreds of people of various ages, indoors and out, blithely absorbed in just "being around." Small, flailing figures are "Exiting" or "Viewing" or "Sauntering." It assigns a ripe and timely emphasis on the child's *being* a child rather than *becoming* a grown-up.

Graham, Bob. *Has Anyone Here Seen William?* **Illus. by the author.** Little, Brown, 1989. $11.95 (0-316-32313-6).
FORMAT: Picture book   GRADES: Preschool–Grade 3.

A highly unsupervised toddler, after taking his first step, frequently causes the members of his family to ask one another, "Where is William?" Luckily, he gets into ponds that are only ankle deep, and into department store window displays instead of the hands of unseemly strangers. Familiarity provides this story with its charm; readers will easily recognize the refrain around which the very funny Graham constructs his story.

Greenberg, Melanie Hope. *At the Beach.* **Illus. by the author.** Dutton, 1989. $11.95 (0-525-44474-2).
FORMAT: Picture book   GRADES: Preschool–Grade 2.

Greenberg's first book is a childlike tribute to the sea, sand, and sunshine of a day at the beach. The colors are as bright as a new set of paints, and the artist sets simple shapes amid flat scenes. An utterly welcome paean to beach life.

Hayes, Sarah, sel. *Clap Your Hands: Finger Rhymes.* **Illus. by Toni Goffe.** Lothrop, 1988. LB $12.88 (0-688-07693-9).
FORMAT: Picture book   GRADES: Preschool–Grade 1.

Jiggling, wiggling, dancing, running, scrambling, beaming—small characters on each page exhibit the finger movements to traditional and modern verses with abandon and plenty of good cheer. This gleeful fare will inspire the most lapbound of readers to join with the breathless energy of the children on these pages.

Haywood, Carolyn. *"B" Is for Betsy.* **Illus. by the author.** Harcourt, 1939. $12.95 (0-15-204975-4). paper avail.
FORMAT: Chapter book   GRADES: 4–6.

This book began the charming series by Haywood, illustrated by her, about Betsy and her friend Billy's first few years in school. They've been called lively, admirable, and delightful. What is true now as then is that the storyteller's ease and her burbling sense of humor are apparent on nearly every page.

Haywood, Carolyn. *Betsy's Winterhouse.* **Illus. by the author.** Morrow, 1955. LB $13.88 (0-688-21090-7). paper avail.
FORMAT: Novel   GRADES: 2–4.

Until her death in the early nineties, Haywood continued to give readers charmingly nostalgic tales of childhood, featuring all the antics that make each day so memorable to the very young. Here, Betsy's idea to build a shelter in the basement provides her friends with snowy day fun the whole season long. For hotter weather, try *Betsy's Busy Summer.*

Hughes, Shirley. *The Big Alfie and Annie Rose Storybook.* **Illus. by the author.** Lothrop, 1989. LB $14.88 (0-688-07673-4).
FORMAT: Storybook   GRADES: Preschool–Grade 1.

Hughes offers her usual clear-eyed view of childhood in a book of stories. Light, unrhymed poems punctuate the stories of a school-age boy and his toddler sister, in a warm neighborhood that almost harkens back to another time. Fans of the other Alfie books or those meeting the family for the first time will be pleased by the real-life situations, jauntily depicted in fresh-faced watercolors.

Hurwitz, Johanna. *Rip-Roaring Russell.* **Illus. by Lillian Hoban.** Morrow, 1983. LB $12.88 (0-688-02348-7).
FORMAT: Chapter book   GRADES: 2–4.

Later to star in such small, witty gems as *Russell Sprouts* and *Russell Rides Again*, Russell makes his first appearance as an attendee at nursery school. For reading aloud or for an early foray into independent reading, this fast-paced story takes a generous view of a preschooler's natural exuberance.

Jabar, Cynthia. *Alice Ann Gets Ready for School.* **Illus. by the author.** Little, Brown, 1989. $13.95 (0-316-43457-4).
FORMAT: Picture book   GRADES: Preschool–Grade 1.

This is an inventive primer on the days leading to that all-important first day of school. This busy five-year-old just can't wait for the big day, and enters into each new experience with gusto, and no small amount of worry. But the people around her reassure her, and the entire bouncing book is so positive and friendly that readers facing that same first day are bound to feel a jolt of happy anticipation with each new page.

Keller, Holly. *Geraldine's Big Snow.* **Illus. by the author.** Greenwillow, 1988. $11.95 (0-688-07513-4).
FORMAT: Picture book   GRADES: Preschool–Grade 1.

Rumor that a big storm is on the way has Geraldine getting ready for the forecasted foot of snow. The snow is delayed, and Geraldine feels derailed, but when it does arrive, no one is happier than she is. The preparations of family and friends for snow bring a cozy glow to the big freeze. Last seen in *Geraldine's Blanket*, this saucy pig heroine is full of her usual high spirits, and children will appreciate her impatient request for a weather report.

Khalsa, Dayal Kaur. *Julian.* **Illus. by the author.** Crown, 1989. $12.95 (0-517-57279-6).
FORMAT: Picture book   GRADES: Preschool–Grade 5.

In more of a dog biography than fiction, Julian joins the other pets on a farm and chases everything: groundhogs, the cats, even his owner's car. The action unwinds across the top of each spread and then hurls back along the bottom of the page—quite new for Khalsa, and refreshingly original. Her colors and patterns, as usual, are boldly harmonious as strong images overlap and collide.

Khalsa, Dayal Kaur. *My Family Vacation.* **Illus. by the author.** Crown, 1988. LB $13.95 (0-517-56697-4).
FORMAT: Picture book   GRADES: Kindergarten–Grade 3.

Khalsa's gifts have been established in previous books; she moves from fresh-faced satire to cheeky looks at childhood with ease. Here May relentlessly pursues souvenirs when her family takes a car trip away from northern snows to Florida. The scenes of this are picture postcard perfect, in near-gaudy colors. Captured in miniature is a litany of moments from any family's vacation: siblings slugging each other, the cramped backseat of the car, motels with pools. Those ordinary scenes, in Khalsa's campy style, are thrown into relief and seem all the more true by contrast.

Komaiko, Leah. *Annie Bananie.* **Illus. by Laura Cornell.** HarperCollins, 1987. LB $13.89 (0-06-023261-7). paper avail.
FORMAT: Picture book   GRADES: Preschool–Grade 3.

Two kooky friends celebrate the good times until one, Annie, has to move away. Komaiko's bouncing verse and Cornell's illustrations prove that separations don't have to mean good-bye.

Leedy, Loreen. *The Bunny Play.* **Illus. by the author.** Holiday, 1988. $12.95 (0-8234-0679-2).
FORMAT: Picture book   GRADES: Preschool–Grade 3.

The *Dragon ABC Hunt* and *The Dragon Halloween Party* are among Leedy's memorable works; in this new book she gives bunnies the same bug-eyed looks of bewilderment that characterized her dragons. The bunnies put on a play. Leedy delves into the behind-the-scenes information with exuberance, letting the bunnies have the run of the book but including a glossary at the end. A nice touch: the classic masks of comedy and tragedy are slightly modified. They have long ears.

Lindgren, Astrid. *Springtime in Noisy Village.* **Illus. by Ilon Wikland.**
Viking, 1988. $11.95 (0-670-82185-3).
FORMAT: Picture book   GRADES: Preschool–Grade 3.

First published in 1965, this is a reissue of a well-loved story. After the long Swedish winter, Lisa describes the joys of the spring season, from muddy walks to the birth of new animals, all shared by the other six children of her village. Infectiously enthusiastic, the book will pry other children out of doors on budding spring days—or perhaps any time of the year.

Mangas, Brian. *A Nice Surprise for Father Rabbit.* **Illus. by Sidney Levitt.**
Simon & Schuster, 1991. paper $2.25 (0-671-73277-3).
FORMAT: Picture book   GRADES: Preschool–Kindergarten.

Honey Bunny and Sonny Bunny wait for their father to arrive home from work on a snowy night, and decide to prepare a tea for him. But after all their hard work, they are sleeping when Father Rabbit finally gets home. Both book and bunnies have a generous spirit that is hard to resist; Levitt's pictures express the gentle sentiments, and add humorous touches throughout. A nice surprise, indeed.

Martin, Bill, Jr. *The Happy Hippopotami!* **Illus. by Betsy Everitt.** Harcourt, 1991. $12.95 (0-15-233380-0). paper avail.
FORMAT: Picture book   GRADES: Preschool–Grade 3.

Bright blue beachcombers-cum-hippopotami deck out the sandy shores, celebrating the warmth, the picnics, and the cool drinks that are part of a grand summer scene. Let the festivities begin.

Martin, Bill, Jr., and John Archambault. *Here Are My Hands.* **Illus. by Ted Rand.** Holt, 1987. $14.95 (0-8050-0328-2). paper avail.
FORMAT: Picture book   GRADES: Preschool–Grade 2.

A surprising celebration of physiological parts and their uses includes "Here is my elbow, my arm, and my chin. And here is my skin that bundles me in." Rand's pictures spill off the page as different children enact the very funny, very pure chant. It's repeatable and rereadable, from the collaborators behind many other books, including *Barn Dance.*

Murphy, Jill. *Five Minutes' Peace*. Illus. by the author. Putnam, 1986. $10.95
(0-399-21354-6).
FORMAT: Picture book   GRADES: Preschool–Grade 3.

All Mrs. Large, an elephantine mother, wants is to have a few minutes
for a quiet bath by herself. But her children, affectionate and inquisitive,
innocently come in the way of her humble plans, and the frazzlement
that ensues will ring true for every family. Winsome illustrations stress
each funny moment of poor Mrs. Large's quest. This family also appears
in *All in One Piece* and *A Piece of Cake*.

***Old MacDonald Had a Farm*. Illus. by Tracey Cambell Pearson.** Dial, 1984.
paper $4.95 (0-8037-0274-4).
FORMAT: Picture book   GRADES: Preschool–Grade 3.

This refreshingly frantic look at a familiar song features Pearson's now
renowned energetic characters, breathless pacing, and rambunctious
scrambling as well as pitchforks full of nonsense. Don't overlook her
illustrations for *A, Apple Pie, Sing a Song of Sixpence*, and *We Wish You a
Merry Christmas* (starring a demanding bunch of carolers), as well as her
own text and art for *The Storekeeper* and *The Howling Dog*.

Omerod, Jan. *Reading*. Illus. by the author. Lothrop, 1985. $4.95 (0-688-04127-
2).
FORMAT: Picture book   GRADES: Preschool.

So what if Father's glasses get knocked a little askew—Baby wants to be
part of everything that's going on, even if it's just a bit of reading. With
one endearing episode per book (the others are *Sleeping, Messy Baby*, and
Dad's Back), these four capture the world of the very young with affectionate good spirits.

Oxenbury, Helen. *I Can*. Illus. by the author. Knopf, 1986. $3.95 (0-394-87482-
X).
FORMAT: Picture book   GRADES: Preschool.

Oxenbury makes children the center of their own universes in four books
about perception that in addition to *I Can* include *I See, I Hear*, and *I
Touch*. Winsome and inventive, these are sure to get a gurgle and a smile
from any child under three, and most older lookers-on as well.

**Oxenbury, Helen. *Say Goodnight; All Fall Down; Clap Hands; Tickle,
Tickle*. Illus. by the author.** Aladdin, 1987. $5.95 each (0-02-769010-5; 0-02-
769040-7; 0-02-769030-X; 0-02-769020-2).
FORMAT: Board books   GRADES: Preschool.

Looking over these books is akin to being in the middle of a room full of
toddlers. An oversized format and the large scale will invite and divert.

The text isn't particularly memorable; instead, these are a showcase for the always winsome, this time multiracial Oxenbury babes, who spill on each other, sing together, play with adults, bounce on beds, clap hands, and play with fingers or toes. Lively and oh, so user-friendly.

Prelutsky, Jack. *The New Kid on the Block*. Illus. by James Stevenson. Greenwillow, 1984. LB $14.88 (0-688-02772-3).
FORMAT: Poetry   GRADES: Preschool–Grade 3.

More than 100 merry poems celebrate all things odd, in rollicking, rhythmic chants and accompanied by frenetic illustrations. Always funny, always worth poring over.

Rey, H. A. *Curious George*. Illus. by the author. Houghton, 1941, 1973. $12.95 (0-395-15993-8). paper avail.
FORMAT: Picture book   GRADES: Preschool–Grade 3.

A favorite title about the inquisitive monkey who unintentionally wreaks havoc on an entire city just by poking into things. For modern readers, George's kidnapping from the jungle may seem severe. But this is a grand adventure, for any time.

Rosen, Michael. *We're Going on a Bear Hunt*. Illus. by Helen Oxenbury. Macmillan, 1989. $15.95 (0-689-50476-4).
FORMAT: Picture book   GRADES: Preschool–Grade 4.

A father and his four children—a toddler, a preschool boy, and two older girls—go on the traditional bear hunt, based on the old camp chant. It's a fantastic journey—real or imagined?—and the interaction among the children is fun to follow on every page. Readers accustomed to Oxenbury's board books will find a different style here, of puddles of color and sweeps of light and shadow. The scale of the pictures and the ease with which the text can be shouted aloud make this ideal for families or groups to share.

Rylant, Cynthia. *Birthday Presents*. Illus. by Suçie Stevenson. Orchard, 1987. $13.95 (0-531-05705-4). paper avail.
FORMAT: Picture book   GRADES: Preschool–Grade 2.

On the first five birthdays of one small girl, five different cakes are baked—star cake, clown, train, robot, and dinosaur cakes, respectively. Before the sixth birthday, the small girl has learned to offer her parents gifts on their birthdays. A celebration of love, this book is as delicious as a chocolate cake and oh, so funny. Stevenson's folk are joyful and charismatic, with puffed, rosy cheeks. Angelic and winsome.

Sandberg, Inger. *Dusty Wants to Borrow Everything.* **Illus. by Lasse Sandberg.** R&S, 1988. $6.95 (9-12-958782-4).
FORMAT: Picture book   GRADES: Preschool–Grade 1.

Dusty is a toddler of very few words. "Borrow this?" he asks, pointing at an object. The answer from his grandparents is usually yes. By the end of the day, Grandpa and Grandma are worn out, but Dusty is still appropriating household items. Spirited, adductive illustrations admirably reflect the world of a curious, creative two-year-old. Evident in text and art is the persistence of preschoolers, and the play habits that make them happy.

Schroeder, Alan. *Ragtime Tumpie.* **Illus. by Bernie Fuchs.** Little, Brown, 1989. $14.95 (0-316-77497-9).
FORMAT: Picture book   GRADES: Preschool–Grade 3.

Just because this is a biography of the childhood of Josephine Baker, should it rightly appear in a more orderly chapter? No. A surge of bounteous energy and happiness show how "Tumpie" had to dance, couldn't let anything stop her, and held on to the dream that would someday propel her to world fame. The pages are as light-filled and joyous as a honky-tonk cafe.

Soto, Gary. *Neighborhood Odes.* **Illus. by David Diaz.** Harcourt, 1992. $15.95 (0-15-256879-4).
FORMAT: Poetry   GRADES: 4–7.

Pleasure-filled—indeed, joyous—notice is taken of life's most mundane objects and ordinary people and events; tortillas, pets, grandparents, weddings are center stage in Soto's beautifully observed, perfect poems. A celebration of real life, this may send readers on to his short story collection, *Baseball in April.*

Steptoe, John. *Baby Says.* **Illus. by the author.** Lothrop, 1988. LB $13.88 (0-688-07424-3). paper avail.
FORMAT: Picture book   GRADES: Preschool.

In this snug vignette, the baby in an African-American family wants the attention of a big brother, and wants it *now*. The humor comes in a gentle unfolding of affection between the two, mostly conveyed in the warmth-infused, realistic paintings.

Stevenson, Suçie. *Christmas Eve.* **Illus. by the author.** Dell, 1992. paper $3.99 (0-440-40729-X).
FORMAT: Picture book   GRADES: Preschool–Grade 2.

Elly and Violet, stars of the summery *Do I Have to Take Violet?*, are back in a winter story with their baby sister Mae. And their conversations over the right and wrong ways of preparing for Christmas are eerily real. Generous in details as well as holiday spirit, Stevenson gives the story of these rosy-cheeked bunnies and their zestful participation a healthy dose of sibling squabbles. The book is both funny and dear.

Tulloch, Richard. *Stories from Our House.* **Illus. by Julie Vivas.** Cambridge Univ. Pr., 1987. $11.95 (0-521-33485-3).
FORMAT: Picture book   GRADES: Preschool–Grade 2.

Here are four glimpses of one busy household, like the stories children tell about their own homes. Messes, chaos, and distractions enliven these funny anecdotes, elevated by vibrant watercolors, wild and lively action shots, and pictures of mischievous children.

Tusa, Tricia. *Stay Away from the Junkyard!* **Illus. by the author.** Macmillan, 1988. $14.95 (0-02-789541-6). paper avail.
FORMAT: Picture book   GRADES: Preschool–Grade 3.

Old Man Campton runs the best junkyard Theodora has ever encountered; he and his pet pig Clarissa befriend the girl, and no one can convince *her* to stay away. Tusa's affectionate illustrations are expressive and funny.

van der Beek, Deborah. *Superbabe!* **Illus. by the author.** Putnam, 1988. $9.95 (0-399-21507-7).
FORMAT: Picture book   GRADES: Preschool–Grade 1.

Not to be confused with John Burningham's *Avocado Baby,* this book reveals the disconcerting problems of having an infant superhero in the house. It's a blithe look at babies, with a breezy rhyme to read aloud and illustrations crammed with genuinely childlike touches.

Van Leeuwen, Jean. *Tales of Oliver Pig.* **Illus. by Arnold Lobel.** Dial, 1979. LB $9.89 (0-8037-8736-7). paper avail.
FORMAT: Chapter book   GRADES: 2–4.

Simple, winning stories in an easy-to-read mode tell about the childhood of a cheerful pig and the homey, Lobel-created surroundings of his family life. Ebullient, yes, but quietly so; the humor comes from the recognition that these are real folk, living lives remarkably like our own. Children will find their own foibles in these pages, and be comforted in the discovery that they are not alone. Caldecott-Medalist Lobel also illustrated *More Tales of Oliver Pig.* Later books about this family, all by Van Leeuwen, were illustrated by Ann Schweninger, and the winsomeness is contagious.

Wabbes, Marie. *Rose Is Hungry; Rose's Picture; Rose Is Muddy; Rose's Bath.* **Illus. by the author.** Messner, 1988. paper $3.95 each (0-671-66611-8; 0-671-66613-4; 0-671-66610-X; 0-671-66612-6).
FORMAT: Picture books   GRADES: Preschool.

In four small books, Rose meets and masters several situations that would slay a lesser pig. This sweetly independent preschooler is capable of imaginative play, but still requires a nudge from her mother here and there. Watercolors, as rosy as the heroine, show the too-tall backgrounds of a child's world, and Rose moving through these large places with ease.

Wells, Rosemary. *Max's First Word.* **Illus. by the author.** Dial, 1979. paper $3.50 (0-8037-6066-3).
FORMAT: Picture book   GRADES: Preschool–Kindergarten.

It is almost impossible to choose just one book to explain how funny and tuned-in Wells is to the concerns of young children. Any of the board books starring Max and his sister Ruby will do—*Max's Bedtime, Max's Birthday,* and others—but this one, in which Max attempts to learn to speak, will be a hit with toddlers and parents alike. There simply isn't a Wells/Max book out that can't be wholeheartedly endorsed for its humor and unembellished joy in childhood undertakings.

Additional Titles

The following titles, annotated elsewhere in this book (see index), could also fit the "Whirlwind Fun" category.

Carlstrom, Nancy White. *Jesse Bear, What Will You Wear?*
Coxe, Molly. *Louella and the Yellow Balloon*
Donnelly, Elfie. *A Package for Miss Marshwater*
Dubanevich, Arlene. *Pigs in Hiding*
Estes, Eleanor. *The Moffats*
Greenfield, Eloise. *Honey, I Love and Other Love Poems*
Henkes, Kevin. *Chester's Way*
Komaiko, Leah. *Annie Bananie*
Komaiko, Leah. *Earl's Too Cool for Me*
Leedy, Loreen. *A Dragon Christmas*
McCord, David. *The Star in the Pail*
Pearson, Tracey Campbell. *The Storekeeper*
Samuels, Barbara. *Faye and Dolores*
Sawyer, Ruth. *Roller Skates*
Walsh, Ellen Stoll. *Mouse Paint*

17: *Comedy Without Laughter*

Soft and Gentle Humor

Beyond the provincial and the trivial, humor may point to a universal *sensibility* shared by children and adults. Untheatrical humor (deep, subtle, placid) relies not on the big laughs of vaudeville, stereotypical finger-pointing, nor grotesquely funny images, but on a feeling from the reader—with a smile—that "yes, I recognize that." The author doesn't have to say much to "get laughs," and the applause sign isn't needed. The reader watches events and images unfold with uncanny familiarity and satisfaction ("How did she know that about me? Here it is, here I am, in a book!") and responds with a serene smile of amusement and recognition.

Such inarticulate delight is as much a part of the humor equation as its noisier relatives, because it is what children carry around with them in their waking hours. Few people can long maintain a state of knee-slapping, side-splitting hysterical laughter (and there may be laws against such behavior); but fewer children walk around in a continued state of gloom and despair, either. Instead, this mode of gentle humor often carries the day; a delight without reason, or motive, that is wholly childlike, and most wholly human. Adults tend to lose this attitude, but it is always there, particularly in children's literature, making the phrase "humorous books for children" very nearly redundant.

Bawden, Nina. *Henry.* Illus. by Joyce Powzyk. Lothrop, 1988. LB $13.95 (0-688-07894-X).

FORMAT: Nonfiction   GRADES: 3–up.

The author of *Carrie's War* and *Kept in the Dark,* among other books, recounts the true story of a red squirrel adopted by her small brother,

Charlie, and her mother during World War II. A spirited tale of a beloved pet, this is also a chronicle of a less-familiar era—the lives of Londoners in exile, adjusting to a country life.

Bemelmans, Ludwig. *Madeline.* **Illus. by the author.** Viking, 1958. $14.95 (0-670-44580-0). paper avail.
FORMAT: Picture book   GRADES: Preschool–Grade 3.

When 12 little schoolgirls and their dear headmistress set out for the streets of Paris, almost anything can happen, and almost everything does. For many readers, the romance with boarding school stories begins here. Energetically conveyed in the simplest of pictures, which have been woefully oversimplified in a TV version of the book.

Blume, Judy. *Tales of a Fourth Grade Nothing.* **Illus. by Roy Doty.** Dutton, 1972. $11.95 (0-525-40720-0). paper avail.
FORMAT: Novel   GRADES: 4–6.

Peter narrates the trials and tribulations that are part of having a toddler brother; again, the treatment is light, but readers come away feeling as if their concerns are being taken seriously. No child reads Blume forever, but few grow up without sampling and enjoying her. The follow-up to this is *Superfudge*.

Brooks, Martha. *Paradise Cafe: And Other Stories.* Little, Brown, 1990. $14.95 (0-316-10978-9).
FORMAT: Short stories   GRADES: 7–up.

In a riveting collection, Brooks writes vivid, convincing portraits of teen-agers in the throes of first love, facing the death of a beloved old dog, muddling through and then achieving miracles in single-parent families, and much more. Enticing and revelatory, each story opens with a remark-ably rounded cast of characters, poised around a pivotal moment and then released to behave in hapless, human ways through the denoue-ment. Fine writing, a mature outlook—welcome.

Brown, Margaret Wise. *Willie's Adventures.* **Illus. by Crockett Johnson.** HarperCollins, 1954. LB $11.89 (0-06-020769-8).
FORMAT: Storybook   GRADES: Preschool–Grade 3.

Brown, known for *The Little Fur Family, Runaway Bunny* and, of course, *Goodnight Moon,* created this small gem about a small boy's three imagina-tive adventures. Her other books tend to be softer and more seriously childlike; this one harbors a sense of humor as well. Johnson is the creator of the well-loved *Harold and the Purple Crayon.*

Byars, Betsy. *Bingo Brown and the Language of Love.* Viking, 1989. $12.95 (0-670-82791-6). paper avail.
FORMAT: Novel   GRADES: 3–7.

Bingo, that incomparable optimist, returns with even bigger issues to challenge him and charm readers. Melissa, the love of his life, has moved away, and Bingo is hit first with an enormous long-distance telephone bill and then with the empty feeling that his is a fickle soul. Bingo, with his wry, self-mocking tone, is just enough of a stumblebum to bring laughs, and enough of a thoughtful, considerate person that he defies all expectations readers may have about boys in books. He's a wonderful romantic, and a heartbreaker to boot. Encore!

Byars, Betsy. *The Burning Questions of Bingo Brown.* Viking, 1988. $12.95 (0-670-81932-8). paper avail.
FORMAT: Novel   GRADES: 3–7.

Introducing one of Byars's most unforgettable male characters. Bingo is a fairly ordinary sixth-grader, with a number of extraordinary questions. Three girls have won his heart, and he is shuffling around, trying to understand the next phase of affection. In the meantime, Bingo's favorite teacher has started to speak out inappropriately in class, asking the children for help they are too young to give. Without resorting to the knee-slapping hysteria of her last few books, Byars gives Bingo a wry, winning dignity, and will inspire readers to seek out the other books about him.

Cameron, Eleanor. *A Room Made of Windows.* **Illus. by Trina Schart Hyman.** Little, Brown, 1971. $15.95 (0-316-12523-7). paper avail.
FORMAT: Novel   GRADES: 7–up.

This acclaimed book may have been many readers' first meeting with Julia Redfern, about whom Cameron wrote several more books. A wryly affectionate look at generations, this novel will surprise those who met Cameron through her lighthearted fantasies such as *The Wonderful Mushroom Planet*.

Carlson, Lori M., and Cynthia Ventura, eds. *Where Angels Glide at Dawn: New Stories from Latin America.* **Illus. by José Ortega.** HarperCollins, 1990. LB $13.89 (0-397-32425-1).
FORMAT: Short stories   GRADES: 7–up.

This is an unusually funny and worthy collection of stories, about the land where angels glide at dawn, magical rabbits take over the wished-for state portraits of a dictator, and a bear moves through the pipes of an apartment house, fondly overseeing the tenants. With an evocative, wistful introduction by Isabel Allende, this too-brief collection will stir children with its diverse images, amusing ideas, eclectic observations, and sometimes solid, sometimes lilting prose.

Christian, Mary Blount. *Penrod Again.* **Illus. by Jane Dyer.** Macmillan, 1987. $11.95 (0-02-718550-8). paper avail.
FORMAT: Chapter book   GRADES: 1–4.

At the close of the endearing *Penrod's Pants*, Griswold Bear is heading off for a long winter snooze. So now that it's spring, Penrod Porcupine is ready to roll up his sleeves and start cleaning. In five easy-to-read stories, Griswold's sorely tried patience and Penrod's blithe good intentions are winningly conveyed; the further adventures of these roly-poly pals will be embraced by all.

dePaola, Tomie. *Merry Christmas, Strega Nona.* **Illus. by the author.** Harcourt, 1986. $14.95 (0-15-253183-1). paper avail.
FORMAT: Picture book   GRADES: Preschool–Grade 3.

There are times for magic, and there are times when it simply won't do. The Calabrian witch knows the difference and sticks to her decision not to use her talent to fix the Christmas feast. A surefire giggle-getter, and best of all, there are more books about her and her assistant, Big Anthony.

dePaola, Tomie. *Strega Nona.* **Illus. by the author.** Prentice Hall, 1979. $13.95 (0-671-66283-X).
FORMAT: Picture book   GRADES: Preschool–Grade 3.

This is the first book about Strega Nona, the powerful witch of Calabria. DePaola's whole heart appears on the pages of this, and subsequent, tales about her. He imbues each sunny page with lively color, and leaves readers a text that is wonderful to listen to out loud.

Dupasquier, Philippe. *Our House on the Hill.* **Illus. by the author.** Puffin, 1990. paper $3.95 (0-14-054227-2).
FORMAT: Picture book   GRADES: Preschool–Grade 3.

In lively, action-filled scenes, the author of *Jack at Sea* shows the seasonal changes that take place in a landscape of hills, pastures, ponds, trees, and a large house, center stage for the natural cycle from January to December. The artist views the house from a fixed perspective throughout the 12 months, thereby emphasizing nature's transitions through time while one place, home, reliably remains unchanged.

Duvoisin, Roger. *Petunia.* **Illus. by the author.** Knopf, 1950. LB $9.99 (0-394-90865-1).
FORMAT: Picture book   GRADES: Preschool–Grade 3.

For any child who ever wondered what's the big deal about books, meet Petunia. She is a somewhat silly goose who believes that simply having a book will make her a knowledgeable bird. Terrifically naive, and generous in spirit.

Enright, Elizabeth. *Gone-Away Lake.* Harcourt, 1957. paper $4.95 (0-15-231649-3).
FORMAT: Novel   GRADES: 4–6.

Summer vacation becomes ripe with potential when Portia and her cousin discover a hidden colony of neglected lakeside cottages. Enright's books, including *Return to Gone-Away* and *Four-Story Mistake*, have provided children with hours of solid reading pleasure for more than 30 years.

Gardam, Jane. *A Few Fair Days.* Greenwillow, 1988. $11.95 (0-688-07602-5).
FORMAT: Short stories   GRADES: 5–up.

Wistful and childlike, Gardam's collection focuses on large and small crises in Lucy's life, such as wandering away from her home by the sea (in "The Wonderful Day"), getting terribly wet, meeting her elderly aunts, and returning home in time for bath and tea. In this place, those grand aunts appear like angels to a child, and just as suddenly become ordinary. The atmosphere is blissful, but Lucy's childhood is not without mishap, and from the stories comes the revelation that if the fair days are few, they are rich and of lasting importance. The writing has an uncommon depth, and elegant, free-flowing language; each setting in an idyllic past is garnished with timeless concerns.

Gerstein, Mordecai. *The Mountains of Tibet.* **Illus. by the author.** HarperCollins, 1987. LB $13.89 (0-06-022149-6). paper avail.
FORMAT: Picture book   GRADES: 2–up.

The kindly woodcutter whom readers see grow up in these pages passes away, but has the chance to return to earth in the form he wishes, to the place he wishes. Gerstein's series of choices presented to the man reveal the contentments of a life well lived; he chooses Tibet, and his village, and becomes the new baby girl of a young couple. Reading this is similar to watching the graceful flowering of a bud, except that it runs full cycle. Understatedly amusing.

Greenwald, Sheila. *Give Us a Great Big Smile, Rosy Cole.* **Illus. by the author.** Little, Brown, 1981. $12.95 (0-316-32672-0). paper avail.
FORMAT: Chapter book   GRADES: 3–5.

Rosy has problems—she's just self-aware enough to know that she doesn't really belong in a book about talented children, but not sure enough of herself to approach the author (her uncle) with her doubts.

The other Rosy books are equally deft, balancing lighthearted and serious concerns, but this plot may appeal to today's overscheduled, under-pressure children even more than when it was first written.

Hall, Barbara. *Dixie Storms.* Harcourt, 1990. $15.95 (0-15-223825-5). paper avail.
FORMAT: Novel   GRADES: 7–up.

At first, it is an old story: the beautiful cousin from the city, Norma, comes to visit her hick cousin Dutch in the country. But Dutch is not all good and Norma isn't all bad; circumstances conspire against their better natures. Dutch is as genuine an article of adolescent torment and reluctance as readers are likely to come across these days, living amidst a throng of troubles and a spirited Southern family muddling through heated times. A quiet delight.

Hathorn, Elizabeth. *The Tram to Bondi Beach.* Illus. by Julie Vivas. Kane-Miller, 1989. $12.95 (0-916291-20-0).
FORMAT: Picture book   GRADES: Preschool–Grade 3.

Pluck wins the day in this tale from Australia, about a boy's mastery of his paper route. Hathorn's story, set in a bygone era, is a simple tale of a child's longing for those things just beyond his reach, and the ways that dreams enliven everyday events. Vivas's characters seem to defy the space constraints of a square page; they reach out to readers, or squabble and taunt one another, filling up backgrounds and engaging in activities that will invite a closer look.

Heine, Helme. *The Marvelous Journey Through the Night.* Illus. by the author. Farrar, 1990. $14.95 (0-374-38478-9).
FORMAT: Picture book   GRADES: Preschool–Grade 3.

A journey through the night leads to a richly evoked paradise of dream-bringing sleep. Heine's watercolors are comical, but convey an atmosphere that suits bedtime telling perfectly.

Houston, Gloria McLendon. *The Year of the Perfect Christmas Tree.* Illus. by Barbara Cooney. Dial, 1988. LB $14.89 (0-8037-0300-7).
FORMAT: Picture book   GRADES: Preschool–Grade 3.

The Armistice has been declared, but still there is no sign of Ruthie's father in their little town in Appalachia. So, in accordance with the traditions of Pine Grove, it falls to Ruthie and her mother to bring home the perfect Christmas tree to donate to the town. An accomplished, fluid telling garnishes this simple story, as do Cooney's moonlit paintings. Readers will experience delight as events unfold in a harmonious blending of text and pictures.

Johnson, Crockett. *Harold and the Purple Crayon.* **Illus. by the author.**
HarperCollins, 1955. $11.89 (0-06-022936-5). paper avail.
FORMAT: Storybook　GRADES: Preschool–Grade 3.

In a very deliberate shade of purple, Harold's adventures unfold as he takes a crayon on a walk. The purely fantastic consequences of Harold's drawings have delighted children for decades, and this book spawned several equally charming sequels—*Harold's ABC* and *Harold's Circus* among them.

Kent, Jack. *Round Robin.* **Illus. by the author.** Simon & Schuster, 1989. $12.95
(0-671-66698-3). paper avail.
FORMAT: Picture book　GRADES: Preschool–Grade 3.

Kent's now-typical humor shines through this early work, about a robin too fat to *fly* south, but who finds a unique way of migrating. Other charmers are *Joey* and *Joey Runs Away.*

Kimmelman, Leslie. *Frannie's Fruits.* **Illus. by Petra Mathers.** Harper-
Collins, 1989. LB $12.89 (0-06-023164-5).
FORMAT: Picture book　GRADES: Preschool–Grade 3.

A family's produce stand is the centerpiece of a summery tale of enterprise and togetherness. The stand is named for the family dog, but everyone pitches in; the pictures convey a shimmery sort of Saturday when it's hot, but it's supposed to be—it's summertime! Children will love the ins-and-outs of the business day, the celebratory feeling among patrons and workers alike. The story is as wistfully pleasant as a day at the beach.

Lattimore, Eleanor Frances. *Little Pear.* **Illus. by the author.** Harcourt, 1931.
paper $3.95 (0-15-652799-5).
FORMAT: Storybook　GRADES: 2–4.

At the beginning of this nearly worn-out century, there was a little boy in China, and his name was Little Pear. This understated story is full of smiles and quietly comic moments, sure to enchant.

Levy, Elizabeth. *Keep Ms. Sugarman in the Fourth Grade.* **Illus. by Dave**
Henderson. HarperCollins, 1992. LB $12.89 (0-06-020427-3).
FORMAT: Novel　GRADES: 3–5.

Levy writes affectionately of a very specific period in fourth-grader Jackie's life: when her energy and imagination are finally appreciated by an adult—a teacher who has just been offered the principal's job. Jackie is the most vocal opponent of change. The minor ambitions of this miniature character study are achieved with an admirable ease; readers will admire both Jackie and Ms. Sugarman, and perhaps gain perspective on any shortcomings of their own.

Lindbergh, Anne. *The Prisoner of Pineapple Place.* Harcourt, 1988. $13.95 (0-15-263559-9). paper avail.

FORMAT: Novel   GRADES: 3–7.

Jeremiah Jenkins, introduced to readers in *The People of Pineapple Place*, is tired of being a nine-year-old and a fourth-grader, never to grow old. And so he gets to work. The logic of the story is flawless as Lindbergh gracefully explains away magical occurrences and surprising developments. As for the folk of Pineapple Place, who bore poor Jeremiah, they will intrigue and charm the most skeptical of readers. Both books are fine

Lindgren, Astrid. *The Tomten.* **Illus. by Harald Wiberg.** Putnam, 1961. $14.95 (0-698-20147-7). paper avail.

FORMAT: Picture book   GRADES: Preschool–Grade 3.

The humor in this is still and quiet, as an elflike creature of Scandinavian legend watches over farms and fauna at night. For more laugh-out-loud adventures by this author, look to *Pippi Longstocking* and other stories about the red-haired orphan.

Lionni, Leo. *Six Crows.* **Illus. by the author.** Knopf, 1988. LB $12.99 (0-394-89572-4).

FORMAT: Picture book   GRADES: Preschool–Grade 3.

There is a war of scarecrows between a farmer and six cows, but as it escalates, the owl interferes and convinces both sides to talk peace. This moral tale eloquently depicts the pointlessness and futility of the ancient war of fear. Lionni's primitive art and abstract forms appeal both to the naive perceptions of children and the universal sensitivity of all readers.

McCloskey, Robert. *Blueberries for Sal.* **Illus. by the author.** Viking, 1948. $15.00 (0-670-17591-9). paper avail.

FORMAT: Picture book   GRADES: Preschool–Grade 3.

Readers watch curious Sal and her bear cub counterpart hasten into the blueberry bushes one dewy morning, where a mix-up over whose mother is whose is brushed away with the breeziest of plots. Delightful, perhaps even more so when readers know there really is a Sal, and she still lives in Maine.

McCloskey, Robert. *Make Way for Ducklings.* **Illus. by the author.** Viking, 1941. $13.00 (0-670-45149-5). paper avail.

FORMAT: Picture book   GRADES: Preschool–Grade 3.

Now these charming ducklings—in bronze—really do reside in Boston's Public Gardens, but for children who stay closer to home, the book's the thing. Mama duck and her children need not worry about their safety crossing streets and the like. They are cared for by guardian angels (in the shape of a traffic cop, for example) at every turn.

MacLachlan, Patricia. *The Facts and Fictions of Minna Pratt.* Harper-Collins, 1988. LB $11.89 (0-06-024117-9). paper avail.

FORMAT: Novel   GRADES: 3–7.

Minna is technically an excellent cellist, but she wants to find her vibrato. The process of its discovery is elusive as the thing itself. As are many of MacLachlan's heroines, Minna is serious and questioning, counting objects and categorizing them, and wondering why her mother's fiction-writing isn't considered outright lying. While Minna's musings make much of this sobering and philosophical, the language is playful and intensely poetic over such familiar things as a pair of unmatched socks. It is impossible not to be swept into the world of Minna's concerns, and to find, among the more absorbing aspects, a plainly sweet story.

Miller, Mary Jane. *Upside Down.* Viking, 1992. $13.00 (0-670-83648-6).

FORMAT: Novel   GRADES: 4–7.

Sara Kovar, her older brother Jon, and their mother have managed to put Mr. Kovar's death the previous year behind them, although they all experience lingering sadness. Then Mrs. Kovar starts dating the father of Adam, Sara's worst enemy in the sixth grade. She has too much conscience, which she attempts to overcome in several witty scenes, to sabotage the romance. The difference between Adam-at-school and Adam-at-home is a sharp piece of irony—funny, subtle—like this book.

Modesitt, Jeanne. *Vegetable Soup.* **Illus. by Robin Spowart.** Macmillan, 1988. $13.95 (0-02-767630-7). paper avail.

FORMAT: Picture book   GRADES: Preschool–Grade 1.

Theodore and Elsie are two rabbits in trouble; their carrot sack is empty on their first day in their new house and the market is closed. They resort to the kindness of strangers—their new neighbors—and from the humble offerings, make soup to be shared by all. Generous and quietly engaging, this brings subtle lessons from a hospitable neighborhood.

Peck, Robert Newton. *A Day No Pigs Would Die.* Knopf, 1972. $19.00 (0-394-48235-2). paper avail.

FORMAT: Novel   GRADES: 7–up.

A Shaker boy, just 13 years old, takes on the responsibilities of adulthood in Peck's graphic, gripping novel. For those only acquainted with the author's *Soup* and all its sequels, this is a harsher tale, blending Yankee values, a droll wit, and a look at life in the country that is beyond the idyll most city slickers imagine. Strong stuff.

Ringgold, Faith. *Tar Beach.* **Illus. by the author.** Crown, 1991. LB $14.99 (0-517-58031-4).

FORMAT: Picture book   GRADES: Preschool–Grade 3.

An effusion of good spirits pour forth from this story of wishfulness. From the tar paper-covered roof of their Harlem apartment building—they call it Tar Beach—Cassie's family while away summer hours. She dreams of flying out over the city, and the scenes of her exultation are composed of arresting perspectives and angular, distant cityscapes.

Rylant, Cynthia. *Mr. Griggs' Work.* **Illus. by Julie Downing.** Orchard, 1989. $12.95 (0-531-05769-0).

FORMAT: Picture book   GRADES: Preschool–Grade 2.

A simple idea reigns here: it is possible to take pride in and, in fact, relish what others may believe is the humblest of tasks. Mr. Griggs is the one-man show at a small-town post office. His entire life is weighing parcels, selling stamps, wondering about those that have gone astray. When he gets sick, he misses his work terribly—he feels like a dead letter. Pictures show his gentle exuberance in the smallest details of his job. Dignified, but not doddering, he will nurture in readers a need to know more about the people who work around them.

Sieruta, Peter D. *Heartbeats and Other Stories.* HarperCollins, 1989. LB $13.89 (0-06-025849-7). paper avail.

FORMAT: Short stories   GRADES: 7–up.

Assuming as many different voices as there are short stories in this collection, Sieruta proves himself an apt student of the form. Whether he is writing as the bemused younger brother in "25 Good Reasons for Hating My Brother Todd," or as the streetwise boy proving himself on his first job, the author has an uncanny ear for the undercurrents that are part of everyday conversation. High school life, and all the players, are represented in these pages. Some seletions will whet readers' appetites and make them wish that Sieruta's next work expands on any of the small universes in this book.

Steig, William. *Amos and Boris.* **Illus. by the author.** Puffin, 1977. paper $3.95 (0-14-050229-7).

FORMAT: Picture book   GRADES: Preschool–Grade 3.

A mouse and a whale are friends in a wry and witty story that some have compared to Aesop.

Steptoe, Michele. *Snuggle Piggy and the Magic Blanket.* **Illus. by John Himmelman.** Dutton, 1987. $9.95 (0-525-44308-8). paper avail.

FORMAT: Picture book   GRADES: Preschool–Kindergarten.

Snuggle Piggy is one cute pig—no wonder his Aunt Daisy sewed him a cozy blanket "full of all the creatures in the universe." At night, they come out to play with him. But when the blanket is left on the clothesline overnight, Snuggle Piggy thinks he can hear the creatures on the blanket—his friends—calling for help, and he saves them. This has a lovable poignance that will make believers of most who encounter it.

Stevenson, James. *Higher on the Door.* **Illus. by the author.** Greenwillow, 1987. LB $11.88 (0-688-06637-2).

FORMAT: Picture book   GRADES: Kindergarten–Grade 3.

Stevenson's people and landscapes have the simple forms of distant memory in a sequel to *When I Was Nine*. With them he proffers a friendly, quite gentle invitation to his childhood, perhaps answering the youthful query of "What was it like in the olden days?" The text is minimal, mostly amusingly on-the-mark observations about kids. The vigor of the remembrance is in the art—some of the strokes of color are so unaffected and abstract that readers are forced to fill in the details. Full of humor and the tender irony of hindsight, this is an achingly sweet look back.

Van de Wetering, Janwillem. *Hugh Pine and Something Else.* **Illus. by Lynn Munsinger.** Houghton, 1989. $12.95 (0-395-49216-5). paper avail.

FORMAT: Novel   GRADES: 3–up.

In another fond story about that curmudgeonly, upright-walking porcupine, Hugh and Mr. McTosh happily set out for New York City on vacation. They, and readers, are equally relieved to get back to the Maine woods. Hugh's wisdom lacks a little of the pungence in which he has based his reputation (*Hugh Pine* and *Hugh Pine and the Good Place*). However, there are singular delights among the pages, not the least of which is Hugh's succinct clobbering of a Pekingese.

Webster, Jean. *Daddy Long Legs.* Puffin, 1989. paper $3.95 (0-14-035111-6).

FORMAT: Novel   GRADES: 4–up.

The classic story, in economical paperback, tells of the misunderstanding and affection that spring up between an orphan and her mysterious benefactor. Keep even older children away from the Fred Astaire/Leslie Caron musical and give them this sure hit.

Yorinks, Arthur. *Hey, Al.* **Illus. by Richard Egielski.** Farrar, 1986. $15.00 (0-374-33060-3). paper avail.

FORMAT: Picture book   GRADES: Preschool–Grade 3.

A janitor, Al, and his dog lead lives of quiet desperation until a jaunt to Paradise convinces them, as Dorothy was also persuaded, that there is no place like home. Egielski's work won the Caldecott Medal. The author and illustrator have collaborated on many books, and while they are not all likely to induce belly laughs, they inevitably make readers smile. All are noted for their comic storytelling style.

Additional Titles

The following titles, annotated elsewhere in this book (see index), could also fit the "Soft and Gentle Humor" category.

Alexander, Martha. *Nobody Asked Me If I Wanted a Baby Sister*
Auch, Mary Jane. *Cry Uncle!*
Barton, Byron. *I Want to Be an Astronaut*
Bate, Lucy. *Little Rabbit's Loose Tooth*
Browne, Anthony. *Look What I've Got!*
Carter, Peter. *Borderlands*
Crutcher, Chris. *The Crazy Horse Electric Game*
Freeman, Don. *The Chalk Box Story*
Gallo, Donald R. *Connections*
Greenberg, Melanie Hope. *At the Beach*
Honeycutt, Natalie. *Invisible Lissa*
Khalsa, Dayal Kaur. *Sleepers*
Kitamura, Satoshi. *What's Inside?*
Lattimore, Deborah Nourse. *The Prince and the Golden Axe*
Lionni, Leo. *Alexander and the Wind-Up Mouse*
Lobel, Arnold. *Uncle Elephant*
MacGregor, Marilyn. *On Top*
Seidler, Tor. *The Tar Pit*
Selden, George. *The Cricket in Times Square*
Ungerer, Tomi. *Moon Man*
Young, Ed. *The Other Bone*
Zindel, Paul. *My Darling, My Hamburger*

Author Index

Illustrator Index

Title Index

Subject Index

Birthdays

The Apartment House, 42
Attaboy, Sam!, 100
Birthday Presents, 190
Happy Birthday, Dolores, 177
Happy Birthday, Moe Dog, 57
Ice Cream Soup, 175
Lizzie's Invitation, 25

Boston

Make Way for Ducklings, 201

Britain

A Few Fair Days, 198
Mary Poppins, 30
The Ruby in the Smoke, 104

Bugs

Nicholas Cricket, 6

Bullfighting

The Story of Ferdinand, 116

Bullies

Ada Potato, 13
There's a Boy in the Girls' Bathroom, 163
Willy the Wimp, 87
*Wonder Kid Meets the Evil Lunch
    Snatcher*, 13

Camp

Arnie Goes to Camp, 3

Canada

Anne of Green Gables, 116

Cancer

The Moon and I, 88

Careers

SEE ALSO Commerce; Jobs

Bea and Mr. Jones, 164
Bill Peet, 129

The Giraffe and the Pelly and Me, 90
I Want to Be an Astronaut, 67
Mr. Griggs' Work, 203
Whose Hat?, 78

Caretaking

Horton Hears a Who!, 9

Cartooning

Bill Peet, 129

Chaucer

Chanticleer and the Fox, 127

China

The Five Chinese Brothers, 144
Little Pear, 200

Christmas

The Best Christmas Pageant Ever, 149
Christmas Eve, 191
A Dragon Christmas, 76
Emma's Christmas, 108
How the Grinch Stole Christmas, 140
Merry Christmas, Strega Nona, 197
The Santa Clauses, 113
Santa Cows, 172
The Year of the Perfect Christmas Tree,
    199

Circuses

*The Amazing Amos and the Greatest
    Couch on Earth*, 50
Big, Small, Short, Tall, 76
Louella and the Yellow Balloon, 36
The Piggest Show on Earth, 37

Civil War

Little Women, 2

Collective nouns

Animals Galore!, 59

Colors

Commerce

Community

SEE ALSO Neighbors and neighborhoods

Conformists

Country life

Cousins

Creativity

Folktales—African

How Many Spots Does a Leopard Have?, 76
Why the Crab Has No Head, 75

Folktales—African-American

The Knee-High Man and Other Tales, 99

Folktales—Australian

Tiddalick the Frog, 161

Folktales—Jewish

How Many Spots Does a Leopard Have?, 76

Foster families

SEE ALSO Adoption; Orphans
The Pinballs, 3

France

The Beast of Monsieur Racine, 124
Madeline, 195
Ooh-La-La (Max in Love), 97

Friendship

A, My Name Is Ami, 27
All But Alice, 6
Amos and Boris, 203
Angelina and Alice, 14
Annie Bananie, 58
Arnie Goes to Camp, 3
Arthur's Pen Pal, 73
"B" Is for Betsy, 185
Babe, 98
Ben and Me, 76
Bently & Egg, 159
Betsy's Winterhouse, 186
The Bigger Book of Lydia, 32
Bill and Pete Go Down the Nile, 70
The Boy in the Moon, 99
The Brave Little Toaster, 47
The Brave Little Toaster Goes to Mars, 47

Captain Snap and the Children of Vinegar Lane, 28
Charlotte's Web, 83
Chester's Way, 5
The Cricket in Times Square, 9
Delphine, 169
Dogs Don't Tell Jokes, 15
Earl's Too Cool for Me, 59
Fast Friends, 29
Fat, 31
George and Martha, 26
George and Martha Round and Round, 27
Giant Story/Mouse Tale, 93
The Goats, 144
Gorilla, 46
Hangdog, 104
Harry's Smile, 155
Heaven to Betsy, 5
Henry and Mudge, 42
Herbie Jones and the Class Gift, 25
The House at Pooh Corner, 49
Hugh Pine and Something Else, 204
The Hundred Dresses, 145
"I Can't," Said the Ant, 46
Ice Cream Soup, 175
Invisible Lissa, 5
A Job for Jenny Archer, 69
Josie's Beau, 24
Just Be Gorgeous, 31
Just Friends, 25
Let's Be Enemies, 108
Little Bear's Trousers, 48
Lizzie's Invitation, 25
Lucky's Choice, 136
Maxie, Rosie, and Earl, 147
M.E. and Morton, 21
Mismatched Summer, 19
Mr. Nick's Knitting, 10
Mrs. Huggins and Her Hen Hannah, 22
Mostly Michael, 28
My Darling, My Hamburger, 10
Nancy, 2
Nellie, 46
O'Diddy, 29

Orphans

SEE ALSO Adoption; Foster families

Anne of Green Gables, 116
Behind the Attic Wall, 21
Daddy Long Legs, 204
The Great Gilly Hopkins, 123
Lucie Babbidge's House, 21
Mrs. Goose's Baby, 166
No Flying in the House, 35
Uncle Elephant, 26
Where the Lilies Bloom, 3

Pacifism

The Story of Ferdinand, 116

Parents

Give It Up, Mom, 15
I Can Take a Bath!, 10

Patterns

Look! Look! Look!, 73

Peer groups/clubs

SEE ALSO Adolescence; School

Invisible Lissa, 5
Sixth Grade Secrets, 15

Peru

Tonight Is Carnaval, 183

Pets

SEE ALSO Animal stories

Bad Boris and the New Kitten, 159
The Big Pets, 164
Custard the Dragon, 176
Dial-a-Croc, 172
Dog Crazy, 4
Gulliver, 81
Henry, 194
Henry and Mudge, 42
Henry and Mudge and the Long Weekend,
  8
Julian, 187

Lily Takes a Walk, 98
Mrs. Dunphy's Dog, 103
No Plain Pets!, 169
Perfect the Pig, 159
Pig Surprise, 75
Rotten Ralph, 146
Ruthann and Her Pig, 176
Wanted . . . Mud Blossom, 88

Pigs

Geraldine's Big Snow, 186
Oink, 184
Perfect the Pig, 159
The Pigs Are Flying!, 177
Porcellus, the Flying Pig, 156
Rose Is Hungry, 193
Rose Is Muddy, 193
Rose's Bath, 193
Rose's Picture, 193
Ruthann and Her Pig, 176
Snuggle Piggy and the Magic Blanket,
  204
Tales of Oliver Pig, 192
Tommy at the Grocery Store, 158

Pirates

The Not-So-Jolly Roger, 105
The Wonderful O., 108

Playtime

All Fall Down, 189
Baby Says, 191
Clap Hands, 189
Dusty Wants to Borrow Everything, 191
Geraldine's Big Snow, 186
Harold and the Purple Crayon, 200
Ned and the Joybaloo, 79
Say Goodnight, 189
Seeing, Saying, Doing, Playing, 184
Tickle, Tickle, 189

Poetry

SEE ALSO Rhymes

Annie Bananie, 58
The Book of Pigericks, 59

Robots

Alexander and the Wind-Up Mouse, 49
Robot Raiders, 48

Rock 'n roll

Journey to Boc Boc, 133

Romance

SEE ALSO First love

B, My Name Is Bunny, 175
Beautiful Losers, 31
Bingo Brown and the Language of Love, 196
Box and Cox, 36
The Boy in the Moon, 99
The Burning Questions of Bingo Brown, 196
Connections, 23
The Dancing Skeleton, 133
Dear Lovey Hart, I Am Desperate, 171
Fat, 31
The Girl Who Invented Romance, 22
Handsome as Anything, 23
The Lady's Chair and the Ottoman, 51
Let Me Tell You Everything, 20
Love Among the Hiccups, 106
Love Is the Crooked Thing, 31
Marci's Secret Book of Dating, 172
My Darling, My Hamburger, 10
My Underrated Year, 28
Ooh-La-La (Max in Love), 97
Simple Pictures Are Best, 109
Snow Woman, 49
Sorotchintzy Fair, 94
The Things I Did for Love, 22
A Three Hat Day, 172
Wonderful Me, 32

Royalty

The 500 Hats of Bartholomew Cubbins, 129
King Bidgood's in the Bathtub, 118
King Change-a-Lot, 156

The King Has Horse's Ears, 166
Ordinary Princess, 128

Runaways

From the Mixed-Up Files of Mrs. Basil E. Frankweiler, 115

St. Patrick's Day

Jeremy Bean's St. Patrick's Day, 9

Scandinavia

The Tomten, 201

School

A, My Name Is Ami, 27
After Fifth Grade, the World!, 14
The Agony of Alice, 102
Albert's Alphabet, 82
Aldo Applesauce, 25
Alice Ann Gets Ready for School, 186
Alice in Rapture, Sort of, 102
All But Alice, 6
Among Friends, 144
And the Green Grass Grew All Around, 149
Angelina and Alice, 14
Arthur's Nose, 20
Bea and Mr. Jones, 164
The Big Pink, 148
Buffalo Brenda, 104
The Cat Ate My Gymsuit, 23
Charlotte the Starlet, 96
The Cinderella Show, 153
The Cut-Ups, 116
The Cut-Ups Carry On, 116
Dinah for President, 78
Dogs Don't Tell Jokes, 15
Freckle Juice, 169
Heaven to Betsy, 5
Herbie Jones and the Class Gift, 25
The Hundred Dresses, 145
Invisible Lissa, 5
Jeremy Bean's St. Patrick's Day, 9

Character Index